The River Ki

SAWAKO ARIYOSHI

Translated by Mildred Tahara

KODANSHA INTERNATIONAL
Tokyo · New York · London

Note: All Japanese names in this novel are given in the Japanese order —surname first, followed by the given name.

Originally published by Chuokoronsha in 1959 as *Kinokawa*.

Distributed in the United States by Kodansha America, Inc., 114 Fifth Avenue, New York, N.Y. 10011, and in the United Kingdom and continental Europe by Kodansha Europe Ltd., Gillingham House, 38-44 Gillingham Street, London SW1V 1HU. Published by Kodansha International Ltd., 17-14 Otowa 1-chome, Bunkyo-ku, Tokyo 112, and Kodansha America, Inc. Copyright © 1980 by Kodansha International Ltd. All rights reserved. Printed in Japan.
First edition, 1980
First paperback edition, 1981

92 93 94 95 12 11 10 9

LCC 79-66240
ISBN 0-87011-514-6
ISBN (Japan) 4-7700-1000-1

THE AUTHOR: Sawako Ariyoshi was born in 1931 in Wakayama City. As a student she developed a deep interest in the theater, both modern drama and traditional Kabuki, and her own plays are widely performed in Japan. Many of her novels have also been adapted for the stage, the cinema, and television.

Ariyoshi first rose to prominence in the 1950s as a writer of short stories, but has since built an impressive reputation as a novelist dealing with crucial social issues. Among her themes have been the problems faced by women in the traditional Japanese household (*Hanaoka seishū no tsuma*, 1967, translated as *The Doctor's Wife*), racial segregation in the United States (*Hishoku*, 1964), and environmental pollution (*Fukugō osen*, 1975). Her *Kōkotsu no hito* (*The Twilight Years*) was published in 1972 and sold over a million copies in less than a year.

Translations of her books have appeared throughout the world and include a French translation of *The Doctor's Wife*, which was a bestseller in France in 1981; *The River Ki*; *The Twilight Years*; and *Her Highness Princess Kazu*, awarded the prestigious Mainichi Cultural Prize in 1979.

Ariyoshi died in 1984.

THE TRANSLATOR: Mildred Tahara is Associate Professor of Japanese Literature at the University of Hawaii at Manoa. Her publications include *Tales of Yamato* (University of Hawaii Press, 1980) and translations of three Ariyoshi works: *The River Ki*, *The Twilight Years*, and *Her Highness Princess Kazu*.

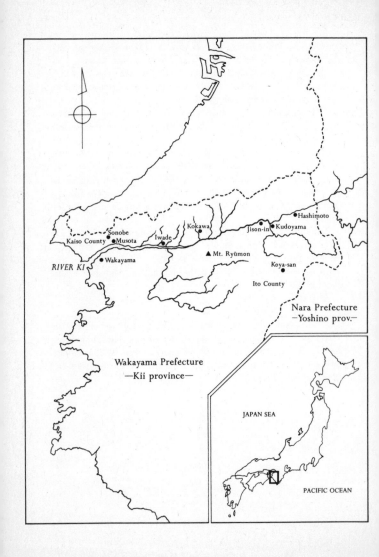

PART
I

GENEALOGICAL CHART OF
THE PRINCIPAL CHARACTERS

THE KIMOTO FAMILY

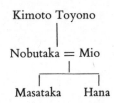

Kimoto Toyono
|
Nobutaka = Mio
|
Masataka   Hana

THE MATANI FAMILY

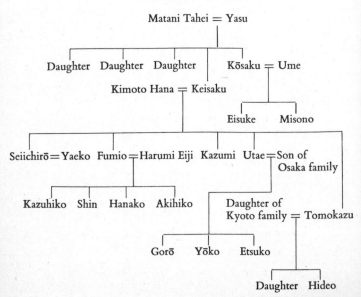

Matani Tahei = Yasu
|
Daughter Daughter Daughter   Kōsaku = Ume
Kimoto Hana = Keisaku
Eisuke   Misono

Seiichirō = Yaeko Fumio = Harumi Eiji Kazumi Utae = Son of
Osaka family

Kazuhiko Shin Hanako Akihiko   Daughter of
Kyoto family = Tomokazu

Gorō Yōko Etsuko

Daughter Hideo

Toyono stepped firmly up the stone steps, leading her granddaughter by the hand. She would soon be seventy-six, and her gray hair, long neglected professionally, had been done up three days earlier by a hairdresser summoned from Wakayama City. The sidelocks were fluffed out and the hair swept up in back protruded a trifle too far for a woman of her age. Thick and lustrous, though now completely gray, her hair gave more than a hint of its former dark beauty. Toyono, dressed in a lined kimono with a fine print, walked hand-in-hand with Hana. The matriarch of the Kimoto family conducted herself with such dignity that it seemed that the old woman was helping the young woman up the stone steps. Toyono had a special air of determination about her on this particular day, for her granddaughter was to leave the family and be married.

The morning mist of early spring veiled Kudoyama. Conscious of her grandmother's strength in her left hand, Hana silently made her way up the stone steps. Her glistening hair had been combed up into a high bun and her face was flushed and aglow under the heavy powder. She was wearing a long-sleeved formal kimono of purple silk crape, and the decorative tassle hanging from the wallet tucked into her kimono fold shook and tinkled faintly. Hana was so tense she could hear the soft, musical sound. Toyono intended her firm grip on her granddaughter's hand to communicate to Hana that once she was married, she would no longer be considered a member of the Kimoto family, and her home for the past twenty years would no longer be hers. At the same time, the handclasp showed her regret that they would soon be parting.

The head priest of Jison-in, who had been informed the day before about their visit, stood waiting in front of the Miroku Hall. He was not, however, in formal priest's robes, for Toyono had specifically stated that the purpose of their visit was not to hear him intone the sutras. He bowed politely, as was only to be expected when addressing the matriarch of an important family in his parish.

"This is indeed a most auspicious day. My sincerest congratulations," said the priest, extending his best wishes.

"Thank you. Forgive us for coming so early," said Toyono, graciously greeting the priest.

He informed them that the hall had been left open and that if they had need of his services they should summon him by clapping their hands. He then walked back to his quarters on the northern side, remembering Toyono's earlier request that she be left alone with her granddaughter.

Toyono watched the priest walk away, then slowly turned to her granddaughter. She looked up at Hana, who was rather tall, and nodded with satisfaction. Together the two women made their way to the Miroku Hall, the mausoleum in which the mother of Saint Kōbō was enshrined.

"Women aren't allowed to climb all the way to the top of Mount Kōya, but they may come as far as Jison-in. That's why they call this place the 'Kōya for Women.' You knew that, didn't you, Hana?"

"Yes."

"Are you familiar with the story of how Saint Kōbō appeared in Kishin's dream and said: 'Rather than worship me ten times, pray nine times to my mother'?"

"Not in detail."

"Being a woman is no excuse for being ignorant."

"Yes, I know."

Toyono quietly pressed her hands together in prayer and closed her eyes. Hana too pressed her hands together, but some breast charms on a pillar caught her attention and she forgot to close her eyes. The charms were made of cotton wrapped up into balls in pieces of *habutaé* silk; the center of each was pinched and tied to represent a nipple. These charms, part of the breast cult popular among the people in this area, were offered for a safe delivery by women at the mausoleum dedicated to the mother of Saint Kōbō and to Miroku Bodhisattva. They hung from the top of the pillar, some life-sized, some tiny, a bare inch in diameter.

Two or three were still very white, but the other charms had been darkened by the elements and by age. Hana had seen such charms ever since she was a child, but she was especially struck by them on her wedding day, probably because she knew that she herself—like her mother when she was pregnant and like Toyono several decades earlier when she was carrying Hana's father—would be offering a similar charm in the near future. Hana, who had been educated at Wakayama Girls' School, firmly believed that the role of women was to bear children in order to preserve the family line. Because of the early death of her mother, Hana had been brought up by Toyono. She felt she understood why her grandmother had wanted to be alone with her at Jison-in on this particular day. Hana quietly closed her eyes. She was still a virgin and had no special request at this shrine which protected expectant mothers; her sole desire at this moment was to be one in spirit with Toyono who stood at her side.

"The head priest has kindly invited us to go into the Worship Hall. Shall we go in?"

"Yes, let's."

Toyono and Hana entered the hall and seated themselves on the tatami straw matting in front of the altar. Once again, they pressed their hands together in prayer. To the right of the altar was a portrait of Saint Kōbō, and to the left, one of his mother. Legend had it that they were by Saint Kōbō himself: one was a self-portrait which he painted by studying his reflection in a pond at a time when he had secluded himself on Mount Kōya; the other was a mandala which he had painted upon seeing in a dream his mother reborn as Miroku Bodhisattva. Like almost everything else she knew, Hana had learned about the origin of these paintings from Toyono.

"I have no further advice for you," said Toyono in a low voice as she looked back at Hana. "Take good care of yourself."

"I shall."

"I won't be seeing much of you any more, since you'll be going far away to be married. I don't have anything special to say to you, but I wanted you to come with me so that we could be alone together."

Ever since this morning, Toyono had begun to address Hana more elegantly and politely than usual, as though she already regarded her granddaughter as a member of another family. But this may have in fact been Toyono's way of expressing her intense loneliness at having to part with her beloved granddaughter. Hana, feeling her grandmother's eyes on her forehead, remained silent. Ever since Hana was a little girl, Toyono had done everything in her power to keep her by her side every minute of the day; her love for her granddaughter was profound. Rumor had it that the matriarch of the Kimoto family had cared for neither her own son Nobutaka nor her grandson Masataka and that was why she lavished her affection on her granddaughter. It was her idea to have Hana, like her brother, spend a few years in Wakayama City attending college, most unusual at the time for a girl. During those years, Toyono, though she was not accustomed to city life, had lived in the city so as to be with Hana. Everyone was sure that Toyono planned to adopt a husband into the family. Otherwise, they reasoned, she would not have given her granddaughter the kind of education which was suited only to a woman scholar. Besides, Toyono's own husband had been adopted into the family. It was obvious that she had her heart set on the best possible man in the east, for the young Kimoto girl was endowed with beauty, intelligence, and an irreproachable character. Toyono had in fact once entertained such thoughts. She still remembered Mio, Hana's mother, who had died young; Mio had been so terrified of Toyono that she had cowered in her presence. Toyono did not want Hana to undergo that kind of hardship. Hana was an only daughter; Toyono prayed that, by teaching Hana all that she herself had been taught, she would make it possible for Hana to lead a rich and rewarding life. The famous Kimoto family of Ki province had reached its full flowering in Hana, and Toyono had seen to it that she was brought up wisely and well. Hana had been thoroughly trained in the art of the tea ceremony and she wrote a beautiful hand. She had also received a certificate for her skill in playing the koto and she had learned under Toyono's tutelage to speak with grace and behave elegantly. Having thus mastered all the arts expected of a daughter of a distinguished family, there was nothing left for her to learn. It was not surprising that numerous marriage offers came pouring in from Kudoyama Village, Jison-in Village, and other villages near and far.

But Toyono rejected every single proposal. She never said a word about bringing a husband into the family and setting up a branch family, but always managed to point out some fault in the other party which enabled her to decline the offer. Her principal dissatisfaction was with the social status of the families of the applicants. When Hana's hand was sought for the second son of the Ōsawa family, an old family in Jison-in Village, Toyono opposed the match, saying her younger sister had married into the same family, making the two young people cousins and therefore too closely related. Nobutaka, the nominal head of the Kimoto family, was of a retiring disposition and a dutiful son, completely under Toyono's influence. He lacked the courage to argue with his mother and even refrained from asking if she really intended to adopt a husband for Hana.

> In Kishū, the province of Ki,
> Grow many trees;
> When you take a wife,
> Choose the loveliest blossom—
> The Kimoto girl of Kudoyama
> Is the loveliest of all.

Children sang this song while playing together. The tune was an old familiar one and the lyrics had been transmitted from generation to generation, but the subject was changed from time to time. It was also sung as a lullaby. When Toyono was young, there had been a young beauty in Sudanoshō. The last lines of the song in those days went:

> When you take a wife,
> Choose the loveliest blossom—
> Sakae-san of Sudanoshō
> Is the loveliest of all.

The name of this beauty was Sakae. Toyono, even then willful and proud, had been intensely jealous of this beauty whom she had never seen. She herself had been pretty, but not quite as beautiful as Sakae of Sudanoshō.

Hana more than compensated for the chagrin Toyono had endured in the distant past, and she had the highest hopes for her. Her affection was so strong that she would have been reluctant to let Hana go, even if the shogun's family were to ask for her. Toyono doted so much on her granddaughter that she could not decide what to do. In the meantime the children's song was being sung throughout Ito County.

In 1897 when Hana was nearly twenty, two proposals came simultaneously during a break in the steady stream of marriage offers. One was from the new Suda family that had formerly owned Suda-no-shō and was now one of the richest families in the region. The proposal was made through the Niu family, related distantly to the Kimotos. Though Sakae-san of Sudanoshō was famous for her beauty, she had not come from a family with any social status—in fact, she had been a maid in the Suda household. Now Hana was being sought after by the whole Suda clan.

"Please give your consent, for Hana is almost past the marriageable age," said Nobutaka cautiously. This was the first time he had ventured to ask his mother about her plans. It was not considered unusual at this time for a girl to be married at the age of fourteen or fifteen. As Hana was no longer eighteen, the age at which girls were considered most eligible, it was natural for Hana's father to be deeply concerned. He urged Toyono not to let her affection for her granddaughter become the cause of Hana's future unhappiness.

Toyono continued to oppose the match.

"I can't allow Hana to go to the Sudas."

"Why not?"

"Why not? Think for a moment about the match. The River Ki flows from east to west. If someone from the Kimoto family goes to the Suda family, she will have to travel from west to east against the flow of the river. Brides from families along the Ki must never travel upstream. I will never allow Hana to marry into the Suda family."

"If you keep on being so unreasonable, we're going to find ourselves in trouble."

"I'm not being unreasonable! My mother came here from Yoshino. Your mother came from Yamato. Both women traveled downriver. To go against nature is a serious crime."

"Hana will never marry if you keep making objections. What will become of her? Have you thought at all about her future?"

"Of course I have. I'm going to send her to the Matanis."

So casually did she inform Nobutaka of her decision that he was quite taken aback. The Kimotos had received a marriage proposal from the Matani family of Musota in Isao Village, Kaisō County, down on the lower reaches of the River Ki. The proposal had been made through the Kita family of Ryūmon.

The Kimoto girl was going to Musota. The rumor had spread throughout the neighboring villages before many days had slipped by. Everyone wondered why Hana had to go to Musota, when people living along the upper reaches of the river were always considered superior. Isao Village itself was by no means in the same class as Kudoyama. It was quite true, all the same, that the Matani family were the most important people in Musota. No one could complain about the status of the family, especially since the request for Hana's hand had come from the main branch. Still, it was generally felt that the Matanis were definitely not worthy of the Kimoto daughter.

As head of the Kimoto family, Nobutaka felt that it was his duty to oppose his mother's decision.

"Mother, you're talking nonsense. You can't discuss turning down the Sudas and sending Hana to the Matanis in the same breath."

"Why not? The Sudas have nothing to do with Hana's being married into the Matani family."

"We must consider the two proposals separately. We have to turn down the Matanis for the same reason we've turned down other proposals."

"Why must we?"

"Don't you think their family status is inferior?"

"Why?"

"Why? Just look at the contrast between Kudoyama and Musota."

"Nobutaka-san, you're talking like an old man."

It was a custom in the Kimoto family for even the parents to address their sons respectfully. Toyono thought that her son was terribly old-fashioned and curtly retorted that Hana was marrying the Matani son, not the family status.

"You've sent both your son and daughter to be educated in Wakayama City. I can't believe that you haven't heard of Matani Keisaku. After graduating from the Normal School in Tokyo, he immediately began helping his father Tahei as the assistant village headman. Now at twenty-four he's the headman. You can search high and low along the River Ki, but you won't find a more suitable husband for Hana. After all, everything hinges upon the man who heads the family."

Nobutaka was so taken aback by his mother's argument that he could not utter a word. Since he himself was the headman of Kudoyama, he had indeed heard of Matani Keisaku, an up-and-coming young man of boundless energy. But as far as Nobutaka was concerned, it was far preferable to have the Sudas as relatives than to have this Keisaku, who was merely the headman of a tiny village, as his son-in-law. Though usually deferential toward his mother, Nobutaka this time stubbornly opposed her.

"If it's unlucky for a bride to travel against the flow of the river, you can just as well argue that a bride mustn't cross over to the opposite side of the river, because its waters are meant to keep people apart. Remember how tragic it was when the branch family took a bride from Myō-ji?"

Toyono's uncle had established a junior branch of the Kimoto family. Not long after his son's bride had come from across the river, the family fortunes began to decline and in time every member of the family died.

"It was wrong in the first place to have the bride come from Myō-ji to Kudoyama. You're familiar with the Brother-Sister poem in *The Collection of the Myriad Leaves*, aren't you? Brother Mountain is located in Kasedanoshō and Sister Mountain on the opposite bank. In other words, the bride should come from our side of the River Ki. The junior family met with great misfortune because they went against tradition. Nothing will go wrong if the bride crosses from the Sister Mountain shore to the Brother Mountain shore."

Toyono was a great debater and she felt that she had to win every argument even if she failed to make any sense.

Toyono had the habit of bringing the Meiji Restoration of 1868 into every discussion. On this occasion she concluded her argument by saying:

"The country's not run on feudal lines any more. There shouldn't be all this fuss and bother just because a girl is about to be married."

Nobutaka still would not give in. He sent for his daughter and asked her what her own wishes were. Hana gazed steadily at her father with her round eyes and replied:

"I would like to marry into the Matani family, because Musota is closer to Wakayama City than Suda."

Toyono looked up at the ceiling and laughed when she heard from Hana's maid, Toku, how Hana had answered her father. The years Hana had spent in Wakayama City had not been without effect. It was obvious to Toyono that Hana had heard of Matani Keisaku; she was very pleased with her granddaughter.

The womenfolk looked forward eagerly to the marriage once

the proposal made by the Matani family had been formally accepted. Nevertheless, the Matanis had to wait for nearly two years after the exchange of engagement presents; the Kimotos needed that much time to prepare for the wedding. Toyono took Hana and Toku with her to Kyoto where she ordered various items for Hana's dowry and trousseau. It took over a year to prepare the exquisite Kyoto lacquerware—from the first layers to the finished articles. Toyono gave careful instructions as to the quality of the lacquer and the nature of the gold lacquer designs for Hana's palanquin, koto, mirror stand, and chests. Toyono also took Hana to meet the masters of the Urasenke School of tea ceremony and the Koryū School of flower arrangement. Nobutaka was astonished by the remarkable change in his mother, who had always been extremely conservative in her tastes and frugal with household expenses; she seemed to have been transformed into a woman of the most flamboyant tastes. Nobutaka sighed helplessly, convinced of the truth of the old adage that any family that has three daughters, like the Matanis, faces financial ruin. To make up for what she herself had never experienced, Toyono, whose husband had moved into her house, planned a magnificent wedding procession for her granddaughter.

Because this was her last chance to live together with Hana, Toyono remained in Kyoto with her granddaughter for over three months, which the two women spent visiting temples and gardens. One day when they were viewing the maple leaves in the Ryōan-ji Garden, Toyono turned to Hana to express her admiration. She chose this moment to remark in a serious tone:

"Your future husband has had to wait for two years, but he hasn't complained in the least. I've no doubt that he's an exceptional man. You needn't worry about him."

Two autumns had slipped by since Toyono decided to send Hana to the Matanis, and she was trying to convince herself that she had made the right decision.

"Yes, I know," said Hana, raising her head. Toyono gazed at Hana's lustrous hair, combed up in a high bun. Presently, Toyono straightened Hana's kimono collar and whispered, "How enchanting you are!" Her eyes were wet with tears. Hana's eyes were also brimming and she held her breath lest she give way to her emotion.

Toyono remained silent, for she had nothing more to say. Her life had been intertwined with Hana's for more than twenty years. All the same, Hana would now be separated from the Kimotos and would not share the same grave as her grandmother. At the thought that she would be free of all family ties and a totally independent woman, Hana felt all the closer to her grandmother.

The morning mist slowly cleared and the sun began to shine.

"Look! The river is such a lovely shade of green!"

The sparkling expanse of celadon green extended before the eyes of the women, who had come out of the Miroku Hall to begin their descent of the stone steps on the east of the temple.

"It's beautiful!" breathed Hana, expressing her wonder.

"It is beautiful!" echoed Toyono, clasping tightly Hana's left hand.

Hand-in-hand the two women descended the stone steps, where they were immediately surrounded by the people who had been waiting for them. The boats were ready to depart. It seemed that everyone in Kudoyama Village and Jison-in Village had turned out to see the bride off.

Saki, the hairdresser, rushed up to adjust Hana's hair. Toku went to open the door of the palanquin which had been set down near the landing. That very convenient vehicle, the ricksha, had recently been introduced to Japan but, in keeping with the status of the family, a lacquered palanquin was used for the bride.

"My very best wishes," said Toyono formally. Hana looked down wordlessly. She drew her sleeves to her and got into the palanquin. Toku carefully placed a doll on her mistress' lap, as it was the custom in this part of the country for a bride to set out for her new home carrying an Ichimatsu doll.

The two palanquin bearers, ordered from Wakayama City, gave a loud shout as they lifted the palanquin in which Hana was seated and carried it aboard the boat moored at the landing. They set the palanquin down in the middle of the boat and stationed themselves at the stern.

"She's a beauty!" said one of the men.

"A little doll," whispered the other. In the meantime the boatmen were calling out one to another.

"All set?"

"All right!"

The bride's boat left the shore. The go-betweens sat side by side like mandarin ducks in the lead boat, which had been loaded to capacity with presents for relatives and gifts sent in return for engagement presents. Toku waited on her mistress in the boat carrying Hana's palanquin, the second in the procession. Toku was fifty years old, and her face, heavily made up for the occasion, was tense. Though Ki province is relatively warm, the air over the river this early March morning chilled the women's skin, even though they were dressed in crested kimonos of silk pongee with matching sashes.

The third and fourth boats carried Nobutaka, Masataka, the members of the main and junior families of the Niu clan, who had earlier proposed a boy from the Suda family, and the relatives of the Kimoto family. No sooner had the boats left the landing than the passengers broke out into lively chatter. Sitting in the last boat, their knees touching, were Saki, the hairdresser, and the servants.

"It's all so magnificent, Nobutaka," someone said. "There hasn't been a bridal procession as elegant as this since the Meiji Restoration."

"Look!" added another member of the party. "People are lining both sides of the river. And the dowry in nine large chests carried along the embankment! No wonder the Kimoto bridal procession is the talk of the whole region!"

Nobutaka had no reason to feel badly about being teased in this manner by senior members of the Niu family. He had spent the whole of the night before drinking and was still slightly inebriated. His face was redder than usual. He smiled and said good-naturedly:

"There's no chance anyone will ever forget the Kimotos of Kudoyama."

The waters of the Ki were blue and silent, but the river flowed fast, and the five boats raced along without any need for the boatmen's help. The villagers waved from the banks of the river as the wedding party sped by. It was already common at this time for a wedding procession to consist of nothing more than a line of rickshas, so an old-fashioned procession of five boats with the bride hidden in a palanquin was enough to make people stare in amazement.

"Toku."

Hearing her mistress's voice, Toku went up to the palanquin.

"Please help me open the door," said Hana in a low voice.

Toku, embarrassed not to have done this without being asked, hurriedly opened the door from the outside. She felt she had failed both Toyono and Hana by not having opened the palanquin door in time for Toyono, still at the landing, to catch a final glimpse of her granddaughter.

"Is this all right?"

"Yes, thank you."

Hana looked out at the budding green leaves on the southern shore of the river. She felt more comfortable now than she had before, cooped up inside the palanquin. But even though a small window was open, the view was obscured by the reed blinds hanging down. The figure of her grandmother quickly disappeared from sight. Hana, her mind preoccupied by the separation, remained tense and was aware only of being borne along on the water.

The Ichimatsu doll on her lap, which gazed wide-eyed at Hana, was dressed in the elaborate garments of a fine gentleman: a haori jacket of *habutaé* silk, a sash, and white socks. Its glossy skin and slightly parted red lips gave it the look of a precocious child. Hana lifted the doll to straighten the crest on the haori. She noticed it was the Matani family crest.

A little boy doll in the arms of a bride on her way to her new home showed the bride understood that, once married, she would bear children and do everything she could to bring about the prosperity of the family. Holding the doll to her breast, Hana wondered what kind of children she would have. Hana recalled that whenever a marriage proposal had been rejected, Toyono had said that it was, after all, a woman's business to bear children. She had looked meaningfully at her granddaughter—was this to indicate that they would have to be careful in selecting a husband who would be the father of the children? Matani Keisaku had finally been chosen. The two young people had met just once two years earlier, but Hana placed her trust entirely in the man selected by her grandmother. Under Toyono's influence, she had gradually persuaded herself she was fond of Keisaku. Now she was sure she was deeply in love with him. Hana clasped to her breast the Ichimatsu doll, feeling that it symbolized her departure from the Kimoto family.

On the southern shore, several washerwomen were lowering into the water their baskets of green bamboo. Calling out to one another, they pointed at the five boats sweeping majestically downriver.

"Isn't that the Kaseda welcoming party?"
"Why, I believe it is!"
Dressed in happi coats, the menservants of the old Kaseda family came to greet the wedding party. Recognizing the men, Toku and the palanquin bearers called out to them. Here the wedding party would rest and have some refreshments. It was not yet noon.

The main branch of the Kaseda family had opened up their new riverside residence and had made elaborate preparations to welcome the party. Mrs. Kaseda made much of Hana's beauty and was impressed by the gorgeous design on her long-sleeved kimono.

"Did your grandmother select that design of orchid, chrysanthemums, plum, and bamboo? She has always had exquisite taste."

Daintily sipping her tea, Hana asked:

"Is Brother Mountain visible from here?"

Hana explained to Mrs. Kaseda about nearby Brother Mountain.

"You probably mean Mt. Narutaka," said Mrs. Kaseda.

"No, I don't. Brother Mountain isn't as high."

Mrs. Kaseda listened politely but did not inquire further into the matter.

Hana, remembering that she was on her wedding journey and thinking that she should refrain from being too talkative, dropped the subject. Nonetheless, she could not help thinking that the lady's ignorance was lamentable. Though the Kaseda family was very important, they did not believe in educating the girls in the family. Hana decided it was better not to explain to Mrs. Kaseda about the poems in *The Collection of the Myriad Leaves* and *The Collection of Ancient and Modern Poems* which drew upon the legend of the Brother and Sister mountains. Very much disappointed, she realized that she had indeed left her grandmother.

They arrived next at Kokawa where they had their noon meal. Their hosts were the members of the Kojima family. Kokawa Temple, the third temple on the pilgrimage route through the western provinces, was located in this village, whose wealth had diminished greatly with the passage of time. The villagers here seemed not in the least perturbed by the wedding party. Hana was able to take a good look at Mt. Ryūmon, which soared gracefully into the clear southern skies. The mountain, referred to as the Mt. Fuji of Ki province, wore a thin mantle of snow and its sides sloped gently downward for a great distance.

"Why, you can see Mt. Ryūmon from here!" exclaimed Toku.

"It's because of the glorious weather we've been having," responded Mrs. Kita, the go-between, in a buoyant mood.

But thin wisps of clouds, resembling silk-floss bridal veils, trailed here and there in the heavens and the chilly air they had felt earlier that morning had melted into mild springlike weather.

The hours slipped by. At three in the afternoon the wedding party arrived at Iwade Village, where they had been eagerly awaited by the Yoshiis. Following the Sino-Japanese war of 1894, the Yoshii family had become wealthy. Honored to have been asked to provide a resting place for the bridal party, the entire village had turned out to greet them. It had not occurred to Hana that Toyono might have had a special reason for singling out the old, well-established families along the northern bank of of the river. However, she could not help but notice that, as they made their way downriver, the families were prosperous even though the land itself was obviously poorer. She also discovered that each area had its own peculiar characteristics and wondered about those of Musota.

As night fell the menservants lit the lanterns with the Kimoto crest aboard the five boats.

In Musota a huge crowd had turned out along the bank to greet the bridal party. The lanterns with the Matani quince crest danced about in the twilight shadows. As the crests of the two families bobbed about, the menservants burst into song.

> On the young pine branches
> The pine needles
> Grow luxuriantly.

The bridal procession with the nine large chests containing the dowry wound its way slowly and with many a diversion along the dark road before entering the grounds of the Matani mansion in Agenogaito. The Matanis, fully prepared to receive the party, immediately conducted Hana into a small room, entrusting Toku and Saki with the task of dressing her in her bridal robes. The Ichimatsu doll was placed in the alcove in the front room.

Toku breathed a sigh of relief when she finished dressing the bride in a long white outer robe over a bridal kimono of white figured silk.

"I've assisted at many a wedding, but the bride has never been so lovely," remarked Saki. Toku gazed at her mistress in silent rapture. Then, radiant with joy, she retorted:

"Why, naturally! She's the girl all the children have been singing about."

The two middle-aged women were enchanted by Hana. Reluctant to hide her lovely face, they hesitated to put on the bridal veil.

The wedding ceremony was held in the inner drawing room. Mrs. Kita formally united the couple. Matani Tahei and his wife, Yasu, exchanged nuptial cups with Hana, thereby formalizing their relationship as her parents-in-law. Keisaku exchanged cups with Nobutaka. Mrs. Kita, dressed in a blue hood and a pale green outer robe, exuded an aura of elegance and charm, and Hana, taking note of this, tried to relax. When she peered from under her veil at Keisaku, the young man squared his shoulders and gazed directly into her eyes. Hana felt her whole body grow warm. The tiny quantity of saké which she had had a while back seemed to set her heart on fire.

Hana removed her veil. When she returned to the front room where a banquet had been prepared exclusively for the men, the guests toasted her with their saké cups. The geishas from the licensed quarters of Wakayama City fluttered like butterflies around the individual dining trays of the thirty-eight guests.

The Kimotos had had the ceremonial bowls for the dining trays made to order by the lacquer craftsmen of Wajima. The exquisite lacquerware gleamed darkly under the countless lamps which had been lit, and each quince-crest design in gold lacquer appeared to be floating upward from the dining tray.

Hana's relatives sat proudly in a group, calling out congratulatory greetings. When Hana left her place for a change of robes, they whispered among themselves.

"Isn't she ravishing?"

"Keisaku must be happy he waited for her."

"She's quiet for a girl who graduated from the Girls' School."

"After all, she's a Kimoto, a cut above the others."

Hana changed into a gorgeous outer robe with a design of pink winter plum blossoms in the Kōrin style woven on a gray ground, which she wore over a robe of figured silk with gold thread embroidery. Forgetting for a moment to see to the guests, the geishas stared in wonder at Hana's magnificent attire.

"Pour me another drink," shouted Kōsaku, Keisaku's younger brother. With his back to the guests, he had rushed up to his brother. The members of the Matani family blanched, terrified that Kōsaku might be too drunk to behave properly. Keisaku, however, smiled and handed his brother a saké cup into which the geisha at his side deftly poured some saké.

Covers were placed over the bowls of clear clam soup and the formal dinner was served to the guests, each one of whom grew tipsier by the minute. When once again the bride left her place, the person seated next to Kōsaku whispered:

"Don't you envy your brother?"

"Why should I?" said Kōsaku, growing increasingly pale as lines of irritation etched his forehead. The guest immediately regretted having addressed him so carelessly and muttered:

"After all, the bride is a beauty."

Downing his saké in one gulp, Kōsaku thrust out his cup and called to the geisha to pour him another drink.

"What's so extraordinary about her?" he spluttered, draining his newly filled cup.

The geishas played congratulatory pieces on the shamisen. There were many businessmen among the patrons of the licensed quarters, but not one was present at this banquet. The Wakayama geishas of the first class appeared to be ill at ease serving wealthy farmers and landowners.

The bride changed her attire several times in the course of the evening. Each kimono she wore was darker in color than the one before, as dark hues were considered auspicious. Finally, she changed into a black kimono with a design on the hem. It was then quite late and the banquet hall was in considerable disorder.

When Hana made her final appearance, a young man seated in front of Keisaku abruptly asked:

"Are you really a graduate of the Girls' School?"

"Yes."

So clear and direct was the bride's reply that the young man was taken aback. Nodding his head drunkenly and brushing aside a lock of hair from his forehead, he said in an intimidating manner:

"Even an educated woman is no better than a fool. I'll tell you this much, your husband is a special person. Take good care of him or you'll have me to answer to."

"What a pest!" laughed Keisaku and silenced the man. He then grinned sheepishly at Hana, who felt her whole body grow numb. This was the first time he had looked unguardedly at her. She was now sure that he was indeed a man in whom she could place her trust. Flustered, she sat stiffly, trying to appear composed. Hana studied intently the quince crest on the dinner tray which she had not even touched and vacantly wondered about the ancient tradition of family crests. On the lining of the outer robe she had worn earlier that evening was a white quince crest. Hana recalled that when it arrived from Kyoto, Toyono had looked it over carefully and said:

"What an ugly crest!"

No matter how tiny the crest was, it looked awkward on a woman's kimono.

Summoned by the go-between, first the bride and then the groom stole away from the banquet. An observant member of the Matani clan noted their departure and shouted:

"Go to it, Keisaku!"

The members of the Kimoto clan frowned. Even if these vulgar words had not been uttered, the Kimotos already regarded the Matanis with contempt for their bad manners. Nobutaka and the other members of the family found the entire evening painful in the extreme. The nine chests containing the dowry, which had also made the journey from Kudoyama in lacquered palanquins, had been duly received in Musota. As Nobutaka had foreseen, the Sudas and the Matanis were as different as the hills and the sea. Tahei, the groom's father, wore his hair up in a topknot; the corners of his eyes drooped because he had drunk too much. As far as Nobutaka was concerned, Tahei was just a lowly farmer. In general, an owner of mountain land looked down on an owner of rice land; Nobutaka was no exception. Toyono took the matter of family status more seriously than anyone else. Had she been present to see the utter chaos in the banquet hall, she would certainly have been filled with remorse. Nobutaka personally felt that Toyono should have come along, since she was going to pay a formal call on the bride the next day anyway. For the first time in his life he resented his mother, who always had things done her way. But it was too late now to complain. At that very moment Keisaku and Hana were exchanging nuptial cups in an inner room.

The altar was decorated with Kōshū plums and dried cuttlefish. The go-between, with a look of utter serenity on her face, had the bride and groom take up the saké cups, treating them like children.

Excusing herself, the go-between said, "Have a good rest."

What transpired afterward remained but a fragmented memory in Hana's mind. For the first time in her life she had been left alone with a member of the opposite sex. Her upbringing had been such that that in itself was a traumatic experience. Toyono had handed her a wallet into which she had slipped an Utamaro print, referring to it as a charm. Not having enough presence of mind at that moment to recall the print, Hana remained rigid as her husband swept her up into his arms. In her pain she pressed her head against the wooden pillow but took care not to ruin her elaborate coiffure. The prenuptial instructions she had received had been very sketchy indeed. Hana did as best as she could to cope.

Keisaku's experience with women had been far too limited for him to be sensitive to her response. He was simply a young man of twenty-six, overcome by the beauty of his bride.

"I've had to wait so long!" murmured Keisaku after his passion had subsided. Having been instructed to obey her husband's every wish, Hana could only silently express her feelings of shame. Closing her eyes in the dark, Hana marveled that her unease had not taken a noticeable form.

In this part of the country the women paid the bride a formal visit the morning after the wedding to extend their congratulations. At the wedding reception the night before the men had stared at her as she sat with her head bowed, unable to distinguish one guest from another. On this day, however, Hana fixed her eyes on each woman introduced to her, doing her best to memorize the woman's face and name. She struck all her visitors as being extremely intelligent.

Yasu rushed over to Hana after the departure of one of the guests and said:

"Her family branched off from ours three generations ago. All branch families take on the name Handa; we're the only family in Musota with the name Matani. Long ago when this area was the domain of Negoro Temple, the head of the Matani family was included among the Negoro One Hundred. The family was given the name Chōfuku-in, which became shortened to Chōkui."

Hana knew all this, but it was another matter to be told of the history of the family by her mother-in-law. Chōkui had an ancient ring to it; it was difficult for Hana to imagine that it was a corruption of Chōfuku-in. Recalling how her father had made fun of the Matanis by referring to them as the Musotas, Hana could not help but be amused.

The women of the branch families of the Kimoto family also came to call on the bride. Each was wearing a fine-patterned kimono as though they had all agreed in advance to dress alike. The ladies were astonished to see Hana sitting serenely next to her mother-in-law as if she had been a member of the family for many years.

"Madame will not be attending the banquet," said the mistress of the branch family. She had been asked by Toyono, who had given her advanced age as an excuse for not coming, to extend her formal greetings. A banquet was customarily held for the women the day after they paid their respects to the bride. Toyono, then, was not making an appearance even when only women would be present.

"Please extend to her my best wishes," said Hana.

That these cool, polite words were uttered by Toyono's beloved granddaughter startled not only the mistress of the branch family but Hana's mother-in-law as well. It would not have been out of place for Hana, in this instance, to have expressed her sadness or regret.

"I suppose she's being a dutiful daughter-in-law."

"She's very wise."

"Her grandmother brought her up very strictly, you know."

These observations were made by the ladies at the banquet in their honor. Under their scrutiny, Hana, attired in an outer robe with a pine cone design embossed on a green ground, sat sedately.

"Look! She's wearing a scarlet kimono."

"What an exquisite creature! She's a little doll."

Hana's outer robe, lined in scarlet figured silk, had a padded hem two inches thick. The figured silk kimono worn underneath was of the same shade. Hana's fair complexion appeared flushed as she looked down to avoid the attention focused on her. She emanated all the delicate fragrance of a bride.

"How shrewd Keisaku was to have chosen a bride with a dowry large enough to fill nine chests and with good looks as well! The bride, too, is extremely lucky," commented the women.

It was the custom in this region for newlyweds to visit the bride's family on the fifth day following the wedding ceremony. However, it had been decided that Hana and Keisaku would not adhere to this practice, since Kudoyama was so far away. This, of course, had been Toyono's idea. And yet Toyono, though she should have been the first person to visit the bride, had not come.

"What could Madame be thinking of?"

Toku, the only person who had accompanied Hana from the Kimoto household, was terribly unhappy. Saki, the hairdresser, had remained five more days to help dress the young bride. Now it was time for her to leave and Toku was very reluctant to see her go.

"Must you leave so soon, Saki?"

"Yes, I must. Come and see me when you're in the city."

"Thank you, I shall. By the way, Saki, don't you think my mistress is behaving strangely?"

"Why do you ask such a question?"

"Here I am feeling utterly miserable at the thought of your going away, and yet she hasn't even mentioned her grandmother or Kudoyama."

Saki smiled.

"Oh, but isn't this the best time of her life? Surely you remember what it was like to be newly married."

"Nonetheless, she's among people who until recently were complete strangers. I should think she'd feel a little homesick," complained Toku, as she saw Saki off as far as the approach to Musota Bridge. The bridge spanned the lower reaches of the river near Shinrotsukai Dam. People called it One-Rin Bridge because a toll was collected. There the waters of the Ki gushed noisily from the dam, and a sound was produced different from anywhere else along the course of the river.

Toku heard koto music coming from the greenery surrounding her mistress's room when she returned to the mansion. Smiling smugly at the houseboys and maids of the Matani household whom she passed in the courtyard, she entered the house. Her mistress was doubtless the only bride in Musota who was an accomplished koto player. Toku wanted to shout it to the world that Hana had received a certificate of achievement from the Yamada School. Heedless of what people might think of her, she openly regarded with disdain the other members of the household. This devoted servant was intensely proud of the Kimotos. If she had her way, she would have gone about boasting that her mistress had been sought by far better families. Had Toku listened closely, she might have deciphered Hana's true feelings in her music, but, unfortunately, Toku did not have an ear for music.

Removing the picks from her fingers, Hana felt guilty about idling the hours away so soon after the wedding. She would never question the accepted principles governing the behavior of a wife. It was perfectly clear to her that her foremost duty was to adopt the customs and ways of the Matanis. But for some reason Hana's place in the household was elevated far above that of the other members.

Keisaku, the headman of Isao Village, had a bright future. Having been educated in Tokyo, he was somewhat of an idealist. Even stubborn old men listened attentively to his advice. He was, moreover, extremely busy. He was an important landowner, and he visited the homes of the tenant farmers in his spare time, getting them to develop an interest in new agricultural methods. He experimented in his own fields with various methods of cultivating tomatoes and other vegetables newly introduced from the West. He also showed visitors from other villages around the greenhouses he had had built behind his mansion. It hardly seemed possible that one man could do all that he did.

Meanwhile Hana's duties were very simple. She had to get herself dressed before her husband awoke in the morning, serve him his breakfast while he read books and magazines in English, and see him off. Tahei dozed all day long in the sun and Yasu did some sewing or patched some old clothes, whiling away the time seated quietly on the floor. Tahei entertained those who came to call. Yasu would occasionally appear to exchange a few pleasantries, and then return immediately to her customary spot. No special duty was assigned to the bride. Toku did the housecleaning and laundry, and Yasu took charge in the kitchen. There seemed to be no place for Hana in the Matani household.

Keisaku, returning home exhausted at the end of the day, was as kind a husband as Hana could hope for.

"Shall I play the koto for you?" asked Hana one day.

Her husband had taken a bath and was now reading the newspaper. Not in the habit of being so entertained, Keisaku stared blankly at his wife. He rebuked her gently, reminding her of the lateness of the hour. The beautiful koto, lacquered in gold along its entire length, was of no use at all in this household.

"It's like casting pearls before swine," complained Toku. Even though Toku did not have any real appreciation for music, she had been trained by Toyono and was proud of her mistress's accomplishments. Considerably disgruntled, Toku expressed her scorn for the Matanis, for not a single member of the family appreciated Hana's playing.

One day Kōsaku shouted from the front room:

"What was that you just said?"

"I said a man would never step foot in the kitchen in Kudoyama."

Toku had been terribly offended when Kōsaku came into the kitchen to draw some water. If he had clapped his hands, said Toku curtly, a servant would have prepared some tea for him. After all, wasn't he the second son of the Matani family?

"What nonsense! Remember, we're not members of the nobility. No maid in this household would pay any attention if I clapped my hands."

"I'm telling you that I would."

"Tea prepared by you would taste terrible."

Hana listened silently. Toku was at once giving vent to her frustration and trying to raise the level of refinement in the household to that of the Kimotos. Nonetheless, she was being impudent.

"Toku."

The maid bowed deeply.

"I'm sorry, but please go to Kudoyama for me," said Hana.

Hana slipped a letter into an envelope, instructing Toku to deliver it to Toyono. She also told Toku to take along the necessary personal effects for a lengthy stay.

Bewildered, Toku asked:

"Won't you be lonely?"

Hana, growing pale, ordered Toku to prepare her things.

"But I really don't want to go. Wouldn't it do just to mail the letter? Why do I have to deliver it in person?" Toku muttered to the maids. Her apprehension was not without reason, for when Toyono finished reading Hana's elegantly written letter, she burst into laughter.

Looking Toku directly in the face, Toyono said:

"You've been dismissed."

"Whatever for? What have I done wrong?"

Toyono could not help smiling as she tried to soothe the ruffled feelings of this loyal maid.

"Don't worry, everything will turn out all right. Now you can rejoin the Kimoto household. It isn't as though you were a bride being sent home in disgrace, you know."

Toyono moved closer to Toku, who had been deeply hurt.

"Tell me, is she expecting?"

"Not yet. She had her period this month."

Summer had come. A persimmon tree grew in the middle of the Kimoto garden. Toyono gazed at its luxuriant leaves and the carpet of green under the tree on this lovely afternoon.

"Oh, I see," she commented absentmindedly.

Even more than she longed to see her first great-grandchild, she looked forward to having Hana come to offer breast charms at Jison-in.

"Don't sulk so. Now tell me all about the wedding," said Toyono.

All went well, with the exception of one unfortunate blunder. No words can express my heartfelt apology. I have duly received the returned item.

Yours sincerely

Hana smiled to herself when she read Toyono's formal letter.

Showing no emotion on her face, she handed the letter to Kei-saku.

"Weren't you being a little harsh on Toku?"

"But I can easily take over her duties. I'll never feel that I'm in Musota if someone like Toku continues to do all the chores."

Keisaku studied Hana with an expression of surprise on his face, but he did not say a word. Immediately following the wedding, he spent each day hard at work. At night he embraced his wife with a young man's passion, but never did he discuss his work with her. This was considered perfectly natural, and Hana did not feel in any way neglected.

"It's warm tonight, isn't it?"

"It is indeed. How good it'd be to have a little rain."

His wife's words caused Keisaku to look up from his newspaper. He had recently been very much worried about the crops during this long period of drought. Nonetheless, he put the paper aside to discuss an entirely different matter.

"Are you acquainted with the Yoshiis of Iwade?"

"Yes, I am," replied Hana. She was too embarrassed to explain that she had stopped in Iwade on her wedding day.

"They're thinking about arranging a marriage with the daughter of the Handa family of Nishidegaito."

"Do you mean the main Yoshii family?"

"No. They're only remotely related to the main family. But they are encouraging a match with the Handa girl."

"That's good news!"

Hana suddenly recalled what Toyono had said about a bride moving against the flow of the river. Aware of her duty as a wife to be compliant, however, she felt herself unable to mention it to her husband.

"We'll have to think about a bride for Kōsaku soon."

"Yes, we will."

Hana remembered that the branch family of the Ōsawa clan of Jison-in Village had a daughter three years younger than she. The Ōsawas would feel offended if they had to negotiate directly with

Hana, who had earlier rejected a proposal from the main family. Nevertheless, if another family were to act as go-between, the branch family would probably be delighted to consider Kōsaku as a prospective bridegroom.

Hana suggested the possibility to Keisaku, who had someone sound out the Ōsawa family. Everything was done at a slow and leisurely pace in Ki province, and so it was not until the end of the year that they received a reply. The Ōsawas were casual about the proposal. Toyono encouraged the match and everyone was impressed with Hana. It was suggested that in time the young Mrs. Matani would become a brilliant matchmaker.

In the presence of his parents Keisaku casually said to Hana: "Please broach the subject with Kōsaku."

Hana's mother-in-law, narrowing her eyes over the brazier, commented:

"What a good idea! It'll be best to have Hana speak to him."

Tahei, never one to present an objection, was perfectly satisfied with whatever his son decided to do. Hana gave a deep bow and said she would speak to her brother-in-law.

Hana was embarrassed to see that the Matanis, fully aware of the difficult relationship between Kōsaku and herself, went out of their way to be tactful. Toku's impudence may have initially caused the estrangement, but, whatever the reason, it was obvious that Kōsaku had been treating his sister-in-law very coldly. Furthermore, the members of the Matani family had always tried to avoid a confrontation with Kōsaku. Hana did not know why the relationship with Kōsaku was so strained. Keisaku, a man of action, spent every minute of the day dashing from one place to another. On the other hand, Kōsaku, though he was a clerk in the village office, spent practically every day at home reading, frequently receiving packages of books from Tokyo. Having been brought up by Toyono who loved books, Hana had indeed been delighted to discover a person like Kōsaku in the Matani family.

"Kōsaku, do you compose *waka* poetry?"

Hana asked this question one day when she noticed a copy of

The Collection of Ancient and Modern Poems on the veranda, but Kōsaku ignored her question altogether.

Keisaku also had books sent from Tokyo, but they were highly specialized books on agriculture and cattle breeding. The scholarly tomes on economics and politics on his bookshelves did not appeal to her in the least. To alleviate her boredom, she longed to borrow books by such modern poets as Kitamura Shūya. Nonetheless, when she asked to borrow a volume, Kōsaku brusquely replied that he did not like to let his books out of his own hands.

Hana was painfully aware of Kōsaku's hostile feelings toward her. Her husband's request that she talk to Kōsaku about the marriage proposal was a difficult one indeed. However, she would have failed in her duties as a wife had she become the cause of further disharmony in the family; therefore, Hana, choosing her words very carefully, spoke to Kōsaku about the Ōsawa girl. Kōsaku listened quietly to all that she had to say.

"Do you mean the branch family of the Ōsawa clan of Jison-in Village?" asked Kōsaku, wanting to be sure he understood correctly which family she was referring to.

"What was his reaction?"
"He has apparently heard about them."
"He didn't refuse outright, did he?"
"No, he didn't."

Keisaku nodded and asked Hana to write a formal letter to Toyono to feel things out, for it was imperative that he give an indication of the family's interest in the match. Hana was both relieved and confident that once Kōsaku met the girl his attitude would change. She knew that the girl was attractive and that she had a pleasing personality.

Toyono's reply arrived together with her New Year's greeting. The status of the girl's family and her character would suit Kōsaku perfectly. How fine it would be to have that part of the province so intimately tied to Musota! At the end of the letter, she said that since the bride would be traveling downriver, the match was a good one. So strong-willed was Toyono that she did not mention her longing to see Hana or her loneliness since parting with her.

The Handa family and the Yoshii branch family of Iwade exchanged engagement presents during the New Year season. Tahei was also very eager to see Kōsaku formally engaged. Nonetheless, Keisaku stated that there was no need to hurry, even though it was he who had brought up the subject in the first place. Listening from the sidelines, Hana began to feel uneasy about the whole affair.

"Kōsaku wouldn't be this obstinate if I had divided up the family property years ago. There's bound to be hard feelings when everything is divided up after my death," said Tahei.

Hana was shocked to realize that when Kōsaku married he would be establishing a branch family. This was the usual fate for a second son, but Hana, who had only one brother, had never really had the harsh reality of this practice brought home to her.

"Hana said that we might ask her father to arrange a banquet at which we could look over the Ōsawa girl," said Keisaku on January 15, while they were having the traditional red bean gruel for breakfast. Hana had formerly taken her meals three times a day with Toyono, it being the custom in the Kimoto household for the women not to eat together with the men in the family. Here in Musota, Tahei, Yasu, Keisaku, Kōsaku, and Hana had breakfast together. A black lacquered dinner tray was set in front of each member of the family. Kiyo, who was over forty years of age, managed to see to everyone's needs. Keisaku and Kōsaku were the youngest of five children. Kiyo had once served eight, including the three older girls before they were married and Tahei's father, who had lived to a ripe old age. She was the most efficient of the five maids in the household and had been unable to get along with Toku during her brief stay.

Kōsaku noisily slurped his gruel. Looking steadily at the tray offered to him by Kiyo, he said:

"No, thank you."

"What's up, Kōsaku?"

"Do you mean the engagement meeting?"

"Yes. I'll go through with it as long as I can say no in the end."

The matchmaker would lose face if the proposal were rejected at that stage. Furthermore, the young girl would be emotionally scarred for the rest of her life. The venom in Kōsaku's words stunned Hana.

"You shouldn't feel that way about the interview," Keisaku answered. "No one can say anything unfavorable about Mr. Ōsawa and, as Hana pointed out, his daughter is a lovely young woman." Keisaku would soon be twenty-seven. A dedicated village headman, he had acquired a good reputation; he was respected for his candidness and not bothered in the least by trivialities. But Kōsaku was a stubborn man.

"The Ōsawas are members of a branch family, aren't they?"

"That's right."

"They wouldn't be able to afford a grand bridal procession with nine loads of dowry, palanquins, and boats. The bride will probably have only five loads of dowry and she'll come in a ricksha pulled along the shore. After all, I'll just be establishing a branch family."

Unable to contain his anger, Tahei shouted:

"Kōsaku, stop talking nonsense. Can't you see how your brother feels?"

Hana had never before heard her father-in-law raise his voice. She put down her chopsticks, feeling that the gruel had formed a lump inside her.

"How Keisaku feels? He's a graduate of a university in Tokyo and village headman. He's married to a girl from Kudoyama, and he'll be the next head of the Matani family. Oh, yes. I understand perfectly how he feels!"

"Fool!"

Kōsaku rose to his feet to leave the room. Turning back, he said in a low voice which contrasted sharply with Tahei's shouting:

"It's fortunate the eldest son isn't a fool!"

Keisaku gazed sadly at his brother's retreating figure. Tahei shook his fist, unable to bear the tension. Yasu, flustered, looked first at Tahei, then followed Kōsaku with her eyes. Hana moaned. Kiyo ran to the kitchen to fetch a dishcloth.

"I'm sorry." Hana, holding back the vomit with the sleeve of her long undergarment, felt herself transfixed by the gaze of her father-in-law and her husband. Without apologizing further, she ran to the privy, sensing that she was going to continue vomiting. The gruel she had helped herself to made its way sluggishly up into her mouth.

Hana had never dreamed that the wedding procession, so painstakingly and lovingly planned by Toyono, had wounded the pride of the younger son. It was understood from the time Kōsaku was born that he would one day establish a branch family. He had developed a gloomy personality from childhood because he knew what the future held for him. In an ordinary household, a girl accepted fully the superior position of boys. But Hana, besides receiving the same education as her brother, had been lavished with all the love Toyono had had to give. She had no recollection of having ever been treated as an inferior. The impact of Kōsaku's words on Hana had therefore been great.

Keisaku noticed that Hana continued to look unwell in the days that followed. One night when they were in their six-mat room which adjoined the sitting room, he gently asked:

"Are you still troubled by what Kōsaku said?"

"I can't help it. Besides, I don't know how to apologize to Father for being sick right there at the breakfast table."

"Don't worry about that."

"Kōsaku has never liked me. I shouldn't have meddled."

"Try not to think about it any more. I intend to give him much more of the property than he expects. I'll also put an end to the practice of having the branch family take on the name Handa and give him the Chōkui title."

"The Chōkui title?"

"Yes. In this part of the country, we're the only direct descendants of a samurai family. Well, I'm going to turn over the samurai status to Kōsaku and become a commoner."

Appalled, Hana listened to her husband's words. It was unheard of in 1900 for a branch family to take on the samurai title. Having been brought up in a status-conscious household, Hana found the idea outrageous and sat up in bed. A whirling sensation in her breast made her feel nauseous and she pressed her sleeve to her mouth.

"Is it morning sickness?" asked Keisaku. Hana looked up in surprise and blushed as her husband stared at her. She herself suspected that her illness was none other than morning sickness. Nonetheless, she lay down in bed without responding.

"It's warm tonight, isn't it?" whispered Keisaku, throwing aside the quilt to look at Hana.

The winter had been exceptionally warm in Ki province and it was difficult to believe that New Year's Day was fast approaching. The custom of celebrating the old Lunar New Year was still being followed in the provinces, though the Western calendar had been officially adopted in 1872. There were only a few families in Musota who, like the Matanis, celebrated New Year's Day on the same day it was observed by the elementary school. The farmers of Isao Village punctually greeted the seasons with the planting of seeds and the harvesting of different crops. At the Lunar New Year, which fell in February, Keisaku called upon the farmers, and the village elders came to extend New Year's greetings to Tahei and Yasu; before returning home they were given some refreshments.

"Today is New Year for us old folks," said Tahei, delighted. When he opened his mouth to cough, one could see that some of his teeth were missing.

"We don't have many years left to celebrate," he added. In spite of the warm weather, Tahei had caught a bad cold because of having celebrated both the Lunar and the Western New Year. He had aged suddenly upon turning seventy.

The engagement of the Crown Prince was announced in the papers not long after the New Year. Kujō Michitaka had received official word that his daughter Sadako had been chosen to be the Crown Princess. Hana read the article again and again, her heart brimming with happiness for the imperial family. Now that she was going to have a child, she viewed the world through rose-tinted spectacles. The Matanis were extremely solicitous and saw to it that she received the best of care. Yasu, who had previously been overwhelmed by the elegant speech and exquisite manners of her daughter-in-law, now followed Hana about all day long. The wall separating the older woman, the mother of several children, and the young expectant mother had crumbled altogether.

"Why don't you visit Kudoyama and pray at Jison-in for a safe delivery before your confinement? I've just been to Daitō-ji in Musota to offer a prayer charm for my ailing eyes," said Yasu good-naturedly.

"Thank you. I'd like very much to see my family," said Hana who had not been back to her father's home since the wedding.

Accompanied by Kiyo, Hana returned to the Kimoto home in May. She was especially careful, keeping her eye on the weather as she made her way along the River Ki. The river was breathtakingly beautiful under the clear blue sky.

Toyono had come out to welcome her granddaughter but found herself at a loss for words, so worn out did Hana look. She looked carefully at the young woman for a little while.

"It'll probably be a boy," said Toyono, breaking the silence. With these words, the Kimoto matriarch and her granddaughter fell back into the comfortable relationship they had enjoyed until a year ago.

Hana could not imagine how Toyono, who had lived each day solely for her, had managed to get along without her. As for Toyono, she did not speak of her loneliness. Delighting in each other's company, the two women simply reverted to their old daily routine.

"Would you like me to read you the newspaper?"

"That would be nice. Even with my glasses I can hardly read."

Hana began to read aloud the headline on the first page of the May 11 issue.

> Balmy breezes and blue skies of early summer. The cranes in the pines at the gate call out joyously on this auspicious occasion.

Hana read smoothly the beautiful lines, then slowly looked up at her grandmother who had been studying her profile. The two women exchanged smiles.

> His Imperial Highness and Crown Prince first appeared in the uniform of an army major, resplendently decorated with medals. At 7:30 P.M. in the Palace Sanctuary, he was attired in ancient court robes. The Crown Prince and the Crown Princess then performed their purificatory rites. Sannomiya Shikibu entered the Palace Sanctuary, followed by the Crown Prince to whom Chamberlain Maruo presented the Jeweled Sword. The Director of the Crown Prince's Household proceeded into the Sanctuary. He was followed by the Crown Princess attended by Ladies-in-Waiting Yoshimi and Shōgenji. . . .

Hana was able to read the article without stumbling over the specialized terms pertaining to the imperial court. The youthful ring to her voice belied the fact that she was in her fifth month of pregnancy. Toyono closed her eyes, trying her best to imagine what her granddaughter's wedding had been like. She had seen to it that her beloved granddaughter had received training in all the feminine arts. Even now Toyono sincerely believed that no wedding ceremony would have been too grand for Hana.

Hana could not bring herself to speak to her grandmother about her estrangement from Kōsaku. She was greatly relieved that Toyono had not asked her why plans were not being made to marry Kōsaku to the Ōsawa girl. She was determined not to bring the subject up, for the sole purpose of her visit was to make a pilgrimage to Jison-in.

"Have you brought the breast charms?"

"Yes, Grandmother. But they're clumsily made."

Hana had made the charms by wrapping a shiny piece of *habutaé* silk around some wadding to form a ball, then pinching and tying the center of each ball to represent a nipple. Studying the charms, Toyono remained silent for a long moment.

"They certainly are tiny," remarked Toyono, cupping them in her hands. Although the matriarch had never done any hard labor in her entire life, her palms were large and thick-skinned and her fingers strong-looking indeed. Held in such hands, the breast charms appeared very tiny.

"Please fetch my ink case."

"Yes, Grandmother."

Hana presently returned with the gold-lacquered ink case, which she had fetched from its customary place next to Toyono's reading stand. Seating herself in a sunny spot on the veranda, Toyono began to prepare some ink.

Nobutaka opened the door and peered into the women's quarters, something he seldom did.

"Please don't monopolize Hana, Mother. After all, I'm her father."

He was feeling lonely and neglected because his daughter, who had been away for so long, had been snatched away by his mother.

"Yes, I'm aware of that. I'll send her to your study in a little while. Please be patient."

Taking a step into the room, Nobutaka bent over Hana and inquired:

"What's that you're working on?"

"Nothing for you to see. Leave the room at once!" said Toyono, rebuking her son, who sheepishly slipped out of the room.

Hana slowly drew out the charms she had hidden under her sleeve. Toyono picked up her brush and wrote: "Hana age 23."

Once again Toyono and Hana made their way up the steps to

Jison-in. In attendance were Toku and Kiyo. It was nearly noon when the four women found themselves in front of the Miroku Hall.

Kiyo, being the tallest, hung the breast charms from a pillar at the entrance to the hall. Hana's tiny charms were dazzling in their whiteness among the older charms darkened by the elements. The May sunshine poured into the hall. Toyono and Hana closed their eyes and prayed.

Toyono stepped forward.

"Let's ask the head priest for a good-luck charm."

Toku ran ahead to the priest's quarters. She found it intolerable that Kiyo, a member of the Matani household, should be serving Hana so closely. As for Kiyo, she flaunted her privileged position before Toku, going out of her way to straighten Hana's collar and looking triumphantly at Toku whenever Hana asked a favor of her. Hana took note of the silent rivalry between the two maids and reminded herself that she was now a full-fledged member of the Matani family. She made up her mind to return home the very next day, even though her mother-in-law had given her permission to take her time with her family.

Nobutaka was terribly disappointed and tried his utmost to persuade his daughter to stay longer. Toyono pursed her lips and looked glum, her feelings deeply wounded. Knowing how stubborn Hana could be, however, she did not voice any protest.

The rice-planting season began the following month, and it rained ceaselessly in the northern part of Ki province.

"What rain!" said Keisaku, clicking his tongue in irritation. It continued to pour with no sign of a letup. However, by August it had become so sunny that everyone was confounded by the strange weather they had been having that year.

On August 25, Itō Hirobumi announced in Tokyo the establishment of a new political party, the Seiyūkai, which had long been in the planning stage. Keisaku was beside himself with joy when he heard the news and read aloud Marquis Itō's declaration.

Hana could not help but be amused: on the one hand, her husband worried excessively about the rain and its adverse effect on the farmers; on the other hand, he pressed the newspaper to his chest in childish glee.

"The baby's going to be a politician," announced Keisaku in an ebullient mood.

"Well then, I'll just have to have a boy."

"It has to be a boy. I've already decided on his name."

"Have you?"

"Yes. I'm going to call him Seiichirō. Matani Seiichirō. Isn't that a splendid name for a politician?"

True to Keisaku's prediction, Seiichirō was born on October 3. The women who attended Hana commented that the delivery had been easy for a first child. Hana did not quite agree. Her knowledge of childbirth, which she had received in bits and pieces, was practically nil; she had had to exert every ounce of strength in her body to have the child.

The Musota midwife forgot to liken the infant to a gem, as custom dictated she should have done. Instead, she described how beautiful the mother looked as she lay asleep in the bedding.

The rain, unconcerned by the joyous celebrations in the household at the birth of the first son, never stopped pouring down. Autumn, the season of melancholy, had arrived. The daughter of the Handas of Nishidegaito went as a bride to Iwade in the rain. Confined to her bed, Hana heard that the bride's dowry had filled three chests that had been covered with oilpaper to keep them dry. Keisaku attended the wedding reception, but Hana was not able to pay the bride a formal call the following day.

"How was the Yoshii wedding?" asked Hana one night when her husband came in to see her, proudly carrying his little son in his arms. Keisaku suddenly became silent and appeared preoccupied. Unable to press him further, Hana studied her husband's profile. A moment later he walked out of the room.

On his way back from Iwade, Keisaku had noticed that the waters of the River Ki were rising. Donning a raincoat, he followed the road to the river and stood on the embankment. In the pouring rain and the darkening light an eerie mist lay over the river. The waters raged at Keisaku's feet. Although he was certain that the embankment would hold, he looked out anxiously over the distant waters.

"Hello-o there!"

A man's voice could be heard from the direction of the river. Keisaku responded tentatively, wondering if he had heard correctly. A dark figure approached him.

"Who is it?"

"Why, aren't you Matani Keisaku?"

"Yes. And you, Kanada Shige?"

"What are you doing out in this storm?"

"I've come to have a look at the rising waters. I've been worried about the possibility of a flood."

"So have I. It started to pour a while back. Will Isao Village be all right?" asked Shige, scrutinizing the face of the young village headman. He was very much relieved to see that Keisaku was as trustworthy as his father.

"I think Isao will be all right," replied Keisaku, looking upstream.

"Look, Shige. Isn't that some lumber?"

"Yes, it is. That's terrible! Do you think the dam at Iwade has burst?"

Shige was only exaggerating, but Keisaku had already appraised the situation. Once lumber began floating downriver, it was only a matter of time before both bridge and dam gave way. There was no one to protect the residents of Musota, but there was one thing the men could do.

"Shige, run over to Sonobe. Tell the young men to gather here with their fire axes. I'll get in touch with Musota and Nōgawa."

"All right."

Running in opposite directions in the rain and darkness, one man headed east and the other west.

The River Ki flooded its banks from late that night to early the next morning, inundating a number of villages. At Musota the young men banded together and removed all the floating pieces of lumber they could reach. Various other precautions were taken, but it was beyond their power to save the dam and the bridge. It was most fortunate that Musota was built on slightly higher land. Moreover, because three years earlier Keisaku had had the embankments reinforced, the waters of the river did not overflow into the village.

A rumor started circulating at dawn the next day that the low-lying lands of Iwade had sustained the worst damage.

"Several houses were swept away, and quite a few people are missing."

"I hear several people died."

Led by Keisaku, a group of young men from Isao set out to aid the residents of Iwade in the afternoon when the rain had abated somewhat. The mother of the Handa girl was beside herself with worry and, ignoring those who tried to comfort her, followed the men.

"The groom was saved, but when he looked around, his bride was no longer there."

"After all, it only takes a second to be swept underwater."

"Poor girl! She probably lost her way. She was a stranger around here, after all."

"Poor girl indeed! Why, the wedding was just ten days ago. I can imagine how her parents feel."

Listening to her mother-in-law and the maids lamenting the loss of the Handa girl, Hana recollected Toyono's words. A bride should never travel against the flow of the River Ki on her wedding journey. How she regretted not having warned her husband about this superstition! Since Keisaku paid little attention to tradition or superstition, Hana was sure that the Handa girl would have gone to Iwade anyway. Nonetheless, Hana was overcome with remorse for not having opposed the match.

On her own bridal journey in spring, the movement of the

river had been quiet and comforting. And then again, how tranquil the river had been in early summer! Hana could not believe that that same river was capable of washing people away. Deeply regretting her reticence, Hana began to have serious doubts about whether submissiveness was really a virtue for women.

"Seiichirō. You're going to grow up to be a great politician, aren't you?"

Keisaku worked day and night dealing with the flood damage. Once he was home, however, he would forget his tiredness and go to see his son. He would waken the baby if it were still asleep. Putting his face close in front of the baby's still-unseeing eyes, he would say:

"Seiichirō. Grow up quickly!" His voice seemed to echo with the excitement of his work outdoors.

Because of his quick thinking during the flood, Keisaku became famous. He was praised by one and all for the way he had gone to aid Iwade.

"Don't play with the child so. You mustn't spoil him," said Hana, stopping her husband from carrying the baby.

"It's all right. He's my son, you know."

"No, you mustn't carry him!"

Keisaku looked at his wife in surprise. Elegant and obedient, Hana was as beautiful as ever. And yet a look or a word was enough to keep her husband in check.

It was a hectic time in and around the Matani household when Hana had her second child. Tahei had intended to have Kōsaku set up a branch family during his lifetime and thereby avoid placing the burden on Keisaku. However, two years earlier—before he could carry out his plans—he had fallen ill and had died at the age of seventy-two. Seiichirō, who was two at the time, crawled innocently about during his grandfather's funeral. Much to the dismay of the adults, he stuffed his mouth with the rice cakes ordered from one of the most famous shops in the west of Japan.

"Let him have what he wants!" said Kōsaku.

Hana was most annoyed to hear Kōsaku speak so coldly on this solemn occasion. As the fateful day on which he would be given his part of the family property approached, Kōsaku resented more than ever the Matani heir, his own nephew.

"Father said he wouldn't let me set up a branch family unless I was going to get married, but I'm already twenty-eight. I'm too old now to be getting an offer to become an adopted son. If war should break out with Russia, I may be drafted into the army. In the meantime, let me at least build a house of my own."

Kōsaku brought up the subject of the branch family in the spring of the following year, which had been greeted quietly by the family, as they were still in mourning.

"I've been thinking the same thing," said Keisaku, nodding. "Whereabouts would you like to build your house?" he asked, turning immediately to the more practical side of the affair.

"I think the area around Okunogaito would be ideal."

"Do you mean the land below Shin'ike? You're right. The air there is nice and clean. It'll do wonders for your health."

Kōsaku gave Hana a piercing look, as if asking with his eyes whether she knew why he spent his time idly at home, whether she was aware of the fact that he had been unable to pursue his chosen course of study because of a lung ailment.

"By the way, now that we're on the subject, I'd like to discuss with you the division of the family property."

Yasu, who had been dozing, opened wide her little eyes and fixed them on Keisaku. Lately she had been complaining about her poor eyesight and a whitish eye discharge. Her eyes were bloodshot. They all looked at Keisaku.

"What is it that you want, Kōsaku? I'll share everything I have with you."

Yasu and Hana sat in stunned silence. Kōsaku bit his lower lip with his small front teeth.

"I'd rather have the hills than rice fields."

"So it's the hills you want. It's just like you. Which ones?"

"All of them."

Keisaku was silent for a while.

"If they're what you want, you can have them. What else?"

"Just give me enough rice land to produce my own rice."

"I'll let you have the land from the bottom of the Matani land proper all the way to Tenjin. Hachirō and Kuma will be your tenant farmers."

"That's poor rice land."

Keisaku remained composed, even though Kōsaku spoke in such a bad-tempered tone.

"Anything else?" he asked, after turning over one-third of the land to his brother.

"No. Just leave me alone from now on."

"Done. Well then, there are a couple of things I'd like you to do for me," said Keisaku, sitting up straight.

"I'd like you to set up a new Matani family. Your name will continue to be Matani, not Handa. All right?"

Keisaku intended to abolish the custom of having the branch family change its name to Handa, a custom which had been observed for generations.

Kōsaku remained unmoved.

"Do you really mean that?"

"One more request. I'd like you to take on the title Chōkui."

This upset Yasu more than anyone else.

"Keisaku, the Chōkui title is virtually the same thing as the Matani name. If your father were alive, he wouldn't allow this."

Hana privately concurred with her mother-in-law, thinking that what Keisaku was proposing was completely out of the question. It was not acceptable for the junior family to strip the main family of its hills and samurai title.

Kōsaku watched as Keisaku's announcement took effect on Yasu and Hana, then turned to his brother, and said brusquely.

"I don't want the title. What use would a samurai title be to the head of a branch family? I'll become a commoner with a social status to match."

Not even thanking his brother for his generosity, Kōsaku rose to his feet as though his business were finished.

"There's no need for you to worry," he said very politely to Hana as he left the room. Keisaku was seething with anger at having been rebuffed.

"Fool! How warped can he get?" muttered Keisaku after he and Hana found themselves in the privacy of their room.

"I feel the same way about him!"

Realizing that her husband was extremely agitated, Hana abstained from expressing further her disapproval of Kōsaku and was careful as to how she dealt with him.

"The way some people talk, you would think that the head of a branch family is treated like an outcast. They don't realize there are any number of main families with no property to divide."

"Yes, I know."

"The second son of the Yamamotos of Miyanomae went to America. Kōsaku must realize that he's also a second son. What does that good-for-nothing have to complain about? Furthermore, if war did break out, a man in his physical condition would never be drafted. Even if he insisted on enlisting, he'd be rejected. What childish gibberish he speaks!"

Hana was taken aback to hear her husband heaping so much abuse on Kōsaku, knowing very well that he would never speak to his brother in the same tone. She watched her husband take off his haori, whip the tatami with the sash he had removed, and stamp his feet in anger as he changed into his night kimono. Her husband was behaving like their son, who was slowly starting to assert himself and who threw a tantrum when he did not get his way. With a smile playing on her lips, Hana quietly picked up the articles of clothing Keisaku had left scattered about, folding them and putting them away in the clothes box.

"Hana."

"Yes, dear."

"Come to bed."

Hana automatically removed the comb from her hair and pressed it against her sidelocks. Her hair was done up in a chignon with not a hair out of place The nape of her neck was of a beauty befitting a woman who had been married for five years. The villagers were now accustomed to addressing her as "Madame." In Musota this title was reserved exclusively for the wife of the head of the Matani family. It made Hana feel uneasy to be called "Madame" while Yasu was still alive. Nonetheless, Keisaku was now the head of the household and Hana was his wife. From about this time Hana took full charge of the kitchen, for Yasu had graciously relinquished her place to her daughter-in-law. Although Yasu still felt constrained toward Hana, she seldom complained. She had always been a modest and kind-hearted woman. After Hana took charge of running the household, the best she could do was to grow old graciously. People said it was on account of Hana's wisdom that there was no discord between the two women.

"Once Kōsaku sets up a branch family, you won't have many problems to deal with. I feel very much relieved, now that I've turned over all that land to him," said Keisaku.

"That was so unexpected! I was really stunned when you said you'd give him the land he asked for."

"Even if I gave all of the land away, I don't think I could perform all my duties as well as I'd like to. And if I didn't perform them, would people come to consult me as they do now?"

What Keisaku suggested was true. He was now thirty and widely recognized as the most efficient man of action not only in Isao but in all of Kaisō County. The prefectural government officials frequently came from Wakayama City to seek his advice. They broadly hinted that they would like him to run as a candidate for the Prefectural House in the near future.

"I may yet become a politician before Seiichirō."

"Perhaps you will."

"What have you been thinking about?"

"Oh, nothing in particular."

"Something's on your mind. Out with it."

"It occurred to me that you will be needing money to go into politics. If you give all your land away . . ."

Keisaku was taken aback. Money was of foremost importance in politics. A landowner sold his land in order to raise money.

Keisaku bit his lip when his wife questioned him about the wisdom of having all his valuable land taken away by the branch family.

"I didn't own many hills in the first place. Anyhow, everything in Kaisō County is still mine."

"Just Kaisō County?"

"What do you mean?" he asked. Hana was smiling serenely, her face illuminated by light from the lamp.

"Why, I thought that all of Wakayama Prefecture belonged to you!"

"Oh, Hana!" cried Keisaku, embracing his wife, happy to hear her express her hopes for the future. Whispering her name again and again, he resolved to run for a government office. Held tightly in his embrace, Hana felt that something had germinated in her husband. She recalled what Toyono had said about a family's social status being determined by the head of the household. Closing her eyes, she let her husband have his pleasure. Hana was certain that Keisaku would one day become the great man her grandmother had imagined he would be.

"Hana."

"Yes, dear."

"Kōsaku is so pathetic. It was all right for me to give him the hills, wasn't it?"

"Yes, I suppose so."

Thinking that he had drifted off to sleep, Hana slipped away from her husband. He then murmured:

"Actually, Kōsaku would rather remain in this house. No doubt about it, he's in love with you."

"What nonsense!"

"I don't blame him. He can't help being so perverse. Since I have you, it's a bargain to give him the good land," Keisaku muttered.

He closed his eyes. Having apparently found some peace of mind after uttering these words, he drifted off to sleep. Presently Hana heard the sound of heavy breathing. Her husband's nose and mouth were large and his face a deep tan. As he slept, his Adam's apple, which protruded considerably, throbbed from time to time. Hana wondered what he was dreaming of.

Dazed, Hana raised the wick of the lamp. She had been completely shaken by the words her husband had so casually uttered. Kōsaku was in love with his sister-in-law. Hana could not believe it, however plausible it in fact was. She had tried not to take seriously the words of the maids who had commented that Kōsaku had become increasingly difficult since she had come into the household. However, little did she dream that infatuation had been the reason behind his strange behavior. It was highly unlikely that Keisaku had thought of this only tonight. That he had not spoken of it in all this time filled Hana with dismay. She reviewed chronologically her relationship with her brother-in-law since her arrival, trying to prove that there was no truth to her husband's statement. This only made her feel more uneasy than ever. Kōsaku had always treated her very coldly. He was aloof and went out of his way to avoid her. Never for an instant had he behaved naturally toward her.

Hana had been a member of the Matani family for five years. She was now twenty-six and the mother of a three-year-old child. That the knowledge of Kōsaku's infatuation made her blush even now showed how greatly it offended the womanly virtues she had been taught to believe in. Hana chided herself for entertaining such fancies and, feeling deeply ashamed of herself, lay down in bed. The large quilt felt extremely heavy that night. She tossed about restlessly, lowering the wick a little at a time. Long after she had blown out the flame, she still had difficulty drifting off to sleep.

That autumn Hana visited her family in Kudoyama for the first time in four years. Eighty-year-old Toyono, in the best of health, came out to welcome her granddaughter.

"There's trouble in store for all of us. It looks like war again," announced Toyono, who continued to take a deep interest in national and world affairs.

"It's inevitable."

"Did Keisaku say that?"

"Yes, he did."

"He's probably right. But Russia is so much bigger than China. Have you read Dostoevsky?"

"Yes, I have," answered Hana.

Gazing into the distance, Toyono shook her head.

"Japan should avoid going to war with a country like Russia that has produced such great men as Tolstoy and Dostoevsky."

Toyono, who read each issue of *Kokumin no tomo* and *Miyako no hana*, was familiar with foreign literature.

"An article in yesterday's paper said that Kōtoku Shūsui and Uchimura Kanzō are going to abandon the antiwar newspaper *Yorozu Chōho*. With society in the state it's in, it'll be increasingly difficult for anyone opposing war with Russia."

"Has Keisaku been telling you this?"

"No, Kōsaku has."

Hana could not find it in her to tell her grandmother that she had borrowed Dostoevsky's *Crime and Punishment*, translated by Uchida Fuchian, from her brother-in-law.

"I understand Kōsaku is establishing a branch family."

"Yes, he is."

"Have they selected a bride for him?"

"No, not yet. He's just going to build his own house."

"That's strange. I wonder why?"

Needless to say, Hana could not very well say that it was because Kōsaku was in love with her. After all, she had no definite proof that what her husband had said was true. Nonetheless, ever since he was given permission to set up a branch family, Kōsaku had become very cheerful and friendly toward Hana. Whenever she asked to borrow new translations or novels by Kitamura Shūya or Nakanishi Baika, he willingly lent them to her. On one occasion he even urged her to read the essays of Abe Isoo.

"I'm glad to hear he's more cheerful these days. He must have made things extremely difficult for you."

Although Hana had never complained to her family, Toyono seemed to know about everything. As they had done four years earlier, the two women followed the road leading to Jison-in. Hana suddenly looked up at a persimmon tree by the roadside.

"This year is a good year for persimmons."

Kudoyama was famous for its persimmons. The large, sweet, rich-flavored persimmons were a bright orange among the dark branches.

"Yes, it's a very good year. But you know pregnant women shouldn't eat persimmons. What a pity you can't have any after coming all this distance."

"They smell so good I can hardly wait to help myself to some."

"How can you say such a thing? It wouldn't do to get a chill in the stomach," said Toyono, once again Hana's grandmother.

In a light-hearted mood, Toyono climbed up the stone steps without the assistance of Toku. On the other hand, Hana, who was already several months into her pregnancy, climbed sluggishly up a step at a time.

"Madame is so full of energy!" exclaimed Kiyo. Toku agreed.

"She's getting older, though. She can't read the paper any more, so she summons relatives from the main house and has them read it aloud to her from beginning to end. Moreover, whoever is summoned is made to read difficult books as well. Everyone complains that it takes all day to please her. And when anyone makes a mistake in reading, she says in a cutting tone that she wishes Hana were here. As for the members of the branch family, they feel rather aggrieved about it all," Toku reported in a low voice.

Toyono was now very hard-of-hearing and could not hear a

word of the maids' conversation. Listening in from the side, Hana realized that the two women were no longer competing with one another over her as they once had and reflected upon the years that had slipped by since she left the Kimoto household. She was now a full-fledged member of the Matani family, enough to make any woman feel satisfied.

The breast charms on which Toyono had written Hana's name and age were much larger than the ones Hana had presented when she was expecting Seiichirō. Having once been through the experience of childbirth, Hana no longer felt uneasy or embarrassed. She looked up at the charms which Kiyo had hung in front of the hall.

"This year will be a good one," declared Hana confidently.

"It will indeed be an auspicious one," responded Toyono lightheartedly.

The four women looked up at the other white charms near Hana's. It was apparent that a number of young women in the area were pregnant.

"It has been a long time. Do come in and have some tea."

The head priest's wife emerged from the priest's private quarters. So earnestly did she urge them to come in that Toyono and Hana accepted the cordial invitation and seated themselves on the sunny veranda. The woman then went to pick some persimmons and served them just as they were in the basket.

Hana was absolutely delighted.

"How wonderful! I'd love to have some."

Toyono reluctantly allowed Hana to taste the fruit.

"I suppose you won't get a chill from eating persimmons served by the priest's wife, but see that you don't overeat."

Hana took up a knife and skillfully pared a persimmon. Toku stared in utter amazement, for she had no recollection of Hana's being able to handle a knife so deftly. Furthermore, she could not imagine Hana working in the Matani kitchen.

After paring the fruit and cutting it into quarters, Hana placed the persimmon on a plate and offered it to Toyono.

"No, thank you, dear. I can't have any."

"Have you got stomach trouble?"

"Not at the moment, but I've made it a point to avoid anything raw, including vegetables and *sashimi*."

Hana ate the persimmon with relish and then wiped her lips clean with a tissue.

"My, that was good! In Musota they say that persimmons are especially delicious if you wait till they're really ripe and chewy. The proper way, though, is to have the persimmons when they're still crisp like this."

Toyono narrowed her eyes as she watched her granddaughter eat the fruit.

"I'll have a branch of our tree cut off for you in the spring. I should have thought sooner of having it grafted with a branch of Kudoyama persimmon."

"Does it really take eight years for a grafted tree to bear fruit?"

"No, it'll take only about five years. Your second child will be climbing the tree to pick the fruit."

Hana tried to picture an energetic little boy climbing the tree in the Matani garden. The baby was due in May of the following year.

Toward the end of the year, Kōno Hironaka, Speaker of the House, censured the Katsura Cabinet in a written answer to the Imperial Rescript. The Nineteenth Congress was recessed and public uproar reached a climax. The situation grew critical as the year drew to a close and finally, on February 10, war was declared. Because of the lack of accommodation for the reserves called up on such short notice, the soldiers of the Wakayama Sixty-first Regiment were billeted in the homes of the wealthy. The Matanis received a list of over ten names. To accommodate the men, they opened up the extra rooms in the house. The family, moreover, lavishly entertained the men as they would soon be going off to war, serving them saké and canapés every night and sometimes even summoning geishas from the licensed quarter.

Although she was in an advanced stage of pregnancy, Hana

worked diligently to see that the men's nightclothes were laundered and that the *miso* soup was seasoned just right so that the young soldiers from Shikoku would have a pleasant stay. The men were truly grateful. A few among them, blind to Hana's ungainly figure, fell in love with her lovely face.

"Madame, will you let us visit you when we return victorious?"

"By all means," replied Hana with a smile.

"But I may die in battle."

"Why should you? How could Russian bullets strike a son of the Land of the Gods?" asked Hana, trying to cheer the man up. Suddenly, his face darkened.

"I'd rather die in battle and become a war hero. If I come back, all I'll get is some rice land and cold treatment from my family."

Hana was overcome with emotion when she realized that the world was full of men like Kōsaku. The eldest son was exempt from military service. The young men billeted at the Matanis' were, without exception, the younger sons of farmers. They had learned from the Sino-Japanese War of a decade earlier that in going off to war, they were virtually going to their deaths. Hana's role was to cheer up these gloomy young men, but she suddenly thought of the sad fate of the child she was carrying. The second son born into the family, now that it no longer owned any hills, would be even more bitter than Kōsaku.

Feeling inferior to the soldiers who exuded good health, Kōsaku failed to make an appearance at the banquets. One day he deliberately snubbed Hana when she passed him in the garden.

"Who's that?"

"My husband's younger brother. He's going to set up a branch family."

The soldiers were in no position to speak ill of a member of a family to whom they were indebted, but they apparently took a dislike to Kōsaku. When inebriated and carried away by the warmth of a spring night, they would strip to the waist.

"Madame, look at the handsome flesh of real men. And then

take a look at that miserable lad over there!" said one of the men, giving his suntanned chest a hefty pounding with his fist to show her what he meant.

Keisaku kept the men company nearly every night, returning tipsy to his room in the dead of night. Hana knew very well that her husband could not hold his drink—one bottle of saké was enough to cause him to walk unsteadily. Nonetheless, Keisaku was a good host and could spend hours at a drinking party picking at his food. Instead of drinking, he would deftly maneuver the drinks to his drinking partner. For this talent, he was much admired by the people of influence in the village.

"Hana."

"Yes, dear."

"Have you visited Kōsaku? He's built himself a most unusual house.

"Really?"

"It's a quaint little cottage. The rooms are so tiny you and I would feel stifled. But he has apparently lavished a great deal of money on it. I had never realized that he was so free with his money."

Hana had been unable to go to the house-warming because of her pregnancy, but from her husband's description of the place, she saw that the house plan suited Kōsaku perfectly. He probably intended to remain a bachelor all his life. Hana remembered coming across the words "Platonic love" when she was a student at Wakayama Girls' School studying English together with Toyono. These words had a special significance for her now, especially since her husband had begun to frequent the gay quarters together with officials of the prefectural government. She felt that Kōsaku's love for her could only be described as being "Platonic." Remembering that she was pregnant, Hana felt thoroughly ashamed of herself for having such thoughts.

"You mustn't come to visit until after the baby is born, for the road leading to my cottage is very rugged. You'll find the architecture very unusual for Wakayama. Nonetheless, it's just big enough for a bachelor."

"You have only to say the word and we'll gladly send over one of the maids. Please don't be so formal."

"Why should I be? After all, I've been a member of the Matani family longer than you."

Kōsaku's mood was likely to change at the slightest slip of the tongue, so Hana commended herself for having made a tremendous effort to get along with him.

"Keisaku mentioned the other day how interesting your house was. I'm most anxious to see it."

"Come with the baby. I've dug a deep well, and so the water is sweeter than it is here."

"Oh good."

"If the baby is a boy, I'd like to make him my heir."

"We'll see. We're wondering if he'll grow up to be a bureaucrat."

"A bureaucrat? Bureaucrats are the most odious people."

Hana had made another blunder.

Studying Hana's advanced state of pregnancy, Kōsaku narrowed his eyes.

"If the baby is born on Boys' Day, I'll give you a special prize. I've already thought of a name for him."

"What do you have in mind?"

"Yūjirō. How does that sound? You'd then have both the Sei and Yū of Seiyūkai in the family."

The first electoral precinct was made up of Wakayama City and Kaisō County. Among the politicians representing the constituents were Tasaki Yusuke and Hoshi Tōru. Both men were vociferous members of the Seiyūkai. It was difficult to gauge to what extent Keisaku's influence had helped to advance the interest of the party in the Kansai area.

"What if Yūjirō turns out to be another Kōsaku?" asked Hana, thinking out loud.

"What do you mean? Yūjirō will be the village headman and Seiichirō, a member of parliament. I'd rather not have another son if he's going to turn out to be a good-for-nothing like Kōsaku."

It was a slightly delayed and very difficult delivery. Early in the morning of May 10 Hana had a baby girl, much to the disappointment of the baby's father.

"So it's a girl."

Keisaku's hopes for a political team of brothers were completely dashed. Hana sensed his deep disappointment when, seated at her bedside, he thanked her formally for her troubles.

"I'll have another baby."

"Of course you will."

Lantern parades commemorating Japan's victory over Russia were scheduled both in Wakayama and in Tokyo. Extremely busy seeing to the details, Keisaku left the house in the morning and failed to return that night. Yasu remained at Hana's bedside all day long. The next morning she hovered about, making a fuss over the baby.

Hana, still stunned by Keisaku's obvious disappointment, had forgotten altogether to thank her mother-in-law for coming to see her. On this occasion, there was none of the intense joy that had filled the house to overflowing at the time of Seiichirō's birth.

"The Kitas of Ryūmon sent us some sea bream. I didn't have any of it served to you, because I was afraid it might stop the flow of milk. However, please remember to acknowledge the present."

"Yes, Mother."

"You don't sound well. A woman is under such strain after childbirth that she often comes down with a strange illness."

"I'll be careful. I just feel utterly exhausted."

Yasu, startled, looked at Hana. Nervously taking out a scarlet silk handkerchief from her breast fold, she pressed it to her eyes. A messenger had arrived late the night before bearing the news of Toyono's sudden death. Yasu wiped her eyes, wondering whether or not to tell Hana.

"Don't worry about me. By the way, Mother, how are your eyes?"

Although she herself was having difficulty breathing, Hana was more concerned about her mother-in-law's well-being.

"They aren't any better, despite the fact that I've been taking Dr. Hirohashi's medicine. Father must be summoning me."

"You mustn't talk like that! How could I show you my devotion if you die?"

Thus rebuked, Yasu looked at Hana with bloodshot eyes. It had moved her profoundly to hear her daughter-in-law wish her a long life. Yasu realized that, if Hana were told about Toyono's death, she would recover from the shock, but, being timid by nature, Yasu was unable to report the sad tidings and spoke instead to her son who returned late that night from the city.

"I didn't have the heart to tell her," she confessed, asking her son to report the news.

"Hana."

"Yes? Oh, it's you. Welcome home. I'm sorry, I was asleep."

Hana hurriedly adjusted her hair as Keisaku looked down at her.

"We've received word from Kudoyama that . . ."

"Yes? What is it?"

"There's been a death in the family."

Keisaku did not mention who had died, but Hana swallowed hard. His dark eyes told her who it was.

"Oh? My, but it was sudden!"

"They say that two days ago, shortly after noon, she somehow fell from the veranda. No one worried at the time, because she didn't injure herself and wasn't in pain. But, when she failed to get up yesterday morning, they went to look in on her and found her dead."

Hana studied her husband's face in silence. Although she nodded each time he paused for breath, there was a terrible ringing in her head which prevented her from hearing every word. She could see in her mind's eye the face of her grandmother when she had refused the persimmon. It had been in autumn that they had sat side by side on the veranda of the priest's quarters.

Getting his things together, Keisaku announced that even though he might not be in time for the wake he was leaving at once. His newly tailored suit was appropriate for a lantern parade, but he had to have a black crested kimono for a funeral. Hana asked Kiyo to fetch the formal kimono from the chest of drawers.

"Has the condolence gift been sent on ahead?"

"I'm afraid not."

Hana had only now been informed of her grandmother's death and could not possibly have sent a condolence gift. Looking down at his wife who was struggling to sit up, Keisaku said gently:

"Don't worry. I'll say prayers for you as well."

"Thank you. I'd appreciate that."

In the still of the night, long after Keisaku's departure, Hana remained in a state of shock. Toyono's death had been so sudden she could not believe that she was gone. As the night grew darker, Hana got up to raise the wick on the lamp. The baby girl, born the day before, lay fast asleep in the tiny bed at her side. The nose and eyes, ears and mouth were still hidden in the soft flesh, but the baby was breathing regularly. She had been so sure that she was going to have a boy that the quilt with indigo and yellow stripes was patterned with helmets and swords, a design appropriate for the Boys' Festival in May. But she had had a girl, Hana reflected absently. It brought a smile to her lips to see the baby girl, who would be brought up elegantly, bundled up in a quilt with a design intended for a boy.

It suddenly occurred to Hana that the baby was the reincarnation of her grandmother. Toyono's spirit had left her body at dawn on the previous day and had been transferred to this child. Of this Hana was certain. When Keisaku had expressed his disappointment that the baby was a girl, Hana had apologized, saying that she would have another child. However, from the time she was thoroughly convinced that the baby was a reincarnation of her grandmother, she no longer felt tired. A wave of elation swept over her and she congratulated herself for having given birth to a girl. Hana leaned forward and looked into the face of the sleeping child, beaming with happiness, the mother of a beautiful baby.

It amused her to realize that she had not yet thought of a name for the baby girl. Her eldest son had had his name chosen for him six months before his birth. But this baby had turned out to be a girl; she could not very well be called Yūjirō. Hana was at a loss what to do. She studied the little baby closely. Tears streamed down her face as she thought once again of her grandmother's death. Returning to her bed, she wept softly.

Keisaku took no interest whatever in choosing a name for his daughter. Nor was this because the baby's seventh-day observance, when it was customary to give a child its name, coincided with Toyono's first seventh-day death anniversary.

As Yasu could barely read, Hana felt she should not ask her to think of a name. If Toyono were alive, Hana could have asked her. She did not feel it proper to ask her father who was in mourning, and so she was left with the task. She pictured in her mind's eye a brush running along the ceiling and writing out different girls' names. In the end, she decided on Fumio.

"A fine name," remarked Kōsaku who seldom praised anyone. He really believed that it was the perfect name for his niece.

"I'm glad you like it."

Because Kōsaku happened to be passing by at the time, she had consulted him first. Hana felt that there was something significant in the fortuitous meeting. Keisaku remained in Wakayama City for the victory celebrations; however, even on the rare occasions when he did return home, he had a number of matters to attend to in the village office. He also felt obligated to visit the elementary schools in Musota and Sonobe to confer with the principals. Therefore, he had little time for his daughter. Keisaku, who had never been interested in literature, became increasingly absorbed in politics. When Kōsaku praised her choice of a name for the baby, Hana felt grateful that at least one person seemed to care.

"Don't you find it inconvenient to be all alone?" she asked Kōsaku.

"On the contrary, it's rather pleasant. I enjoy not being nagged at."

Kōsaku was merely being sarcastic, for no one had bothered him much when he lived in the main house. Hana had grown accustomed to his awkward nature, but the residents of Musota and Sonobe treated him coldly at the village office. Fully aware of their unfriendly attitude toward him, Kōsaku became even more cynical. Hana knew that Keisaku was trying to force his brother to resign as village clerk, because he rarely reported for work. He lived alone after moving into his own house, positive that no maid would want to serve him. Hana felt that if she were his mother she would go to live with him. Anyone would willingly have followed Keisaku, but no one close to Kōsaku wished to go with him. Nonetheless, Hana was his sister-in-law. His own mother trembled in his presence, so afraid of eliciting a sarcastic comment from him that she was rendered speechless.

"Fumio's father won't give her any love. She's a lucky girl to have a doting uncle."

Apparently very lonely living all alone, Kōsaku often came to visit the main family. He adored Fumio, lavishing her with attention. Being skillful with his hands, he personally took care of everything, including—once he had found out where they were kept—the changing of the baby's diapers.

"I guess I love you as I do because I don't have a girl of my own. It'd have been traumatic if you had been a boy. You see, the family no longer owns much land. The lot of a second son would be even more wretched than mine when the time came for him to set up a branch family. It's a terrible thing to have nothing to look forward to except becoming an adopted son. I'm glad you're a girl. Fumio, you're so lucky you're a girl!"

Kōsaku strolled about aimlessly, carrying his niece in his arms. He now had a great deal of time on his hands, for he had resigned from his job. Taking care of the baby was also his way of getting some exercise.

"A cold evening wind has sprung up. Where could they have gone?"

Hana could never feel at ease when Kōsaku was with the children. Thinking that they might have gone to the shrine, she went out to look for them. Just then Kōsaku called to her from the gate.

"Welcome home. I was going out to meet you."

"Hear that, Fumio? Your mother has come for you. She didn't really have to."

"Where did Uncle take you?"

Following a few steps behind Kōsaku, Seiichirō replied:

"We went to see the pond."

"Pond? Which pond?"

"Shin'ike."

Hana was dumfounded. Shin'ike, which was located beyond Okunogaito, was where Kōsaku had built his house. Kōsaku, accompanied by his little nephew, had walked all that distance and back carrying in his arms a six-month-old baby.

"My, you've covered a great distance," remarked Hana, addressing neither Kōsaku nor her son. The road which led to Shin'ike was very steep. For this reason Hana had been unable to go to the house-warming during her pregnancy. She had yet to visit Kōsaku's new home, as she had until then felt weak from childbirth. Hana was surprised that her four-year-old son had grown big enough to walk all that distance and back. Kōsaku was not a strong man, so Hana worried about his having carried the baby so far. She also worried that Fumio might come down with a cold after having been exposed to the cold wind.

"She must feel terribly heavy after carrying her for so long. Come to Mother, dear."

Hana held tightly the small warm bundle wrapped up in the quilt. She and Kōsaku stood very still. Neither made a move toward the house in that brief moment which to both of them seemed an eternity. Then, pricked by her conscience, Hana took a step forward, although it seemed that her feet had been nailed to the ground.

"Look! The grafting has been successful," remarked Kōsaku, looking at the persimmon tree near the gate.

"Yes, it has," Hana answered, at long last able to breathe freely.

The branch which Toyono had sent over in the spring had been successfully grafted to their persimmon tree. However, the Matanis did not anticipate any fruit this year, as this was just the first autumn since the branch was grafted. Small red leaves clung tenaciously to the dark branch. It was obvious that the grafted branch was receiving nourishment from the earth. One could always be certain that there was life in this branch, even if it should fail to bear fruit next autumn as well.

"When do you think it will bear fruit?" asked Hana.

"How should I know? Ask Keisaku." Kōsaku then departed abruptly for home, ignoring her invitation to have some tea and rest a while.

Fumio began to cry in the middle of the night and Hana had a difficult time getting her back to sleep again. Keisaku was awakened by Fumio's crying.

"She cries a lot, doesn't she?"

"I guess she was outdoors for too long."

"So she's been outdoors, has she?"

Hana explained that Kōsaku had taken her and Seiichirō all the way to his new home. Keisaku frowned.

"Don't you think the children will get sick?"

"I'm sorry."

Hana bowed her head meekly, wishing to avoid an argument with her husband. She knew more about Kōsaku's illness than Keisaku. It had been carefully explained to her that the children could not catch Kōsaku's illness, even if he carried them in his arms. It therefore did not bother Hana to be thus reprimanded. She immediately turned to a more urgent subject that she wished to discuss with her husband.

"Seiichirō mentioned seeing a young girl at Shin'ike."

The villagers now referred to Kōsaku's new home as Shin'ike because of its proximity to a place of the same name. Her son had innocently remarked:

"There was a lady at Uncle's house."

Hana had been truly startled. Surely her husband would react in the same manner to this piece of news, she thought.

"I gathered as much," said Keisaku. It seemed that he had known about the girl all along.

"I didn't know about her at all. Is she from this area?"

"No, she isn't. If she were, I'd have known about her right away. He apparently brought her home with him from the city."

"Oh, dear! From the city?"

"Yes. It seems he asked a friend to help him find a maid. He's so intensely private! I don't care for that kind of secrecy. I just hope that this doesn't start any ugly rumors!"

"Is there anything suspicious about the girl?"

"Not that I know of. I haven't yet met her. She's presently serving as a maid in his house."

"Why, that's marvelous!"

"But there was no need to keep it from me. He's such a head-ache! Regardless of what he had said, he should have had a maid from the beginning to keep the house in order. Please check on the situation as soon as you can."

"Yes, dear."

Hana too had been worried. Now completely recovered from childbirth, she could visit Shin'ike if she wished to. This was a perfect chance for her to make a formal call.

One lovely autumn afternoon, Hana, with a small basket on her arm, headed north along the pathway through the rice fields. Most of the fields on either side of her had been harvested and men were busy threshing the rice; the grains were scattered all around them on the ground. They were using a threshing implement with six-foot-long pointed teeth which they pulled over the sheaves of rice to rake off the grains. The golden husks formed tiny mountains in front of the threshing device and the men who were operating it. As Hana looked on, the husks were scooped up and carried away by the women. The grains of rice, exposed to the strong sunlight, exuded a rich smell. In the Japanese art of incense-smelling, one did not "smell" incense, one "savored" it. Hana thought that she could truly "savor" the fragrance of autumn. Apart from Kudoyama where she had been brought up, Wakayama City was the only other place she knew fairly well. Surrounded by mulberry fields and rice paddies, she was now in the autumn of her sixth year since first coming to Musota. Still, the harvest season seemed to have a fresh significance for her. She could practically taste the rich fragrance of autumn rising from the fields which had produced a bountiful harvest.

Dressed in a haori with a fine design over a purplish gray silk kimono, Hana walked briskly though the fields. The tenant farmers paused in their work and called out to her.

"Isn't it a lovely day?"

"Indeed it is. You all work so diligently!"

"How unusual it is to see you out here. Are you heading any-where in particular?"

"Yes. I am going to visit Shin'ike for the first time."

"Oh? Have a pleasant visit."

"Thank you."

Each time a farmer called out to her, Hana stopped and bowed politely before continuing on her way. Her politeness was unaffected and the farmers, who had never been accorded such courtesy by their former mistress, were deeply impressed. They made a great effort to use polite speech, which they were unac-customed to.

"A lovely woman! It's hard to believe she's the mother of two."

"She looked quite a picture with that basket on her arm."

The farmers looked admiringly in Hana's direction long after she had passed. The villagers still talked about her magnificent wedding. They had the utmost respect for the Matani family, which had provided the village headman for generations. They felt, however, that Hana had finally given it some class. Hana's refinement and accomplishments had elicited the respect of the people, not the fact that she was from the prestigious Kimoto family. Even though she was a woman, Hana had won the villagers' affection.

Hana was well aware that all eyes were riveted on her, but she was not at all perturbed. Ever since she was a child, she had been so accustomed to being the center of attention that she did not feel at all self-conscious.

"Is anyone at home?"

Having been told that there was only one road leading up to Shin'ike beyond Okunogaito, Hana arrived safely at Kōsaku's house without losing her way. However, nothing stirred in the grounds of the house. Kōsaku had said that the house was small, but there was a large storehouse out in front and the house itself seemed to have considerable depth. One glance at the wood of the tightly closed front door told her that it was of a superior quality.

"Is anyone home? It's me, Hana," she called out in a loud voice. There was no answer.

Being a close relation, Hana felt that it was all right for her to go in and wait inside, even though no one seemed to be at home. Unlike the ancient, heavy door of the Matani mansion, the front door slid open when she pushed against it lightly.

"Is anyone home?" repeated Hana softly, as though she were speaking to the house. The concrete floor had been swept clean. Placed neatly side by side next to the stepping stone was a pair of clogs whose thongs were being loosened for daily wear. Whenever Kōsaku changed to new clogs, he would wear the new pair for short distances around the house until he had broken them in. The clogs he wore when he came to visit looked so old and worn that Hana had been thinking of getting him a new pair. Indeed, his fastidiousness was in keeping with one who intended to remain a bachelor.

Hana sat down at the entrance and peered into the house. Beyond the latticework door was the kitchen, complete with a modern stove. The sink and water jar were indoors. This impressed Hana, a devotee of the tea ceremony. Although she was eager to see more of the house that Kōsaku had personally designed, she could not very well prowl about an empty house.

Suppressing her curiosity, Hana carefully lowered the basket from her lap and removed the kerchief. The basket was filled with eggs for Kōsaku, who, being of a weak constitution, was in need of the extra nourishment. Keisaku had been successful in breeding a new species of hen that had been introduced from the West. Hana had selected ten of the whitest eggs and had brought them with her. This was not the first time she was presenting her brother-in-law with eggs. Chicken eggs were believed to have the highest nutritional value; therefore, whenever Kōsaku came to visit, Hana had him take home some of the eggs. The only difference this time was that she was delivering them in person. In an attempt to make the eggs look like a formal present, she had covered them with the tea ceremony kerchief she had brought with her as a bride and which she had not had an opportunity to use. The red handwoven brocade, embossed in gold with the Matani crest, was lined with white material on which there was a landscape painting in ink by Komuro Suiun.

Hana gazed at the painting for a while. She then took out an egg from the basket and gently tapped the pointed end with a coral hair ornament which she had removed from her chignon. Hana had no difficulty breaking the shell and leaving the membrane intact, though this required considerable dexterity. She then fitted the hair ornament back in her hair and gently, very gently, broke the membrane with her fingers. Placing her lips to the egg, she threw her head back and drank it all up. The egg white, mixed with the rich-flavored yolk, felt very soothing as it slipped down her throat. She believed that the egg would banish the tiredness she felt from having climbed the steep uphill road without pausing for rest. Hana also remembered that she had brought with her an even number of eggs, and one always presented things in odd numbers. Besides which, she firmly believed that eggs were a panacea.

After helping herself to the egg, Hana suddenly became aware of a pair of dark eyes fixed on her back.

"Who's there?" she inquired as she slowly turned around. Peering through the black, latticework door, she saw a girl standing in a corner of the bright kitchen.

"Who are you?" asked Hana gently, smiling as she rose to her feet. She knew immediately that it was the girl Kōsaku had engaged as a maid.

The girl looked timidly into Hana's eyes and bowed politely. There was nothing particularly striking about her eyes or nose, though she was petite and fair-complexioned. Hana wondered if the girl was totally lacking in manners.

"Are you the maid from the city?"

The girl nodded.

"I have come from the main house. Is your master in? Do you know where he is?" asked Hana in an attempt to get the young girl, who remained speechless, to respond.

"Will he be back soon? I should like to wait for him. Please make me some tea and fetch me a cushion," Hana said. She thereupon entered the house. The girl was back in a moment with a cushion, then withdrew to prepare some tea. Hana examined the girl carefully when she returned to serve the tea and realized that she was very young indeed.

"How old are you?"

"Seventeen."

"In what section of Wakayama City did you live?"

"Bokuhan-machi."

"Oh? Whereabouts in Bokuhan-machi? I lived nearby in Fuku-machi for six years."

Wakayama City was made up of four affluent sections: they were, from east to west, Suruga-machi, Fuku-machi, Bokuhan-machi, and Yoriai-machi. When Hana was a schoolgirl, she had lived with Toyono and Masataka in a detached cottage belonging to a prosperous cosmetics dealer in Fuku-machi. Hana was therefore immediately drawn to this girl from the city, from those four districts where wholesalers and merchants with huge storehouses did business alongside modest sash makers, pharmacists, and confectioners. The girl too seemed more at ease with Hana, who remembered nostalgically the city streets, and answered readily whenever she was asked a question.

Hana learned that the girl's name was Ume. She was a cousin of a friend of Kōsaku whom Kōsaku had known since his days in middle school. Her father had been a small merchant in Bokuhan-machi whose shop had shut down during the depression. Just as they were about to find themselves homeless, they were taken in by relatives. One day Kōsaku had hired her. When Hana asked Ume if she were serving as a maid, the girl nodded. Hana was suddenly filled with compassion for the child.

"How long have you been living here?"

"Since the end of summer."

"Really? No one realized that you were here until fairly recently."

"Yes, I know. My master gave me strict orders not to go out. He absolutely forbade me to show my face to the residents of Musota."

"How cheerless it must have been for you."

"Oh, no."

Kōsaku was probably very strict with Ume, for she trembled with fear at the mere thought of her master. Living together with a difficult man of twenty-nine was undoubtedly trying for a young girl who had seen little of the world. Ume was wearing a plain striped kimono. When she shrugged her shoulders, Hana noticed that the kimono she was wearing was made for a young girl. Hana could not help but be moved by the poor child's plight.

After chatting with Ume for a while, Hana began to wonder once again where Kōsaku might be. Just as she was thinking of leaving, he returned home. His clogs had not made a sound in the garden and he had opened the front door without a noise. The clogs in front of the stepping stone told him that he had a guest.

"So you came in while I was out, did you?" he asked gruffly.

"I'm sorry. I was going to return home, but Ume seemed so lonely I chatted with her about the city," said Hana. She then handed him the basket of eggs, handling it with great care.

"White eggshells may be fashionable these days, but I doubt the eggs have much nutritional value. Tell Keisaku they have very little taste," he said, again in a begrudging tone.

Nevertheless, he did not seem altogether displeased that Hana had come to visit him. When she complimented him on his home, he got up and showed her the various rooms.

The entrance, kitchen, and sitting room were in the sturdy farmhouse style, but his private living room and parlor were elegantly designed. What surprised Hana most was the detached tea ceremony hut with a tiny kitchen. A corridor connected it to the main house. It faced north and was located at the back of the house so that the rooms were darker.

"What a splendid room!" exclaimed Hana.

She bowed slightly before viewing the hanging picture scroll and censers, then sighed. Here was actual proof that Kōsaku had removed a number of antiques from the Matani storehouse. Even after six years of marriage, Hana had not yet been allowed to examine the family storehouse. It was ridiculous that she should suddenly come across those objects in the possession of the branch family. She had been married into the family and was yet to be regarded as a real member.

"Ume, serve us some tea."

"Yes."

"You'll find some bean jelly on the shelf above the chest in the adjoining room. Cut a few slices for us."

"Yes."

Ume jumped to obey Kōsaku's every command. In the past, even Hana had been rendered completely helpless by her brother-in-law on several occasions. She therefore felt very sorry for Ume, who at a tender age had to put up with such a difficult master. As the mistress of the Matani family, Hana felt that it was her duty to provide the girl with better kimonos.

"Ume."

"Yes."

"You know very well I have a weak stomach, so why are the slices so thick? And another thing, does one serve coarse tea with bean jelly?"

"Yes."

"Don't 'Yes' me. What are you going to do about it?"

". . . Yes."

No longer able to look on with indifference, Hana rose to her feet to prepare some fine tea.

"Please don't interfere when I am trying to discipline the girl. Small though it may be, this place is my castle," said Kōsaku. Hana was therefore unable to lift a finger.

Kōsaku continued to grumble about one thing or another. Finally, unable to stand it any longer, Hana sat up, bowed, and hurriedly excused herself. She could have remained longer, as her husband was away with officials of the local government on an overnight trip to Osaka. However, she felt far too uncomfortable to stay any longer.

"Allow me to come again," she said very politely.

"Please take the tea ceremony scarf with you. I've nothing I can offer you in return for it," said Kōsaku. A compulsion to be sarcastic was ingrained in his personality.

Hana made her way outside, where twilight shadows had fallen, heaving a deep sigh of relief. She was wet with perspiration. The kerchief she had slipped into her breast fold felt bulky. She was about to slip it into her sleeve when she felt in the lining of the sleeve the shell of the egg she had eaten at Kōsaku's house. Hana removed the crushed eggshell, the fragments of which were still held together by the membrane. Deciding it was better not to toss it into the rice fields, she waited till she reached a bridge spanning a stream which flowed from the pond and threw it into the water.

The white eggshell bobbed along slowly, turning again and again, before it finally caught on some small pebbles in the shallow waters. Hana stared at the eggshell and was overcome with shame at the thought of Ume having seen her swallow the raw egg in such a rough-and-ready way.

Hana's breasts felt swollen. Suddenly reminded of Fumio who was waiting for her at home, she loosened the front of her sash which was pressing uncomfortably against her breasts and quickened her pace.

On October 10, when the end of the war seemed far away, an imperial proclamation was announced enjoining everyone to persevere. On October 30, it was reported in large print even in the Wakayama newspaper that the Keiō-Waseda baseball tournament had been a thrilling affair.

"Look. The days of the Normal School are gone for good. It's three cheers for Waseda now!" cried Keisaku excitedly.

Hana knew much about traditional culture and international affairs but absolutely nothing about baseball. However, it was clear to her at least that her husband was ecstatic over the victory of his alma mater, once known as Tokyo Normal School but now called Waseda University. After Itō Hirobumi was appointed head of the Privy Council, Saionji Kimmochi became leader of the Seiyūkai. Hana now had serious doubts as to the strength of Keisaku's antibureaucratic convictions. Keisaku liked to think of himself as a tolerant man, one not taken to acts of rebellion. The vehemence of his brother's feelings against bureaucrats was anathema to Keisaku.

Hana told her husband about her visit to Kōsaku's new house.

"That was thoughtful of you. I feel sorry for the poor girl, but I trust you asked her to stay on," Keisaku said. "You know, Hana, Osaka is enjoying great prosperity, thanks to the war. The city has undergone a remarkable change. I'm afraid a person who gets too deeply involved with the affairs of Wakayama will be left behind. All the latest things are displayed in the stores. I bought a few presents. Just look at the things I have here."

Keisaku untied a parcel and took out the objects one by one. He was as delighted with them as a child with new toys.

"This is what they call aluminum."

"Really? Isn't it pretty?"

"Hold it in your hand for a minute. It's extraordinarily light."

"It really is. I can't believe it's as strong as they say it is."

This was the first time Hana had actually seen aluminum, though she had read in the paper about the discovery of this synthetic metal and how it had already appeared on the market. Taking it in her hand, she expressed astonishment in order to please her husband. She compared the two brothers in her mind: Keisaku watched the world change at first hand, just as he was doing now; Kōsaku, ensconced in his home, only read about the changes.

At the end of the year Admiral Tōgō and Vice-Admiral Uemura returned home in triumph. Port Arthur surrendered on New Year's Day of 1905. This marked the turning point of the war.

Carrying two-year-old Fumio in her arms, Hana made her way to Yaito Shrine, which was dedicated to their clan deity. Keisaku, who had accompanied them, listened to the drums of the Mikawa strolling dancers.

"It's the Western New Year we celebrate now. Now at last, the whole of Japan follows the Western calendar. Seiichirō, Japan will be so changed when you're big. How I'd love to be around then!" Keisaku exclaimed in a buoyant mood.

Seiichirō, now six years old, strained his ears to hear the drummers.

"They're in Yagaito. Father, may I go to see them?"

"Yes, off you go. Run along."

Hana smiled as her son ran off, full of the energy of a young boy. She and Keisaku strolled leisurely to their home in Agenogaito. Fumio was dressed in a colorful silk kimono which appeared very bright against Hana's breast.

"She's fast asleep."

"How different she is when she cries!"

When Fumio cried she could be heard as far away as Hinokuchi. Hana had visited the shrine of the guardian deity of children in Sonobe and had walked around its precincts a hundred times praying as she walked according to a prescribed ritual. However, her efforts had been in vain. Fumio still cried so loudly the entire household felt like pressing their hands to their ears. Once she started crying, moreover, it seemed as though she would never stop. Seiichirō had been quiet as a baby and even now was far from strong-willed. Hana watched him playing with the children in the neighborhood, thinking it highly unlikely that he would ever become a bully. But whenever Fumio started crying, her grandmother Yasu would rub her eyes and worry that the child would grow up to be very headstrong.

"Welcome home." Yasu greeted her son and daughter-in-law.

"We also said a prayer for you."

"Thank you. You must be exhausted. I kept an eye on the time and toasted some rice cakes."

Yasu's eyesight was slowly failing. Even during the day, she could no longer see clearly and therefore did everything by instinct. She had groped about to put the grill on the brazier and toast the rice cakes for her daughter-in-law and grandchildren.

One variety was cut into triangular pieces. Another, the *fuku-mochi*, was round and had red beans pounded into it. These two kinds of toasted rice cake had been dipped in soy sauce while piping hot; but even as Hana enjoyed eating them, she worried about Yasu's eyes.

"They're delicious! I'll go and pray at Daidō-ji after I finish my share."

"For my eyes? I've visited the temple three years running and there's no sign at all of improvement. Don't bother about me any more."

"But it's the New Year. Surely the god of healing will try a little harder. I'll go in your place."

Hana left Fumio, who was now wide awake, in Kiyo's care. After greeting the tenant farmers who had come to extend their New Year's greetings, she set out for Daidō-ji Temple. She slipped into her clogs and was hurrying through the garden when she heard the sound of a child crying. Wondering what could be the matter, she looked in the direction of the gate and saw her son. Surrounded by several children, he had covered his face with his hands.

"What in the world happened?" she asked. Seiichirō was weeping so hard she could not get a word out of him. The other children told her why he was crying. They had begun to tease the strolling dancers whom they had been following. One of the dancers was so provoked he shouted angrily and began to chase them. Seiichirō being a slow runner, the dancer had caught him and hit him on the head with his fan.

Seiichirō, the Matani heir, had been protected by his family all his life. His parents had never had to raise a hand against him, for he had always been an obedient child. It had therefore come as a terrible shock for him to be struck on the head by a strolling dancer. Hana, feeling that her pride had been deeply wounded, remained speechless for a moment. She did nothing to soothe Seiichirō, who would not stop crying. On the contrary, she felt a sudden chill in her heart as she watched her eldest son, who had none of Fumio's vitality, wailing in such a wretched manner. Was it normal for a boy to cry like this? What a depressing sight to behold on New Year's Day, she thought, as she set out for the temple.

The votive tablet which Yasu had hung from the lattice in front of the Main Hall of Daidō-ji three years earlier looked old and weather-beaten. It was generally believed that if one painted eyes on it, it would be efficacious in curing ailments of the eye. Yasu had lost her husband. One of her sons was married and the other, the head of a branch family. Practically blind at the age of seventy-one, she must have felt very lonely indeed when she brought her hands together in prayer. Toyono had grown old enjoying the best of health; moreover, her death had been painless and sudden. Hana tried to imagine what the last years of her grandmother—who had said what she wanted to say and done what she wanted to do—had been like. In striking contrast, her mother-in-law's last years, though peaceful and not lacking in material comfort, seemed sad indeed.

The strolling dancers had probably reached Sonobe by now, for the drums could no longer be heard. On her way home, Hana thought of calling at Shin'ike. However, her husband would consider it a breach of etiquette if she, the mistress of the main family, were to go to Kōsaku's house before he came to extend his formal New Year's greetings. Looking to the west as she descended the stone steps, she noticed a man and a woman coming from the direction of Shin'ike. She could see that it was Kōsaku and Ume.

That Kōsaku would even think of visiting the Matanis on New Year's Day accompanied by his maid showed a total lack of common sense on his part. Staring incomprehensibly at the couple, Hana stood stock still for what seemed an age. Kōsaku walked ahead, then turned back to say something to Ume who timidly responded. Presently the couple moved forward again as though nothing had happened. After a while, Kōsaku again came to a stop to speak to Ume, apparently to scold her for being so slow.

Ume looked miniscule as she followed behind her tall, thin master. She all but ran after him but still found it difficult to keep up. Again Kōsaku turned back.

Hana remained rooted to the deserted pathway until the two figures disappeared from view. Her intuition told her at once that the relationship between the two was as intimate as Keisaku feared it was. She felt her heart grow numb, though this revelation should no longer have caused her any surprise. Hana had unconsciously sensed the true nature of their relationship when she first visited her brother-in-law.

Kōsaku was not among those who greeted Hana upon her return home.

"Has Kōsaku already left?" she asked. She was then informed by her maids that he had not yet made an appearance. Hana wondered where the two had gone. They ought to have arrived before her. Had they postponed their New Year's greetings and set out for the city? Hana was pondering these thoughts when Kōsaku alone entered the house.

"Happy New Year!"

"Is that you, Kōsaku? We've been waiting for you. Hana, pour him some saké."

Keisaku was in an ebullient mood, eager to celebrate fully the first New Year's Day since the establishment of the branch family. Kōsaku meekly took up the saké cup as Hana, barely able to control her trembling hands, poured the saké.

"Stay with us until the third. It'll be dreary spending the New Year all alone."

"To tell the truth, I've never cared for the New Year. Like you, I can't drink. And I have no place in particular to visit. And by the end of the year I've had my fill of rice cakes. And anyway, it makes little difference to me whether I'm alone or in a crowd, I think New Year celebrations are a terrible bore!"

"You really do speak your mind, don't you?"

Keisaku laughed, highly amused by his brother's crankiness. When they had lived together, it had often annoyed Keisaku to see his brother's sullen face. However, now that they lived in separate households, Keisaku was happy to greet the New Year in Kōsaku's company.

"I think I'll stay for a few days, after all."

"Please do," said Hana graciously.

"Would you like to toast some rice-cake blossoms, Uncle?" asked Seiichirō. Delighted to see his uncle, he had been hovering nearby. It was strange that Kōsaku, ostracized by adults, should be adored by children.

"If you take down all the rice-cake blossoms on New Year's Day, the next few days will seem so colorless."

"But one branch wouldn't do any harm, would it?"

"I suppose no one will miss a single branch," said Kōsaku. Surely the fact that he could speak in such an easygoing manner to a child was a sign there was something more to him.

The "blossoms" were pieces of rice cake which were suspended like cocoons from willow branches. They were pink or yellow in color and were used to decorate the house over the New Year. Children would eye the tempting morsels hanging from the doorway of each room. They were put up as decoration, and so parents generally forbade the children from taking them down during the first seven days of the New Year. Child though he was, Seiichirō knew that no adult in the household would dare oppose his uncle's wishes. Keisaku narrowed his eyes and looked fondly at his son who licked the rice cakes hanging from the branch. He was convinced that his son would grow up to be a man of great wisdom. On the other hand, Hana felt apprehensive about her son who would not chew the rice cakes properly. A typical boy would even chew glutinous jelly with gusto.

A stream of visitors flowed in and out of the house. Besides the tenant farmers, many villagers had been coming regularly for many years to call on Keisaku. Having heard rumors that he would soon be running for a prefectural office, the village elders came to pay their respects. Things were especially lively because the members of the Young Men's Association were drunk and rowdy. Keisaku was all smiles as he offered saké to one and all, sending them home thoroughly drunk.

Hana got up now and then to see that everything was in order. After greeting her guests, she withdrew to the adjoining eight-mat room. There she joined Yasu and Kōsaku, who were seated around a big porcelain brazier, and listened to Kōsaku.

"You shouldn't always wear your hair in an old-fashioned chignon. How about trying a more fashionable coiffure?"

"Keisaku tells me to do the same thing. Saki also urges me to try a new hairdo on her once-a-month visits. But personally, I feel rather embarrassed about experimenting with something new."

Blinking her eyes with which she could hardly see, Yasu remarked:

"The Kagetsumaki hairstyle seems to be very popular these days."

"Mother, that's an extremely vulgar hairstyle!"

"Is it really?"

"Indeed it is. It became popular among the maids serving in the houses of assignation, so how could it possibly be elegant? It's best to do one's hair up in a stylish chignon. The next time Saki comes, have her do your hair up in a new style."

"I'll think about it."

Hana chatted amiably with them, but she was still thinking about Ume, whom she had seen with Kōsaku a short while ago. She had no particular reason to mention Ume but could no longer suppress her curiosity.

"If you're going to stay for a few days, you should have brought Ume along."

"Whatever for?" asked Kōsaku indignantly.

"For no special reason. I just thought she'd be lonesome by herself over the New Year, that's all. She'd find it more fun to be with the maids," she explained quickly. But it was already too late. Kōsaku had become very glum.

"A maid's duty is to look after the home. I refuse to take orders from the lady of the house on such private matters."

Hana apologized and Yasu interceded, but nothing could keep Kōsaku from stalking out of the house. Keisaku later heard about the incident and was filled with disgust. He could not blithely dismiss the matter with a laugh, saying that his brother was as difficult as ever. Yasu sighed again and again, muttering that her son would never be cured of his willfullness.

Hana now had definite proof that Kōsaku was in love with Ume. Nevertheless, she knew that he would never admit that he loved the young girl he had brought into his house as a maid.

Now that she knew Kōsaku and Ume were on intimate terms, Hana tried to cure herself of her own infatuation. The shame she now felt as she remembered having once been strongly attracted to Kōsaku was as great as the shame she had experienced after being seen by Ume helping herself to a raw egg. But Hana's pride had not been wounded, for she had been the first to detect the true nature of the relationship between Kōsaku and the girl, possibly even before Kōsaku himself.

This past summer when she visited Shin'ike, Hana had noticed that Ume's eyebrows were growing thin, a supposed sign of pregnancy. She now reported this to her husband. Hana had mulled over the situation for a long time. However, feeling guilty about trying to drive Ume away from Kōsaku's side, she felt unable to consult anyone, even Yasu.

"Are you sure about this?" Keisaku was completely stunned. Much to Hana's astonishment, he lost his composure altogether.

"One can't be absolutely sure without asking Kōsaku himself, but I'm reasonably certain."

"What has he gone and done now? It'll be a scandal once it's known in the village. Send Ume home at once. Then we'll discuss what's to be done."

"If you send her home, everyone will hear about it. It's just a matter of whether they find out now or later, that's all."

"You really are cool-headed. If Kōsaku has got the girl pregnant, I'll have to seriously consider resigning as village headman and forget about entering politics."

Keisaku was indeed speaking the truth. In exchange for wielding absolute power, the head of a family had to bear on his shoulders the responsibility for the conduct of each member. Keisaku's reputation would be completely ruined by any indiscretion on Kōsaku's part. His dreams of the future were about to be dashed.

"I'll dole out any sum of money. Please find a solution."

"Then people will say that you paid to have the child aborted."

"We mustn't endanger the mother's life. Let her have the baby. I'll pay to have the child given away."

"Ume's parents are dead. Her relatives will never be satisfied, no matter how much money you hand over."

Keisaku studied his wife's face and saw that she had a plan in mind.

"What do you suggest we do?"

"Ume's family isn't wealthy, but the match is not entirely out of the question.

"Yes. And so?"

"Kōsaku's personality being what it is, no other girl will put up with him. I suggest that we formally welcome Ume into the family as his bride."

"People will talk, regardless of what I do. They'll say that Kōsaku seduced his maid and had to marry her."

"But nobody will say that Keisaku did anything cruel."

Keisaku folded his arms. He was not thinking about whether or not he should go along with Hana's suggestion. It was obvious that she had taken into consideration the well-being of all three people most intimately involved: Kōsaku, Ume, and himself.

Several days later, Keisaku set out for Shin'ike and returned late that night with Ume. Kiyo made her way to Shin'ike the next day to take Ume's place as a maid; she was to serve in that capacity until autumn. In the meantime, Ume was to receive training in etiquette and home-making.

Hana went to Wakayama City to make arrangements for Ume's bridal kimonos at a shop in Yonchō-machi. Needless to say, the kimonos could not be elaborate because it was a rush job. However, Hana did her best to be more extravagant than she would have been for an ordinary maid. The baby was expected within three months of the wedding; therefore, all preparations had to be informal.

Hana was planning to wear at the ceremony a kimono with medium-length sleeves. When she sent out Ume's kimonos to be dyed, she boldly changed the crests to an ivy motif, as she had never been happy with the Matani quince crest. She recalled that Toyono, who had not cared for the Kimoto crest, had selected for herself the ivy crest. From ancient times, the ivy which grew around its own central stem symbolized positive feminine

characteristics. Hana felt that she had every right to change the
crest in this apparently arbitrary way. She was too pressed for
time to think deeply about Toyono's reasons for selecting the
ivy crest, but it did occur to her that Toyono's mother's family
had also had an ivy crest, although of slightly different design.
Or was it that her great-grandmother had not wanted to use the
crest of her husband's family and had therefore designed her own?
How Hana enjoyed imagining what things were like back in the
distant past.

Hana had one of Ume's wedding kimonos dyed with the quince
crest, since she desired above all to avoid being criticized by her
brother-in-law. In the meantime, she thought about an appropriate crest for Ume to use regularly after her wedding. Hana,
who was twenty-eight, worked enthusiastically on the wedding
preparations for Ume, who was ten years younger. She enjoyed
immensely every minute, as though she were the girl's mother.
In time she began to feel kindly toward Kōsaku and treated him
with special care.

Kōsaku stopped visiting Agenogaito altogether after Ume was
taken into the Matani household. He was extremely sullen when
Hana made her way to Shin'ike to discuss with him some matter
involving Ume's relatives. The dark expression on his face showed
that he was not at all sorry to have caused all the fuss. In fact, he
was very much displeased that Hana had not minded her own
business. Furthermore, he refused to answer Hana civilly, turning
angry eyes upon her more openly than during the first years of
her marriage. And when Seiichirō went to visit his uncle, he was
coldly turned away.

The whole village was in a furor. Keisaku therefore postponed
running for a prefectural office and spent each day brooding over
his disappointment, especially after hearing that Hana's brother
was running for an office in Ito County. But this didn't seem to
bother Kōsaku. He remained idle at home, doing nothing when
he felt too agitated to read.

The two brothers were miserable indeed. Hana, however,

looked forward eagerly to the wedding. Just as she had predicted, Keisaku's reputation had not been hurt in the least. On the contrary, everyone sympathized with him, for he had voluntarily withdrawn from the political race. Nor was Kōsaku's reputation, which was not good to begin with, further damaged.

No one expected Kōsaku's bride to be so ordinary, but the villagers extended their goodwill to the girl when they heard that Hana was treating her kindly. In short, everything turned out well because of Hana's efforts.

"Even though you find it difficult at times, don't forget what they say about cleaning the toilet. You want to have a pretty child, don't you?"

"Yes. I'll do my best."

"And after your wedding, be sure to wear your kimono a little longer. As the mistress of the branch family, you must be refined."

"Oh, but no one will call me 'Mistress'!"

"All right, then, you can go on being called the Shin'ike Bride until you're old and gray."

"That won't do!"

The two women laughed merrily.

PART
II

THE GIRL had her head covered with a long white woolen shawl twisted loosely around her neck, one end falling forward and the other trailing in the wind. Her green cashmere hakama skirt appeared somewhat strange; two white stripes ran around the hemline. Over a dress of handwoven striped cotton, she was wearing a silk haori. Her stockinged feet were visible under the short hakama. It was clear to see that she was a student at Wakayama Girls' School. No one could help but stare on seeing her for the first time, striding boyishly across the bridge. Dressed as she was, however, Fumio would not have startled anyone living in this area. The eldest Matani daughter had been an attraction in the village for years. After entering the Girls' School, she, together with her father, had become increasingly famous.

"That's the eldest daughter," whispered the villagers. Sometimes they were critical of the girl, at other times they could do little else but express their bewilderment.

Fumio did not care what people said about her. In fact, she reveled in making people frown. This had certainly been true when she had protested against the practice of wearing maroon hakamas. A classmate, imitating the members of the famous Takarazuka All-Girls' Revue, had once worn a green hakama to school only to be severely reprimanded by the teachers. Fumio had rebelled against the teachers, arguing that, "Nowhere in the school regulations does it say that we have to wear maroon hakamas." She then encouraged her classmates to join her in wearing green hakamas. At this very moment, there was further proof of her rebelliousness. Dangling from the white trimming of her bright green hakama, which she had been wearing for the past year oblivious to all opposition, were twenty Kewpie dolls, each one over an inch tall. She would probably have maintained that, "Nowhere in the school regulations does it say that we cannot wear Kewpie dolls." With typical audacity, Fumio had begun this new protest after a classmate had been reprimanded for pinning fashionable trinkets onto the trimming of her hakama.

Fumio strode on, unconcerned by the dust gathering on her black shoes and mercilessly kicking the hem of her hakama with each step she took. The little Kewpie dolls danced merrily about and rolled their eyes as she crossed Musota Bridge. Under the bridge the blue waters of the River Ki flowed gently as in years gone by.

At the beginning of the Taishō era, the sobriquet of Musota Bridge was changed from One-Rin Bridge to One-Sen Bridge in line with the higher toll. Each time the river overflowed its banks, the bridge was swept away. No sooner was it rebuilt than the men involved would celebrate its completion with a banquet. It was therefore whispered that a new bridge meant another feast for the members of the Prefectural House.

The abundant waters of the River Ki, which was known nearer its source, in Yamato province, as the River Yoshino, flowed to the sea from east to west, taking with them the waters of both Yamato and Ki provinces. The villages along the river's banks were in danger of being flooded whenever the waters rose. However, in all of Kaisō County, Musota had always been an exception. There had never been any landslide near the mountains nor any flood damage along the banks of the river. The residents of Musota had therefore never been too concerned about natural calamities. And if the bridge were swept away by flood waters, no one in the village was so poor he would suffer from giving a hand to help in rebuilding the bridge.

Since Musota Dam in the northwestern sector of Kaisō County was used for irrigation purposes, there was no danger of a flood even if the dams at Musota and Sonobe were breached. Furthermore, Keisaku's grandfather had worked diligently to ensure that nearly all the rice paddies could draw their water from the ponds at the foot of the mountains.

Not even during the Great Drought mentioned in the history of Ki province had Musota sustained any damage.

Upon being elected a member of the Prefectural House in 1906, Keisaku had strongly urged that the rice paddies along the Ki draw their water from the river. He sincerely believed that if his plan were implemented, the damage to the villages on the lower reaches of the river would be greatly reduced in a flood. His wife had often voiced her opinion regarding the flood damage sustained by Iwade, saying "Isn't it because the abundant waters of the Ki aren't made full use of?" That Hana's words had been behind Keisaku's plan, however, was not known to a soul.

Keisaku set up plans for the rice paddies in Isao Village to draw their water from Iwade Dam and went as far as to invest his own money to cover half of the project's cost. To obtain the money for his contribution, he sold part of his rice land. This act of magnanimity made it possible for the irrigation works in Waka-yama Prefecture to flourish. For years the Land Improvement Association and Ki River Water Utilization Association had existed in name only, but they effected noteworthy changes now that Keisaku was a member of the board of directors.

Keisaku's fame grew after each flood. It is said that people will follow a leader who is sincere. No one opposed the choice of thirty-eight-year-old Keisaku as the Speaker of the House. His boundless capacity for work, his generosity in using his own money, and his sincerity inspired admiration among his constituents. This year his eldest daughter was about to graduate from school and he had already served as Speaker of the House for over ten years. The titles he held were too numerous to be printed on a single name card. To begin with, he was chairman of the board of directors of the Water Utilization Association and chairman of the Prefectural Agricultural Association. Even in the remotest mountain village of Wakayama Prefecture, everyone knew of Matani Keisaku.

Reports of Fumio's wild behavior were circulated all the more widely because of her father's fame. The young girl, who had inherited many of her father's characteristics, was neither hated nor resented by anyone. She had her father's panache, which won her a certain amount of admiration, but she was considered a nuisance by many. On one occasion Fumio's behavior reached a point where her mother was summoned to school by Fumio's teachers.

"We are fully conscious of the fact that she is Mr. Matani's daughter and find ourselves unable to reprimand her in front of the other students. However, when we summon her privately into the Teachers' Room to give her a word of warning, she overwhelms us with a flood of words. So we'd like you, please, to try to reason with her."

Having found it difficult to deal directly with Fumio, the teachers now beseeched the girl's mother to take over.

"I am truly sorry that she has caused you so much trouble. By the way," Hana added, "do you think that Fumio is a flirt? That possibility worries me above all else."

"No," one of the teachers answered. "She doesn't write notes to boys at the Middle School; she doesn't seem interested in the opposite sex at all. I once happened to overhear her speaking to her friends. If anything, she is too prim. Despite the fact that she wears green hakamas, she said that she had once seen a performance of the Takarazuka All-Girls' Revue and thought it was positively ridiculous. I may be exaggerating, but what I consider dangerous is her thinking. I suppose she has been greatly influenced by Mr. Tamura, for even now she's always talking about 'democracy'."

"She really did cause a great deal of trouble at that time, didn't she?" Hana again expressed her deepest apologies.

Mr. Tamura was a young Japanese-language teacher who had come to his new post in Wakayama when Fumio first enrolled in the school. A recent graduate of the Faculty of Letters of Tokyo Imperial University, he set aside the textbooks during his classes and expounded upon "freedom" and "democracy." Whenever he opened the poetry journal *Red Bird* he read aloud the new-style poems and enthusiastically encouraged Fumio and her classmates to be modern in every respect. Wakayama Girls' School, whose motto was "Be Good Wives and Wise Mothers," found the presence of such a teacher extremely embarrassing. Despite his popularity among his students, Mr. Tamura was harshly reprimanded on numerous occasions by the administration. Persecuted by his superiors, he was finally expelled from the teaching profession. This had been the "incident" of the previous year. Fumio had been so enraged she rallied together the girls who supported Mr. Tamura and argued with the school administration. Girls of Ki province were by no means weak, but, having been carefully brought up in a mild climate, they were not known for their indomitable fighting spirit. The girls enrolled in Fumio's school were no exception, and, when the situation became too troublesome, they deserted the cause. Fumio had fought in vain, for in the end her cohorts deserted her and Mr. Tamura drifted aimlessly back to Tokyo like a kite whose string had snapped.

Fumio was guilty of organizing the girls in a protest. If she had been an ordinary student, she would certainly not have been pardoned so readily. Nonetheless, her father was president of the Parents' Association of the school. Moreover, the school principal had obtained his post through Keisaku's recommendation. Fearing above all the effects on Keisaku's standing, the school hushed the matter up and Fumio narrowly escaped being suspended.

Hana continued to worry. If it were said that Fumio had been treated leniently because she was Keisaku's daughter, Keisaku would lose face. Furthermore, it would be a black mark on Fumio's personal history and could be used against her when she was considered for marriage. Hana had a premonition that Fumio's marriage would cause her considerable trouble. If it were rumored that her daughter had been suspended from school, an arranged marriage would be completely out of the question.

Hana had therefore made her way humbly to the homes of the principal, the vice-principal, the homeroom teacher, and even the teachers of home-making and physical education. There were those among the teachers and directors who resolutely maintained that it would be a bad precedent and against all principles of education for the school to take into consideration the fact that Fumio was Matani Keisaku's daughter. Nonetheless, they found themselves feeling sympathetic toward the girl's mother. None of them, however, felt they had been cajoled by her. Without taking advantage of her authority as Keisaku's wife, Hana bowed reverentially and entreated each teacher she visited to forgive Fumio just this once, for, from then on, she would keep an eye on her daughter to see that she never misbehaved again.

Hana was the younger sister of a member of the Prefectural House and the wife of the Speaker of the House. In Wakayama, official authority was regarded with utmost respect; therefore, people felt in awe of a woman in her position. Nevertheless, Hana's modesty inspired admiration in one and all. On account of her efforts the matter was quietly settled.

Neither Hana nor Keisaku reprimanded Fumio for her part in the incident. Keisaku's only comment was:

"If only she were a boy!" Hana listened to Keisaku's lament and wondered to what extent her husband was expressing his disappointment in their son, who had just entered the First High School in Tokyo. Seiichirō had maintained an outstanding academic record while attending Wakayama Middle School but was regarded as being somewhat strange, a taciturn and unsociable boy. He had none of his sister's eloquence. It would be difficult indeed for him to enter politics. However, Hana had observed that once her son made up his mind about anything, he refused to listen to anybody else's opinion. In this respect, he was far more clearheaded than his father. And there was reason enough not to be disappointed that he was so unlike his sister.

Hana firmly believed that everything should revolve around the eldest son. Never had Fumio attempted to get the better of her brother at home. On the contrary, she had the utmost respect for her brother's personal character and academic ability. Hana had noticed, however, that he had become rather conceited since going to Tokyo. A second daughter, Kazumi, was born two years after Fumio; Utae, the third daughter, was born two years later. Tomokazu, the second son, was five years younger than Utae. Fumio was adored by the younger members of the family, and in return took good care of them. Hana could find no fault in Fumio as the eldest daughter.

But for some reason Fumio was extremely hostile toward her mother and always highly critical of her. At the time of Mr. Tamura's dismissal, Fumio was infuriated by her mother's intervention.

"Mother, why were you meddling in my affairs? I was determined to fight fair and square, even if I were expelled from school. I would have accepted what was coming to me and fought all my life against injustice of every kind."

If anyone, no longer able to remain indifferent, dared to interrupt, Fumio would burst into tears. "What was wrong with Mr. Tamura? It's the school administration that ought to be questioned for having dismissed him."

Fumio would then go into a long and emotional diatribe, winding up with these words:

"Really, Mother, you're so hopelessly old-fashioned! You're making yourself an enemy of all Japanese women by keeping me in shackles. As a member of the same sex, it's unforgivable. If you weren't my mother . . ."

Overcome with emotion, Fumio would let out a wail. If she were overheard, it would hinder her chances for an arranged marriage.

Hana had no recourse other than to supervise her daughter's education from behind the scenes. She was very strict about having Fumio take lessons in the traditional arts of Japan—the tea ceremony, flower arrangement, and the koto—which cultivated modesty and refinement in a young girl. Fumio openly showed her disdain for such lessons. Once Hana made up her mind about anything, however, her daughter was forced to submit, no matter how violently she opposed the idea. When Fumio expressed a desire to continue her education, Hana said:

"I'll allow it as long as you continue your lessons."

At that time, Hana did not consider the pros and cons of a girl attending college. She insisted upon the lessons because she felt strongly that Fumio's training ought to be completed while she was still at the Girls' School. Kazumi and Utae were unlike their sister in every way: both were of a quiet disposition and had been taught to be modest from the time they were little. Moreover, they worked hard at their lessons without being forced by their mother. Utae in particular had a special talent for music and on her own initiative took shamisen as well as koto lessons.

"If both Fumio and Kazumi say that they don't want your koto, may I please have it, Mother?" Utae begged. She was only fourteen but already very fond of musical instruments.

Utae and Fumio were poles apart. Fumio seemed to have no desire for material goods; she never once expressed a wish for a new kimono or a pair of shoes, let alone a koto. If no one bothered her, she would wear the same old kimono with its sleeves coming apart at the seams. Most of the older girls at school fluffed up their hair to look more attractive, but for four years Fumio continued to wear her hair in the same austere fashion—parted in the middle and tied back. After school, she participated in mock marathon races. She also got together with girls who shared an interest in the novel, discussing with them new trends in fiction. By the end of the day, she was thoroughly exhausted.

"I send her out wearing a lovely kimono made to order, but she returns home so disheveled one would think she had been involved in a bloody vendetta," Hana lamented. Many were the times Hana grieved to see Fumio looking such a mess.

And then a change occurred. Fumio came home with her collar as crooked as before, but from around autumn—shortly after definite plans for her advanced studies had been agreed upon both at home and at school—her energy grew beyond all bounds.

Thoughts of Tokyo Women's College, an institution that had been established in 1918, and her own private hopes filled Fumio's heart and set her dreaming.

"It'll be all right. Seiichirō is in Tokyo. It isn't at all a bad idea to have both of them attending college. After all, I'll soon be going to Tokyo regularly myself," said Keisaku.

Keisaku agreed to let Fumio go, but Hana worried that her daughter would grow wilder still if she were let out of sight.

"What about a school in the Kyoto area? Both Kyoto Normal School for Girls and Higashiyama Normal School for Girls are excellent colleges. And they both have a Home Economics Department."

"But Fumio won't hear of taking up home economics."

"Yes, I know. She's already told me so. If it has to be Tokyo, I'd like to send her to Mejiro. The college there has a fine Home Economics Department."

"Hana, aren't you being a bit too pushy, insisting upon home economics? Remember, you yourself received an education fit for a woman scholar."

"But I'm terribly worried because Fumio takes no interest at all in affairs of the home."

Hana had given her eldest daughter the same kind of education she herself had received and was greatly alarmed by the results. Fumio had been instructed in reading aloud difficult Sino-Japanese texts. Training in this skill called for the kind of intelligence with which years earlier Toyono had impressed Hana. However, Fumio had shown no interest whatever in cultural accomplishments. Even though Hana had had Fumio help her move objects from the storehouse to the sitting room, she had not been at all aware that they were precious antiques nor did she feel any remorse when she chipped or broke valuable objects. She detested above all sewing, a required course of study from the second grade on. In the entrance examination administered by her school, she had drafted an entirely different kimono from the one asked of her. While attending school, she had had all her sewing assignments done by the maids and had taken the finished work to school. Nonetheless, she was not the kind of person who would deceive her teacher, and so she said:

"This is most distressing."

"What is the trouble, Miss Matani?"

"This lined kimono has been sewn far too skillfully."

She then proceeded to rip apart the bottom seam. There was something engaging about Fumio, even though her behavior at times was shocking.

"She'll never be able to graduate from college if she's forced to major in home economics. Mr. Tamura's influence aside, she's best suited for Tokyo Women's College."

Five girls from Wakayama planned to attend the Tokyo Women's College in Mejiro. Had Fumio decided to join this group, Hana would not have worried about sending her daughter to Tokyo. But Fumio stubbornly insisted on traveling to Tokyo by herself. Her mother had nothing to worry about, since she knew the five girls going to Mejiro. Hana wrote to Seiichirō for advice. His reply, written on the back of her letter, consisted of one line: "You should consider Fumio's wishes."

As a member of the Kansai Seiyūkai, Keisaku personally looked after Tasaki Yusuke's constituency. Hana was therefore resigned to asking Mrs. Tasaki to keep an eye on Fumio. She finally gave her daughter permission to go to Tokyo after she promised to continue her lessons in the traditional arts. All this was decided in autumn.

Since then Fumio had been walking on air. In those days there was no difficult entrance examination to study for; therefore, she would chatter endlessly about her future life in Tokyo whenever she found someone who would listen.

After the decision was made to send Fumio to Tokyo, her footsteps sounded different whenever she crossed Musota Bridge. The schoolgirls who were concerned about their appearance tended to wear shoes, but Fumio found wooden clogs more comfortable. She wore them all the time except on festive occasions. Now that she was leaving for Tokyo, however, she made a big effort to wear shoes. The streets of the city were clean and tidy, but the road back to Musota—the trip took about an hour on foot—suddenly became a torment for her from the other side of the bridge. In Wakayama Prefecture, where the climate was mild, there was a ground frost at night in winter, even though it rarely snowed. As it got warmer in the morning, the road became muddy under the feet of schoolchildren and workers on their way to the city. By late afternoon, the country road was covered with a layer of slush. Fumio walked straight ahead, the heels of her shoes kicking up mud which spattered the bottom of her hakama. Being tall and heavy, even under ordinary circumstances she was a striking figure. But as she strode along, swinging her arms like a soldier marching, she could easily be recognized from a distance. Fumio called out to a villager who passed her on the road:

"Good day, Shige."

"Oh, you're back. A little early, aren't you?"

"Yes. Bye now."

Fumio walked on after this brief conversation.

"She's a fine young lady, but her mother must be terribly worried about her. Isn't she a bit too lively for a girl?"

"She does everything a boy does—climbs trees, goes fishing, plays war games. I often wondered what would happen when she came of age. She hasn't changed at all."

"I heard that once someone came from Yamato with a marriage proposal. When he was informed that the eldest Matani daughter was fishing by the canal, he was surprised that she was still such a child and returned home."

Fumio gave no indication that she had overheard their conversation as she continued north along the road without slowing her pace. Presently she entered the gate of the Matani mansion, which was enclosed by a thick earthen wall. The gate was even more imposing than the temple gate of Daidō-ji; its thick black wooden frame contrasted sharply with the white, freshly painted walls. The main gate had been left open. There was a building on the right and the men's quarters on the left, in front of which there always seemed to be a cluster of old men. These "lifetime employees," formerly tenant farmers, had for some reason or other remained bachelors. They led a relatively carefree life working on Matani land and being hired out to people in sudden need of extra hands.

The road led right up to the garden. On the right was the persimmon tree and on the left, a wall enclosing the garden outside the inner drawing room. Fumio skirted the wall, arriving at the entrance.

"I'm back."

Inside, the house was dark. She closed the door behind her. Her mother's voice could be heard from the room at the end of the corridor.

"Is that you, Fumio?"

Making her way to her room on the second floor, Fumio set her things down and took off her hakama. After quickly changing from socks to tabis, she went downstairs. Every member of the Matani family was expected to announce his comings and goings. It was necessary for Fumio to appear before her mother, press her hands to the floor, and formally report her return.

As she had expected, she found her mother applying lacquer to Yasu's teeth. Hana looked at her daughter.

"Welcome home. You're a little early, aren't you? Didn't you have a lesson with Miss Matsuyama today?"

"Miss Matsuyama has a cold, so she canceled today's lesson."

In fact, Fumio had come straight home without going to her tea ceremony lesson. She felt no compunction at all about lying to her mother.

"Really?" asked Hana in a suspicious tone.

Fumio began to feel very uncomfortable, for a slip of the tongue would get her into further difficulty. The only other alternative was to disappear, as it was almost impossible to deceive her mother, who knew her through and through. Completely at a loss what to do, she was unable to move.

The maids were preparing dinner outside by the well, and the fire had not yet been started in the kitchen stove. At this busy time of day, Yasu would say:

"Hana, please lacquer my teeth."

"Yes, Mother."

Hana never failed to answer her mother-in-law. Laying aside whatever she was doing, she would start a charcoal fire in the portable cooking stove. Transferring the red-hot coals to the brazier, over which she threw some ashes, she placed an unglazed piece of pottery containing lacquer over the low flame. She then slowly melted the lacquer, which she applied to Yasu's teeth with a brush held in her right hand. Her left hand was placed on Yasu's lower jaw to keep it steady. The so-called *daidokoro* where she performed this task was not the room in which the meals were prepared. In this part of the country, the *daidokoro* was sitting room not kitchen. The Matani *daidokoro* was a smallish room in the middle of which the two women were sitting down facing each other. This domestic scene had an air of coldness about it which might in part have been due to the fact that Yasu, who would be celebrating her eighty-eighth birthday the following year, was totally blind. Yasu had never been vain about her looks, but she insisted on being neat and tidy as she grew old. Hana had rarely seen her mother-in-law lacquer her teeth in anyone's presence when she first came as a bride. Once in a while she had noticed that the lacquer applied to Yasu's front teeth had begun to wear off, thus exposing the white enamel; however, she had been unable to draw Yasu's attention to it. For her part, Yasu had always felt constrained in the presence of her daughter-in-law, but after losing her eyesight, she began to take advantage of Hana's kindness.

"Hana, please see if there are any stains on this kimono."

"Hana, the rim of my tea bowl is chipped. Please get me a new one in town."

"Hana I'd like to take a little walk in the garden. Please join me."

If she dropped her chopsticks, it would invariably be Hana she called, and if a maid picked them up for her, the maid would be harshly rebuked. Those who had known Yasu as a good-natured and meek woman were bewildered by this dramatic change in her personality. Hana never showed any sign of irritation and cheerfully carried out Yasu's requests. She felt that the least she could do was to take good care of the old woman, who, having lost her place as the mistress of the family, no longer wielded any real power.

As Keisaku's responsibilities became increasingly onerous, his wife's assistance became indispensable. Whenever a constituent was locked up in a police cell in Isao Village or Wakayama City, his relatives would come pleading to Keisaku's home. Hana would then set out in her husband's place to arrange for the prisoner's release. Being highly accomplished and of an unimpeachable character, her dignity and quick thinking made her much more than an ordinary housewife. Furthermore, she had a large family of two boys and three girls. Keisaku's duties kept him away from home much of the time, and so Hana had to take full responsibility for the children's education. She also saw to it that the houseboys and maids performed their duties. Furthermore, she acted as a mediator in disputes involving the tenant farmers and comforted them in times of sorrow.

Yet here was Yasu summoning Hana in the midst of her hectic schedule to ask favors of her. Had Yasu been able to see, she would certainly have hesitated. Fumio was highly critical of her mother.

"It's entirely your fault, Mother. You keep doing everything Grandmother asks you to. You're spoiling her far too much. She takes advantage of you because she's blind. You're so bound up with the idea that a woman should be devoted that you've become a slave to the family."

The picture of Hana next to the brazier in the sitting room intently applying lacquer to Yasu's teeth struck Fumio as being a caricature of women and family life.

"Please open your mouth once more."

Yasu exposed her clenched teeth. Most of her back teeth had been extracted, but she still had her front incisors, four on top and four on the bottom. Yasu had never been considered a beauty, but she had always been proud of her teeth. Every morning and every night, after brushing her teeth with salt, she had applied the lacquer; thus, even at the age of eighty-seven, she had eight teeth in excellent condition. She had been blind for more than ten years. Feeling that she was living to preserve these teeth of hers, she had Hana lacquer them every other day.

Hana used a tuft hair toothbrush dipped in lacquer and brushed her mother-in-law's teeth again and again. The teeth gradually took on a black, metallic sheen. Only recently had Hana become aware of the beauty of lacquered teeth. Wrinkles radiated outward from Yasu's brown lips and from time to time some mucous trickled from her tightly closed eyes. The gray of her hair and eyebrows had a yellowish tinge and Yasu's face was the very epitome of old age and ugliness. Nonetheless, her teeth, on which she had lavished great care, were strong as ever. Hana ignored Fumio's criticisms. As she brushed on the lacquer, she experienced the joy of giving a little energy to the old woman, whose life was slowly ebbing away.

Suddenly Hana realized that Fumio had quietly made her way to the entrance and was putting on her wooden clogs.

"Where are you off to now, Fumio?"

"I'm going over to the Hiratas of Yagaito," Fumio answered, a guilty look on her face.

"Whatever for?"

"To talk about my going to Tokyo."

"Again? You shouldn't overdo it."

"I shan't. I'll be back right away."

Kazumi was returning home from school just as Fumio passed through the gate. The collar of Kazumi's silk kimono was always neat, and sometimes she would have bows attached to her haori. Unlike her sister, Kazumi was very concerned about her looks.

"Are you back already?"

"Yes. I skipped my tea ceremony lesson. Don't tell Mother."

"But Miss Matsuyama won't be giving lessons this month. She said that a relative of hers was getting married."

"Really? I didn't know about that. Then I needn't have lied to Mother."

The two sisters laughed merrily.

"Where are you off to?"

"To Shin'ike. Don't mention that to Mother either."

"I shan't."

"Well, I'm off."

"Please give Uncle my best. Eisuke too."

"Sure."

Fumio folded her arms inside her kimono sleeves like a schoolboy. Her shoulders slightly hunched, she made her way north along the road which led through the rice paddies. For years, Kōsaku had not associated with the main family except to attend Buddhist memorial services. As long as Fumio could remember, her uncle had never voluntarily come to visit Agenogaito; his wife, too, rarely came to pay her respects. Whenever the branch family was mentioned, Hana, who seldom spoke ill of anyone, would knit her brows.

"No couple could be as selfish as those two," was her usual retort.

Fumio had always sensed a strained relationship between her uncle and her mother.

It was through Fumio that the two families had kept in touch. Eisuke, Kōsaku's son, was a year younger than Fumio and a year behind her in school, but the two cousins got along fine. Fumio regularly visited Shin'ike. Kōsaku, as cynical as ever, grew to love his niece as though she were his own child.

"Good afternoon. Is Eisuke home?" Fumio asked, calling out from the entrance in such a loud voice that she could be heard in her uncle's room at the back of the house.

"How good of you to come! Eisuke is inside going over his lessons. Please come in," said her aunt in a gentle voice as she peered out from the kitchen, her hair covered with a towel. Ume, who had always been small, had suddenly put on weight after turning thirty, and now gave the impression she had difficulty walking. However, her face was plump and unruffled, making it hard to believe that she did all the heavy chores around the house, everything from working out in the fields to making the fire to heat the bath water. As her aunt slowly removed the towel from her head and bowed politely, Fumio noticed that her hair had been done up in a casual bun like that of an ordinary maid. Ume was very different from Hana, who always wore her hair in an elaborate chignon.

"Is your mother well? That's good. Please give her my best regards. I've really been so remiss . . ."

Seventeen years had elapsed since Ume, born and raised in the city, had come here as a bride, and she had mastered completely the Musota dialect. Fumio decided not to mention the fact that Hana nowadays felt ill-disposed toward Ume as well. Seeking desperately to change the subject, her eyes wandered about the entrance.

"Aunt Ume, isn't that a bicycle?"

"Why, yes, it is."

Fumio ran up to the bicycle propped up against the wall between the bath and the entrance.

"How marvelous! Did Eisuke get you to buy it for him?"

"Yes."

"That's wonderful. How I envy him!"

Fumio timidly placed a hand on the bicycle handle. She bombarded her aunt with questions. When had it been bought? Could Eisuke ride it? Was he using it to go to school?

"Fumio. Come on in," said Kōsaku as he appeared at the entrance.

Eisuke was locked in battle with a mathematics problem in the sitting room. As his cousin entered the room, he lowered his eyebrows, looking sorry for himself. Kōsaku's two children, Eisuke and Misono, did not do as well in school as their cousins. Both Seiichirō and Fumio had been top of their class at school, but Eisuke was just an average student, much to the disappointment of his father. Not to be outdone by Hana, Kōsaku had begun to educate his children relatively early. Eisuke, who was in his third year of Middle School, was forced to aim for secondary school, but the boy did not react to his father's intense ambition. Hoping to be excused from his studies since his cousin had come to visit, he cautiously studied his father's face.

"Eisuke, can you ride that bicycle?" asked Fumio innocently.

"Not yet. I'm still practicing, though. It's not the easiest thing to master, you know."

"I guess not. Let me practice too."

Kōsaku, who had been listening from the side, interrupted: "Eisuke, have you solved that problem?"

"No, not yet."

Kōsaku rebuked his son. Eisuke, however, merely scratched his head and did not seem too unhappy about the situation.

"Work it out quickly. If you don't, you'll go without your dinner."

"What can't you work out? Is it your homework?" inquired Fumio as she peered at Eisuke's work.

"No, it isn't. I understood perfectly when the teacher showed us how to solve the problem, but I'm finding it difficult to repeat the steps on my own."

"Let me have a look at it. Goodness, the standards are high at the Middle School! I wonder if I can solve it."

Fumio sat down next to Eisuke. Borrowing a sheet of paper and a pencil, she drew a triangle and pondered over the problem. Presently, she wrote out five lines of an equation.

"Is this the answer?"

"Why, yes. That's exactly the way the teacher solved the problem."

Kōsaku, who until this moment had been standing impatiently nearby, stopped scowling and dismissed his son. He knew a great deal about literature and history, no less, indeed, than the Middle School teachers; however, his knowledge of science and mathematics was no better than Fumio's.

As Eisuke left the room with his textbook, Fumio and her

uncle sat down facing each other and gazed out at the garden, over which the evening shadows were falling. Ume quietly served them tea and cakes.

"Fumio, won't you stay for dinner?" she asked.

"We'd invite you to dinner more often if only our meals were better than those served at your home," Kōsaku added.

"Why, I'd love to stay. I enjoy so much the food you cook."

"Such flattery!"

Kōsaku noisily sipped the dark green tea.

"You'll soon be leaving for Tokyo, won't you?"

"Yes, indeed. I'm so happy I could burst. Even after returning home from school, I can't keep still. The house seems so hopelessly old-fashioned. My heart beats wildly at the thought that I'll be leaving it soon."

"But studying in Tokyo won't be as easy as you think, Fumio. If you're too light-hearted about it, you'll find yourself in trouble. Your mother always has her wits about her. Learn from her and go to Tokyo with her courageous spirit."

"But Uncle, what's so courageous about Mother? She never asserts herself and she's always at Father's beck and call. Right now she's in the sitting room lacquering Grandmother's teeth. I feel thoroughly disgusted seeing her comply so meekly with Grandmother's endless requests. And as for my education, it's all tea and flowers and music. She doesn't seem to understand we live in a new age."

"You're a funny girl! I also dislike your mother, but for entirely different reasons. I'm not disgusted by her going out of her way to lacquer her mother-in-law's teeth, nor do I detest her for flaunting her devotion before her husband. What I find unbearable is the way she cleverly conducts herself in an old-fashioned manner."

Fumio stared in amazement at her uncle. Kōsaku sipped the hot soup with its pieces of Kada sea bream, enjoying its delicious flavor as if he were at the same time savoring the abuse he had heaped upon his sister-in-law. Now forty-six years old, Kōsaku

looked much older, thanks, no doubt, to his cynical approach to
life. He had begun to turn gray relatively early. The extraordinarily long hairs of his eyebrows shaded his sharp eyes and the
vertical lines on the bridge of his nose were clearly etched. He
looked at least ten years older than his brother.

"Uncle."

"Yes?"

"I've been meaning to ask you about something for a long
time."

"What is it? Speak up, child."

"Why are you and Mother on bad terms? I can't help thinking
that it's very peculiar."

With her daughter's assistance, Ume began to clear away the
dinner dishes. She kept coming and going restlessly between
the kitchen and the sitting room.

"Let's go into my room. Ume, bring us some hot tea."

Fumio followed her uncle into his study. The two of them
had an unusually close relationship and once they began talking, not even Kōsaku's own children were asked to join in the
conversation. Feeling as though they had been set free, Eisuke
and Misono hurried off to their room and romped about like little
children as they spread out their bedding. Ume did not enjoy
a position of high standing as wife and mother in the household.
Without a word of complaint, she went about putting things in
order while Kōsaku, who was so hard to please, grumbled at her.
Although the house they lived in had been enlarged as the family
grew, they did not have a maid. Kōsaku alone, master of the
house, seemed quite content, and had his wife and children do
all the chores.

"Would you care for some bean jelly?"

Kōsaku opened the small chest near the brazier and took out
the red-bean jelly. With a length of string, he cut the jelly into
five equal parts. Misono came in to serve the tea, which had been
poured into Kutani tea bowls.

"Misono, you have some too," said Fumio.

"Thank you, but Eisuke is calling me . . .," said Misono. Studying her father's face, she hesitated for a moment before scurrying away.

Kōsaku treated his daughter as though she were a maid. With a look of displeasure on his face, he continued to chew silently on a thick slice of bean jelly.

"Fumio."

"Yes."

Kōsaku gulped down his tea, took out a towel from his breast fold, and wiped his lips. Gazing steadily at a spot beyond his niece's face, he asked:

"Do you know what vitality is?"

"If you mean the basic meaning of the word, yes, I do."

"Those endowed with it are strong, and those without it, weak. Your mother is a good example of a strong woman. You can compare her to the River Ki. Its blue waters, flowing leisurely, appear tranquil and gentle, but the river itself swallows up all the weak rivers flowing in the same direction. It also possesses the energy to pour its waters into a strong, promising river. Long ago, the Ki flowed to the area around Kinomoto, slightly north of its present mouth. There happened to be a more powerful river to the south with which the Ki merged, thereby changing its course."

Her uncle's words were laden with meaning. Being cautious not to interpret them wrongly, Fumio did not even nod. She gazed steadily at her uncle, who continued his solemn monologue.

"Your mother wanted to sweep me up into the mainstream. In order to do this, she even tried to overwhelm Ume. I guess she thought of us as being weak rivers totally lacking in vitality. But there are narrow rivers flowing parallel to the Ki, like the Narutaki, which are difficult to swallow up. We're like that. Does this answer your question as to why our relationship is strained?"

"Well then, Uncle, I too am like the Narutaki River. I've been raised by Mother for eighteen years, but I haven't lived up to her expectations."

"That's why you and I get along so well."

"At least we think alike."

"Whom do you think I meant when I spoke of a strong, promising river?"

"I guess you meant Father. Mother says he'll one day become a minister of state. That's why we have to take such good care of him."

"A minister of state? Well, well. The Speaker of the House seems to be an extraordinary man!" Kōsaku snorted.

Fumio was beginning to feel uneasy. She was antagonistic toward her mother, but she could not join her uncle in ridiculing her father. Nonetheless, she had recently heard rumors about her father which troubled her.

"Uncle, I've heard some strange rumors about Father."

"What have you heard?"

"That he's keeping a mistress in the city."

Her father spent two weeks of each month away from home. Fumio had been aware of his lengthy absences for the past two years. It was only fairly recently, however, that she had heard about his mistress, a geisha whom he had ransomed three months previously.

"Is that right?"

Kōsaku folded his arms, deep in thought. His face remained composed, but his brows betrayed his anger. Having severed all ties with the outside world, apart from newspapers and books, Kōsaku rarely heard any gossip. What he had just learned from his niece was news indeed.

"When I think of how Mother, who has done everything to please Father and the family, has been betrayed, I feel that she is the one to blame for allowing him to become so selfish."

"You're extraordinarily logical for a girl, Fumio."

Kōsaku noticed that his tea had grown cold. He drank up what he had left and poured some hot water from the kettle into the teapot. He then poured himself and Fumio some hot tea. Following the movement of his hands with her eyes, Fumio noticed the gracefulness of his fingertips and blushed. She was embarrassed that she had allowed dirt to accumulate under her own long fingernails, which she had not bothered to cut for some time.

Sipping the tea, Kōsaku asked:

"Does your mother know about the other woman?"

"I really can't say. No one thinks of her as being dull about such matters, so I doubt that anyone has told her to her face."

"You're right about that."

"I don't think she'd rebuke Father, even if she knew about it. After all, he's going to be a minister of state some day."

Kōsaku smiled cynically.

"The Women's Rights Society was established more than ten years ago and women are now conscious of their inferior social position. It's intolerable that Mother hasn't changed at all. I can hardly wait to get away from the stifling atmosphere at home. I'm not particularly fired with the idea of becoming an activist for women's rights, but I'll never be old-fashioned like Mother."

Kōsaku listened without comment to his young niece. Fumio's image of her mother contrasted greatly with the image he had of Hana, which filled him with a feeling of deep regret. Nevertheless, they both resisted Hana as best they could and had been drawn to each other. Both Kōsaku and Fumio detested the "ideal woman" known to the world as the elegant wife of Matani Keisaku.

After his marriage to Ume, Kōsaku had broken off all ties with Hana, so as not to be influenced by her. As for Fumio, by going off to Tokyo, she planned to lead an independent life away from her mother. At the subconscious level, both Kōsaku and Fumio had sensed the danger of being swallowed up by Hana if they remained too close to her. Nonetheless, though Fumio condemned her mother at her uncle's house as being old-fashioned, she behaved submissively at home. Hana's bearing was such that she compelled one and all to behave properly.

"I'll be giving you koto lessons starting today," announced Hana one day.

Fumio did not protest. It had earlier been arranged for Fumio to go to a koto teacher in the city after school, but she had lied and deceived her mother about her lessons. During her second year at the Girls' School, she had stopped going altogether. From the spring of her third year, koto teachers had been summoned to the house. Fumio, however, would sometimes be late for the lessons and at other times, not show up at all. When at last she took her place opposite the teacher, she had been unable to memorize the most elementary piece no matter how many times she went over it, for she had absolutely no desire to learn. The teachers had been paid handsomely and treated very politely by Hana, but anyone with a sense of pride went home either highly indignant or seeth-ing with anger. Hana had had to bow low, entreating the teacher to please be patient with her daughter. Three different teachers had come from the city to give koto lessons and no other teacher was available. Hana obstinately insisted that her daughter master the instrument. Her younger sisters had enjoyed their music lessons from the start, but Fumio made no effort to please her mother. Hana felt that her daughter's intransigence was quite unforgivable.

The room attached to the dimly lit hall with the Buddhist altar in it was reserved for koto lessons on Sunday mornings. It was natural for Fumio to feel tense, but Hana ignored the girl's emo-tional state. As though she were teaching a beginner she was strict about each point: how a student should sit down in front of the instrument, the way to put on the ivory picks, and how a student should behave toward the teacher.

> Have you seen
> The Silver Pavilion
> In the capital?
> Its gate of bush clover,
> Its alcove post of nandina?

Without a music sheet, Fumio was expected to learn this old practice piece with which even the koto teachers in the city were probably unfamiliar.

"Once again."

Regardless of how many times Fumio played the melody, Hana was not satisfied. It was incredible that anyone who had been taking lessons for so many years could find it difficult to master this simple piece. With patience surpassing that of any of Fumio's previous instructors, Hana quietly observed her student's total lack of interest in the lessons.

Kazumi and Utae had memorized the piece. Even when they went about the house humming the tune and Utae started learning to play it on the shamisen, Fumio was still unable to play the piece to Hana's satisfaction.

At long last, Fumio managed to pick out the simple tune which accompanied the song. Nevertheless, she played in such a distracted manner that anyone with an ear for music could tell that she had no appreciation for the light quality of the lyrics and the simple elegance of the tune. Hana was determined to wait until her daughter realized that however busily her fingers, fitted with ivory picks, flew over the strings, the koto, which possessed an intrinsic life of its own, would give out a cold sound. The instrument would not produce music for someone who did not listen attentively and had no appreciation for the melody. Without demonstrating some warmth of feeling toward an object, whatever it might be, one could not comprehend its true nature. Unless one spoke from one's heart, one would be denied a direct answer. Hana was trying to get her daughter to appreciate these concepts by means of the koto. If Fumio were mentally prepared to question the concept of "family" and not just blindly rebel against it, she would receive a response overflowing with vitality. Hana was admonishing her daughter who indiscriminately rejected old traditions without probing into the reasons for their existence.

Alas, all Fumio felt was that the woman seated correctly in front of her was an overbearingly strict and extremely obdurate mother who made her suffer and forced her to play the koto. Fumio wondered abstractedly whether the worst blunder she could possibly make would be to cut one of the strings with a pick or to trip over the koto and let out a shriek. Of course, those were fantasies she would not carry out. However, she knew a sure way to dispel her feelings of oppression before they became intolerable. She had already concluded that the basic points in flower arrangement and music lessons were foolish. Therefore, she had convinced herself that—though the lessons at times seemed taxing—she should not express her feelings of disgust. Fumio would stifle her yawns while her mother patiently waited for her to show some spontaneity. She strained her ears if she heard anyone in the adjoining room, and if she heard voices, her attention was drawn to what was being said. When there was nothing to be heard, her eyes wandered around the room from one object to another. In this way she refused to concentrate on the music.

Being a woman of excellent taste in art, Hana occasionally redecorated the rooms in the house by exchanging the scrolls, ornamental objects, and vases with pieces brought out of storage. It was apparent that both her father-in-law and his father had had a deep interest in antiques, for a number of objects of considerable value had been stored away. But it was also apparent that for years the Matanis had not taken out the objects to look at them and enjoy them. Hana had boldly displayed such treasures as the calligraphy of Rai San'yō and hanging scrolls by Takeda in the drawing room. Whenever she had the opportunity, she displayed on the alcove shelves the ornate mirror stand and elaborate cosmetic boxes she had brought with her as a bride.

Whenever she got bored during a music lesson, Fumio looked at these objects, impressed that they were family possessions. A jar that had been stored away long before Fumio's birth, a hanging scroll which had been rolled and unrolled any number of times years before Hana had become mistress of the house, all were objects which had been valued highly and handed down from one generation to another. Tea utensils and a variety of vases. Each object appeared to have been in the family for generations and had become darkened like the thick beams of the house itself.

Fumio had grown so accustomed to the lessons she no longer

found them intolerable, but she nonetheless awaited them unen-
thusiastically.

"Bring the koto with you," ordered her mother.

Hana took up the older koto and made her way along the corridor in the direction of the sitting room. Wondering where they
were going to practice this time, Fumio obediently followed her
mother with her own koto. Hana turned at the sitting room and
carried on to the storeroom at the north of the house, then headed
straight for the main storehouse. The door, as though anticipating
their arrival, had been left open. Hana glanced quickly back at
Fumio. Without uttering a word, she shifted the koto she was
carrying into a more comfortable position and entered.

The place had been cleaned by the maids. Light poured in from
a small open window on the second floor, shone down at the same
angle as a flight of stairs, and illuminated the floor. The interior
had been designed so that the ventilation and the temperature
were naturally regulated, and so the air inside was heavy and
damp even during this early winter season of dryness. Mother and
daughter sat facing each other with their kotos between them. The
mat on which they sat had been placed out of reach of the sun,
but the two women were oblivious to the cold.

"No sound will reach us here, so you won't be distracted. Concentrate solely on playing the koto," Hana said in a solemn tone.
She finally allowed Fumio to progress from "The Silver Pavilion"
to a new selection. Hana played the new piece once all the way
through in order to introduce it to Fumio. Both the tune and the
lyrics were old-fashioned and slow in tempo. Fumio had never
heard the tune before. It did not differ greatly from the earlier
piece: it was a simple tune with little embellishment.

"I'm going to play it again, so listen closely."

Hana played the piece once again with feeling, doubtless because she was remembering her own childhood. In her determination to teach her daughter, Hana herself at some point had become a captive of the instrument she was playing. Her koto was an
old-fashioned one, seven feet long, and quite unlike the fine wood

but inelegant shape of the new koto that Fumio was playing. The side panels were decorated with plovers and waves in gold lacquer. Her koto had been ordered from Kyoto by Toyono and special care had been given to its design. Stretched loosely along the length of the instrument, the koto strings produced a rich sound which seemed to give a nostalgic caress to Hana's penetrating voice.

Seeing her mother thus absorbed, Fumio realized that she was no match for her. She felt extremely irritated. Hana, who had turned forty-four, had worn her hair in the same elaborate chignon for over ten years, but her beauty had not faded in the least. She did not go out of her way to appear younger than she was; on the contrary, she took great pains to dress her age. The dark, purplish gray kimono she was wearing had a fine print woven into the material, and her sash, of a subdued shade of rusty red, also had a fine pattern. Hana's features, in harmony with her taste in clothes, glowed with all the maturity of a woman of forty. In perfect accord with her age, Hana continued to preserve her beauty. She retained her girlhood serenity, a serenity which, in all probability, would remain unruffled in the years to come.

Fumio sighed. Her eyes, which had grown accustomed to the dark, grew rebellious. They darted from one corner of the room to another, taking note of two oblong chests placed side by side— one of black lacquer and the other of red—and the carefully stacked paulownia boxes of varying sizes. She noticed that slips of Japanese paper which noted the contents were attached to the boxes and strained her eyes to read them in order to alleviate her boredom. She saw that the tags were written in her mother's hand: "Ko-Kutani plate with vermilion painting," "Chinese lion of celadon," "decorative object with cloud-and-dragon design."

Hana had almost finished playing the piece through a second time when she suddenly realized that Fumio was not paying attention. She rebuked her daughter severely:

"Fumio, do you still refuse to listen?"

In that instant, Fumio felt a flash of pain on her right hand. Hana had struck the back of Fumio's hand, which was resting on the koto strings. With the force of the blow, the picks on Hana's fingers cut deep into the back of her daughter's hand. The tender skin, broken in three places, began to bleed. Hana and Fumio stared blankly at the oozing blood, which appeared a deep red even in the dark.

As far back as Fumio could remember, Hana had never revealed her feelings in this manner, nor had she ever laid a hand on her daughter. Fumio was taken by surprise. At the same time, she experienced a mysterious sensation which she had no time to analyze. Having seen for the first time the worst in her mother, Fumio had a perverse desire to make her feel ashamed of her outburst. Fumio little imagined, being the young girl that she was, that her mother's irritability had been intensified by her husband's chronic neglect of her. The scars on the back of her hand remained for a long time, and even after the wound had healed, three lines were clearly visible. Whenever Fumio looked at the scars, she thought of her imminent departure for Tokyo.

Nevertheless, Fumio continued to hold her mother in awe and behaved more submissively than ever in her presence. After the incident, she attended her other lessons religiously, telling herself that she had just a little longer to put up with them.

There were no more koto lessons. Hana had been appalled by the fact that she had caused her own child to bleed. She tried to banish the memory of that unpleasant incident from her mind. Nevertheless, less than half a year later Hana again lost her temper, this time in front of her two younger daughters and the servants as well. Fumio was again the cause.

The end of her final semester was fast approaching and Fumio was spending her days blissfully dreaming of Tokyo. She may not have been the easiest person to get along with, but everyone was reluctant to see her go. She continued to make startling statements, shocking the conservative residents of Ki province. However, people were more tolerant than before and were merely amused. Fumio was delighted to be leaving her birthplace, for which she had very little genuine affection. She could not have chosen for herself a new life more suitable than that which the capital of Japan would provide.

School ended at four o'clock, but she always returned home after dark. That day, however, it really was too late, even if she had gone to her lessons.

"Where is Fumio? What in the world could she be doing?" asked Hana, seeing that her eldest daughter was the only one missing from the dinner table. Kazumi, Utae, and ten-year-old Tomokazu, avoiding their mother's eyes, answered evasively.

Hana was the only one ignorant of what Fumio had been up to lately. Fumio's younger brother and sisters and a few of the maids knew, but no one dared to tell on Fumio. It was not that they lacked the courage. They were simply trying their best to keep Fumio's latest activity from Hana, knowing full well that she would be extremely displeased. Instead of returning straight home, Fumio made her way to Shin'ike every day after school. Borrowing Eisuke's bicycle, she practiced riding it in the playground of Musota Elementary School. Lately, this had been the talk of the village. The villagers knew very well that Hana and Kōsaku were on bad terms. Moreover, they were unable to tell on Fumio, as they felt warmly toward her. They all dreaded the day Hana would find out about it.

One Friday afternoon, Fumio herself, little bothered by the concern of others, showed her mother what she had been doing. Having been buffeted by the cold winter wind, Fumio's cheeks were ruddy. She got off the bicycle at the gate and carried it into the garden. Then, supporting herself against the persimmon tree, she got on again and began to pedal away.

"Tomokazu, Tomokazu. Come and see me ride the bicycle!" Fumio cried in a loud voice.

Kazumi and Utae came running out of the house. A few of the maids peered at her from the entrance.

With all eyes on her, Fumio impressed her audience as she

showed off on the bicycle, circling the garden a couple of times. To show that she was in complete control, she looked back and flashed a smile. The Matani garden was covered with matting at this time of year when the tenant farmers presented their rice crop. It was smaller than the school playground but big enough for Fumio to demonstrate her newly acquired skill.

Fumio had recently reverted to maroon hakamas. But when she straddled Eisuke's bicycle, which had a metal bar connecting the handlebars and the seat, and pushed on the pedals, the bottom of her hakama flapped upward in a most unladylike manner. Moreover, she was wearing white socks and wooden clogs instead of shoes that day. The sight of Fumio's sturdy white legs which were clearly visible caused both Kazumi and Utae to feel faint. Fumio's younger sisters had been taught to feel aversion toward any indecent exposure of human flesh. They were therefore distressed to see their sister in such a state.

But Tomokazu innocently cheered his sister on.

"How does it feel?"

"Marvelous! When you race against the wind, the world is completely transformed! I'll tell Father to get a bicycle for the Young Men's Association."

"Will you? Then I'll ask Father to buy me one too."

"You should. I'll put in a good word for you."

"I wonder if I can ride it. Isn't it a little too big for me?"

"No, it isn't. Would you like to try?"

She was about to stop when Fumio instinctively sensed something rushing at her from behind and fell off the bicycle.

"Fumio!"

Hana was standing there. In her haste, she had not bothered to look for her clogs but had rushed out in her tabi socks. Her face was pale and the corner of her right eye twitched nervously.

"Where did you get that bicycle?"

"I borrowed it from Eisuke."

Fumio had no time to think of a plausible lie. Trying to hide her embarrassment, she got up and brushed the dust from her skirt.

"Fumio!" cried Hana, this time shrieking. Hana grabbed her daughter roughly by the arm and dragged her into the house.

"Have you been practicing all this time without telling me?"

"But Mother . . ."

"You've been riding around the village, haven't you, you shameless girl!"

"But Mother . . ."

"How much longer must you insult me to feel satisfied? Just how far do you intend to go?"

"I'm sorry, Mother . . ."

Hana gave Fumio no chance to speak in her own defense. She gave vent to a torrent of almost incomprehensible abuse as she dragged Fumio in the direction of the storehouse. No sooner did Fumio realize that she was going to be thrown into the dark room than she burst into a childish wail.

"Mother, I'm sorry. Please forgive me. I was wrong."

Sliding open the door with one hand, Hana pushed Fumio inside with all her might. That a woman who spent her days in such a quietly civilized way possessed so much strength was astonishing.

"I promise not to ride the bicycle again."

Paying no attention to her daughter, who was crying like a baby, Hana slammed shut the heavy door and fastened the latch. Fumio's voice followed her as she rushed back to the entrance, feeling the cold corridor against the soles of her bare feet. Her heart was pounding. Her anger, which was greater than her shock, had still not abated. Nevertheless, she felt she had better first put away the tabis she had quickly slipped off as she came in from the garden. Not one of the maids, who were still in a state of shock, had had enough presence of mind to pick them up.

Hana gathered up the dirty tabis and went into the storeroom to put on a freshly-laundered pair. She was in the habit of changing her tabis in the morning, in the evening, and whenever she had callers. She had been quick in slipping off the dirty pair, but to put on a fresh pair she went into the storeroom where no one was about to watch her. Then, sitting sideways, she quickly fastened them on. Rising to her feet, she looked down at her white tabis and struggled to regain her composure.

"Mother," pleaded Kazumi and Utae, who were seated at the entrance. "Please forgive Fumio." Tears streamed down their faces.

By this time Fumio, who had been momentarily terrified, had stopped crying. She grew calm when she realized she had nothing to cry about. Being put into a storehouse may be an appropriate form of punishment for a child but definitely not for an eighteen-year-old girl. Fumio laughed at her mother for having lost her temper just because she had discovered that her daughter had been riding a bicycle. She had the feeling that her mother's anger had been as great as it was because the bicycle belonged to Kōsaku, whom she disliked so intensely. Was she that resentful of the Narutaki River which refused to flow into the Ki? Recalling how she had wailed when first startled by her mother's outburst of anger, Fumio could not help but smile sheepishly to herself.

In spite of the entreaties of Fumio's sisters, Hana's anger remained unappeased. Fumio had removed her haori before riding the bicycle. All that physical activity had made her feel warm, but now that she found herself alone in the dark storehouse she felt the intense cold and winced. She recollected how tense she had felt as she practiced the koto in her mother's presence. Suddenly thinking of playing the instrument which had been left in this room, she made her way gingerly toward it in the semi-darkness. She removed the oilcloth cover and saw that the eleventh and twelfth strings had snapped. She did not dare touch her mother's koto. To keep herself warm, she thought of spreading out a quilt. Opening the oblong chest of red lacquer, she found— instead of bedding—things she had not expected to find.

The first object she came across was a big crimson crape cushion. She then unearthed an unusually large folding paper-case and found wrapped inside it an outer robe with crimson lining. It was the light yellowish green outer robe of embossed satin that Hana had worn at her wedding banquet. The small silvery print of pine needles and cones appeared to float upward. Fumio pulled out the cushion and the robe and decided to use them to keep herself warm.

In her search for something of interest, she noticed a bundle of magazines on the shelf under the stairs. Being fond of reading, Fumio took the bundle down and dusted it off. It contained about thirty issues of *Women's World*, a journal Hana had read regularly for a time after her marriage.

Fumio thought that a bright spot was preferable, even though it would be colder, and so she climbed up the steep, ladderlike stairs. She set the cushion down near the second-story window. Then, throwing the robe over her shoulders, Fumio sat down on the cushion and looked intently through the old magazines. One issue contained the 1911 proclamation of the Seitōsha Women's Rights Organization. The writings of such women as Hiratsuka Raichō and Otake Kōkichi, enthusiastically advocating the extension of women's rights, were scattered throughout the volumes. Fumio found it incredible that her mother had once read these articles. How was it possible for Hana to have lived through such a period? After all, she had given Fumio her first lessons in Sino-Japanese texts, essential English grammar, tea ceremony, flower arrangement, and the koto. As she leafed through the pages, Fumio discovered that in both the old *Women's World* and the current *Wives' World*, the basic philosophy of the contributors remained unchanged. Near the end of a 1912 issue, she came across the name Kimoto Hanako in a list of writers of prize-winning essays.

Her mother's essay, entitled "Family Life," had received first prize. Printed very ostentatiously were the writer's words: "Having been graciously informed of this unexpected honor, I take up my brush, my heart palpitating with joy. I truly feel that this is but a dream." Her essay, written in elegant prose, extolled the woman who married and carried within her the spirit of the family. Such a woman should try her utmost to become a slave to and an indispensable part of the family. The essay seemed some-what inappropriate for a magazine whose aim was to enlighten the meek, old-fashioned women and to nurture young women belonging to the modern age. Nonetheless, the editors, in their capacity as judges, were impressed by its lyricism and rich power of expression and praised it glowingly. The prize was five yen, then considered a large sum of money.

Fumio graduated from Wakayama Girls' School in 1921. Afterward, accompanied by her father, she made her way to Tokyo where she took her entrance examination in a temporary building of Tokyo Women's College, then located in Tsunohazu. There were fewer than forty applicants, many of whom were dressed either in plain handwoven kimonos or well-laundered dark blue kimonos with a splashed pattern. Fumio, who was wearing a brocade haori over a kimono made-to-order, felt extremely self-conscious. There were a number of girls over twenty who looked very grown-up to Fumio. Although she was taller than the average Japanese girl, she was painfully aware of the fact that in every respect she was just a country girl. Observing that only half of the girls wore shoes and that the others wore wooden clogs or straw sandals, Fumio felt ashamed: to think that back in Musota she had boasted about the new women's movement!

Her linguistic ability was far inferior to that of the girls who had been brought up in Tokyo and her English examination was, she thought, a total disaster. Nonetheless, the Women's College found a place for her, treating her with unusual generosity. To her great joy and relief, she was allowed to enroll. Furthermore, she registered in the English Department.

The dormitories were filled to capacity, and so the college officials expressed their hope that she find accommodation in a lodging house. Fumio therefore decided to stay at the Muraki-ya, an inn which was located in Tameike, and to commute to school from there. The Muraki-ya, owned by a man from Kii Village, which adjoined Isao Village, was where Keisaku took up lodgings whenever he was in Tokyo. Mr. Muraki said that he would be delighted to look after Mr. Matani's daughter. Only the previous year, Tokyo Women's College had obtained a second campus after taking over the old classroom buildings of the Peer's School in Nagata-chō. The college now owned those buildings along with the ones it already possessed in Tsunohazu. Fumio did not therefore have far to go from her lodgings to her college.

I am writing to formally inform you that I have been in love.

Hana received this disturbing news within three months of Fumio's departure.

But I have been disappointed in love. Only while he was in Wakayama did Mr. Tamura's existence seem so brilliant! I have been utterly disillusioned! I saw with my own eyes how, within two years, the man I idolized had lost his youthful zeal, and was made painfully aware of the cruel changes wrought by time. However, I still have my youth before me. I have been deeply inspired by Yasui Tetsu's lectures on ethics and attend her lectures faithfully. Please do not worry about me, as I am regularly going for my lessons in tea ceremony and flower arrangement.

Hana breathed a sigh of relief as she folded the letter, which Fumio had dashed off with a pencil. She then slipped it into the envelope. Seiichirō's letters were shorter, but his calligraphy was smaller and neater than Fumio's terrible scrawl. Hana continued to worry about whether it had been wise to send her daughter to Tokyo. She had received word from Mrs. Tasaki that she would keep an eye on Fumio. Even then, Hana's anxiety was not dispelled.

The Matani household was filled with the tranquillity of spring.

Kazumi and Utae were quiet girls who did not rebel against their mother. Unlike Seiichirō when he was little, Tomokazu was mischievous; he was reprimanded severely whenever he trampled the neatly arranged plants in the garden. He would clamber up the persimmon tree on the south side of the house within the walled enclosure, shouting:

"This is the siege of Port Arthur. Charge!" He would then shout orders to the children in the neighborhood whom he had rounded up.

It seemed incredible that a branch of Kudoyama persimmon had been sent over to be grafted to the tree. With its healthy branches, the tree did not even shake, though Tomokazu climbed it with great aplomb. Fumio had been the only other of Hana's children to climb the tree. As she watched her son at play, Hana thought of her daughter in Tokyo. She remembered that when she had been pregnant with Fumio, Toyono had predicted that the child would be climbing the tree. Hana was suddenly assailed by memories of her grandmother, who had been dead for eighteen years. "Please tell me how Fumio will turn out," Hana asked in vain.

Ume arrived at the gate on an errand for her husband. Seeing Hana, she grew flustered.

"I've been terribly remiss. I hope that you have been well," she said, bowing low.

"My, but it's been ages since I last saw you. I, too, have been remiss. I do hope you've been well, Ume."

Hana had not seen Ume in years, and so, overcome by nostalgia, she greeted her warmly. Ume entered the house and rubbed her hands nervously over the empty brazier. She was as well disposed toward Hana as before, but she could not very well say that Kōsaku kept her from displaying any warmth of feeling. She therefore sat there feeling awkward and embarrassed.

"I'm afraid these didn't turn out very well. I don't know whether or not you'll find them palatable, but please try some," Ume said. Removing the towel covering the plate, Hana saw that her sister-in-law had brought some homemade *sushi*. Ume's culinary skill was recognized throughout Musota. After chatting informally for some time, Ume turned to the real purpose of her visit.

"My husband sent me over to ask you for Fumio's Tokyo address."

"Fumio's address? What business does he have with her?" inquired Hana, with a cautious look on her face.

"We'd like to send her some *bariko* when they're in season. Kōsaku says that he'd like to send her a package containing various Wakayama delicacies."

"The season is still a long way off. Please tell Kōsaku not to worry about Fumio, as she is living in an inn where she can eat her fill of such delicacies."

Bariko was a kind of fish caught in the waters off the western coast of Ki province which was cut open and dried. It was considered a great regional delicacy. When broiled, fish and bones could be crunched and eaten. It had a wonderful aroma and tasted delicious. People living along the western shores of the province were fond of this tiny fish with its large eyes and tiny mouth. The *bariko* was, moreover, highly regarded by the gourmets of Osaka. It was in season from the end of autumn to winter, and so Hana found it strange that Ume spoke of sending some of this delicacy to Fumio at this time of year. Furthermore, Fumio had insisted that she be left alone, so Hana coldly turned Ume away.

Ume hunched her plump shoulders. She appeared extremely worried about the prospect of having to report her failure to carry out her mission. Watching Ume cross the garden and head for home, Hana wondered why she was trying to monopolize her daughter. She also wondered why she had not taken this golden opportunity to resolve the long-standing estrangement between Kōsaku and herself. How narrow-minded she was in turning away poor Ume, who had come to visit her in such a friendly spirit!

Hana removed her jade hair ornament and scratched the back of her head with the pointed end. She had a bald spot under her chignon which was done up in a married woman's coiffure.

Keisaku returned home earlier than usual that day. He had been busy in the Lower House polishing up a proposal for improvements in the River Ki project. He was hoping to have Tasaki Yusuke present the proposal to the House of Representatives of the National Diet within the year. Lately, however, there had been a break in his normally hectic schedule.

"Welcome home."

"What's new?"

Keisaku had been away in Wakayama City for about five days. Feeling guilty about his long absence, he avoided looking directly into his wife's eyes and played instead with Tomokazu who demanded his attention.

"There was a letter from Fumio."

"Oh? What did she say?"

"She asked us to send her an Ōshima kimono and some money. She also mentioned that Tokyo is more of a cultural center than Wakayama. That was the gist of her letter."

"She's a strange one. I wonder how far she'll go in expressing herself. Send her the money she asks for. We can trust her."

"But we already send Seiichirō seventy yen every month. Fifty yen should be more money than she actually needs."

"Don't worry about it. I'll manage somehow."

Hana remained silent for a while, remembering that it was an indication of a man's financial success to keep a mistress. She abruptly changed the subject.

"Your work here has been piling up. Is there something in Musota that you find unpleasant?"

"Oh, no. It's just that I usually get through late in the day, so I remain in the city. I'm even thinking of buying a little house."

Actually, Keisaku had already bought a house for his mistress without first consulting his wife.

"But you couldn't possibly buy a little house."

"I suppose not."

"I hear that Mr. Karaki is looking for someone to buy his mansion in Masago-chō. You will disgrace your name and position if you buy a house that is any smaller."

Keisaku had also heard that the imposing mansion, occupying almost a half an acre of land, was up for sale. However, it had never occurred to him to buy the place for himself. It surprised him that his wife, who worried about the seventy yen for Seiichirō and the fifty yen for Fumio, should speak so eagerly about buying a new house. He was more taken aback than impressed by the astuteness of his wife who felt that a mansion in town was a worthwhile investment for the future.

The tiny cottage he had bought for his mistress was located in Masago-chō. What was really behind Hana's words? Had she mentioned Masago-chō on purpose or just by chance? Hana had not once in all this time complained about the nights he spent away from home, and yet here she was urging him to buy this spacious mansion in Masago-chō. Keisaku could not help suspecting that his wife's words were inspired by jealousy.

"That would be splendid. I wouldn't want to be thought of as Matani of Musota for the rest of my life."

Keisaku said these words casually, but he realized that sweat was pouring from his armpits. Hastily taking up his tea bowl, he gulped down some tea and complained that it was cold.

Keisaku rarely complained, as his brother did, about the tea being either too dark or too light. Now, however, he was speaking out of desperation. Hana sprang to her feet.

"I'm terribly sorry. It was thoughtless of me."

With quick steps she disappeared into the kitchen with the teapot. Keisaku slipped his hands into the opening of his kimono sleeves and touched his wet armpits.

"How would you like to live in a house in the city?" he asked Tomokazu.

"A house in the city? That would be great. Musota is so provincial," his son said with a precocious air. Keisaku, relaxing for the first time since his return home, laughed boisterously.

In the election for member of the Lower House for the constituency of Wakayama City and Kaisō County, Tasaki Yusuke,
member of the Executive Council of the Seiyūkai, had con-
sistently been chosen by an overwhelming majority of the voters
in past years. Nonetheless, the general election of 1924 had been
an unusually hard battle, for immediately after the split in the
Seiyūkai, the Sakai family—until then staunch Tasaki sup-
porters—suddenly went over to the rival side with Mr. Sakai
himself running as a candidate. Tasaki received 3,478 votes and
was reelected; however, he won by just thirty votes.

"The time has come for Matani Keisaku to take over," murmured the veteran politician to himself, greatly relieved upon
hearing the results of the ballot count. In his capacity as chairman
of the party's election committee, this seventy-year-old politician
had rallied his men about him in an impressive manner. He had
been nominated minister of state a number of times but had been
in no great hurry to attain national fame. His sincerity and honesty
showed in his noble profile. Listening to the cheers of victory in
his election headquarters, Tasaki pondered the fighting spirit dem-
onstrated by Keisaku in the recent election. It would not have
been an exaggeration to say that Tasaki was entirely indebted
to Keisaku for his reelection.

The election results strengthened the feeling throughout the
prefecture that it was now time for Matani Keisaku. His mansion
in Masago-chō was most imposing, all but confirming the rumor
that he would run. The Western-style iron gate opened to reveal
a gravel road which led for about 120 feet to the entrance. Visitors
were constantly streaming in and out of the one-storied building,
which occupied 908 square yards, and menservants and maids ran
busily about the place on their errands.

Hana was at the center of all this activity. After the family had
moved to the city, she was addressed by all as madame. In keeping with this title of respect, she started wearing kimonos with

smarter designs. Hana, now aged forty-seven, still retained her former beauty. She looked only about forty; but she made sure her kimonos were not too conspicuously youthful. On the contrary, she had such an air of refinement about her that people found it difficult to believe that she was a country girl who had made her way to the city.

When the excitement of the May election had subsided in the Matani household, Hana suddenly found herself extremely busy. There was a possibility of a marriage for Fumio, who was still attending Tokyo Women's College. Having successfully completed her first year of preparatory courses, Fumio had been accepted into the regular undergraduate program and was currently a third-year student majoring in English literature.

For the past two years, Hana had been very worried about her daughter's chances for marriage. She herself had married Keisaku when she was twenty-two, but she was determined to marry Fumio off before she turned twenty-one. Hana deeply regretted having allowed Fumio to attend college in Tokyo, for her daughter was gleefully striding in the opposite direction from that which Hana had in mind.

Keisaku often made his way to Tokyo on official business, as he was now the head of the Wakayama branch of the Seiyūkai. On his return from one of his trips, he found himself alone with his wife.

"You know, Hana, Fumio has found herself in quite a predicament." His eyes twinkled as he studied his wife's reaction.

"What do you mean by that?"

Hana knew that her husband was only teasing her, but she could not help worrying endlessly about her daughter. When Fumio first went to Tokyo, she had written regularly describing enthusiastically her new life. Within six months, however, she wrote but rarely. When she sent an occasional postcard to her parents, it was a request for more money. Seiichirō had failed in the diplomatic service examination and was still ensconced in his Tokyo boarding house. His letters—formal and to the point—were also requests for money. The Matanis quickly forwarded the amount requested, as they accorded their eldest son the highest respect. Neither Keisaku nor Hana had ever worried about how their son would spend the money, for they knew that most of it would be used to buy books and presents for his brother and sisters when he returned home for the holidays. Seiichirō was not at all an impetuous youth and would never squander money to buy the favors of geishas or to pay for expensive visits to a house of assignation.

On the other hand, Fumio's demands were puzzling. In the first place, a girl about to be married should not be spending her father's money so freely. Secondly, she described in detail the exact sum she needed and how she planned to spend it. Seiichirō had never asked for a particular amount of money, although he would send an urgent letter by special delivery if the amount forwarded had been too small. Whenever that happened, Hana would nervously send a larger sum than he could possibly use. As for Fumio, she wrote the exact cost of each item and requested a given total. That in itself was all right, but Fumio, who was a lavish spender to begin with, listed each item and her reason for wanting it. Furthermore, her requests for money came far more frequently than her brother's.

"Fumio has been leading quite an exciting life."

"Really?"

"Yes, indeed. She says that since men and women have equal rights, women should go to places frequented by men. Therefore, she goes regularly to cafés."

"Goodness! Does she really?"

"I heard Fumio herself boast about it. She's really amusing."

"I don't think it's at all funny," Hana retorted, silencing her husband. Keisaku sheepishly shrugged his shoulders. After moving to the mansion in Masago-chō, he often found himself face to face with his wife. Shortly before the family moved in, he frantically bought off his mistress, who had been installed in a house less than a block away. In deference to his wife, his amorous dallyings became extremely discreet. While he was in Tokyo, the clerks of the Lower House took care of official business, but Hana saw to the more obscure duties of a politician which could not be classified as business. In her capacity as the wife of Matani Keisaku, Hana carried out her obligations admirably. In time she had become indispensable to her husband, and so he listened carefully to her opinions.

"It's no joke."

Keisaku's expression suddenly grew serious, and he thoughtfully folded his arms. He was not a heavy drinker, and therefore his daughter's words had amused him at the time. Now that he thought again about her remarks, they certainly were not funny. Leftist thought which was considered very dangerous was currently widespread among the young, especially among students. It was foolish for Keisaku to have abandoned his daughter.

"Dear, you should start thinking about finding a husband for Fumio."

Being the daughter of Matani Keisaku, Fumio would not be lacking in candidates for her hand, despite her reputation for being somewhat wild. Almost immediately the name of an only son of an old family in Hidaka County was mentioned as a prospective bridegroom. Then, through an intermediary, the Sakai family of Kaisō County asked if their second son, who would be setting up a junior line, might have the hand of Keisaku's daughter. For Fumio to marry into the Sakai family would be an ideal means for reconciling political rivals. The two marriage offers were the results of Keisaku, the Speaker of the Prefectural House, announcing during a recess in the official proceedings:

"Do you know of anyone interested in marrying my daughter?"

Keisaku and Hana decided to reject the proposal from the Sakai family; however, the Hidaka proposal sounded promising. As a formality, photographs of Fumio had to be handed over.

"Hana, please go to Tokyo. You're better than I am at reasoning with Fumio."

"No, I'm not, but I'll try my best."

That summer Hana made her way to Tokyo and saw the capital of Japan for the first time in her life. Mrs. Tasaki came to greet her at Tokyo Station and saw to it that she was comfortable during her stay. A year had passed since the Great Kanto Earthquake and Tokyo had not yet been rebuilt to the extent that one could go sightseeing. But, of course, Hana was far too busy to pass the time in such a leisurely manner.

Fumio, who remained in Tokyo even during the summer vacation, worked together with other students to produce a coterie magazine and was completely absorbed in writing articles. The words "women's rights" appeared frequently in her essays. A few short stories were included in the journal, but it consisted mainly of critical essays. All of Fumio's articles expressed her feelings of indignation toward a society dominated by men. In her essays, written in a very involved literary style, she vehemently attacked "members of the same sex who allow men to oppress them." Her articles, which were bitter attacks on the apathy of Japanese women, described actual examples taken from society.

The Muraki-ya in Tameike had fortunately escaped being destroyed by the fire that followed the earthquake. The guests staying there were, without exception, respectable people. In keeping with its guests, the inn itself—from the stepping stone at the entrance to the fine quality wood of the corridors—was well constructed. The place was immaculately clean, having been wiped and dusted from corner to corner. However, Fumio's room was in a state of complete disorder. And it was so filthy Hana could hardly believe it was a room in the Murakis' inn. Hana sighed and set down *Women's Rights*. She saw at a glance that the money for lessons in tea ceremony and flower arrangement—which Fumio had promised to continue—had been pocketed. The elegant writing table which Hana had personally selected for Fumio looked as though it had not been dusted for months. A cottonlike layer, far thicker than ordinary dust, covered the table, on which were stacked several English-language dictionaries. Scattered about the room were such magazines as *The Rehabilitation of Women*, *Japanese Women*, and *Women's Opinions*.

Fumio was not in the habit of reading or writing at her elegant writing table. Instead, she used as her desk a board balanced on two tangerine crates. Even now she was seated at this makeshift desk. Placing her hands on her lap, she declared:

"Mother, I think you'll understand me better after you read those magazines. I'm leading a full life as a student, you know."

Fumio was brimming with self-confidence. The expensive formal kimono she had slung over her shoulders was torn at the shoulder and lap. Hana could not imagine how her daughter had managed to tear her kimono in such unlikely places.

Hana was not one to nag. She remained silent and promptly set to work putting the room in order. When she asked one of the maids to bring her a broom and some rags, the proprietress, very much flustered, came rushing in.

"Madame, please tell us what you would like to have done. I'll have the maids do the actual cleaning."

Thinking of all the trouble Fumio must have caused at the Muraki-ya by inviting her classmates over and making a noise well into the night, Hana politely declined the offer. Getting Fumio to help, she began the onerous task of cleaning the room. When she opened the closet, a stench struck her nose. Month after month Fumio had thrown her soiled undergarments into the willow luggage.

Without telling Fumio the reason for her visit, Hana took her the very next day to Mitsukoshi department store in Nihombashi. At the beauty parlor, Hana had Fumio's casual bun combed out and put up into a fashionable young girl's coiffure with a parting. Fumio sat very still, letting the hairdresser do her hair. However, she was bathed in a cold sweat when the woman scraped her scalp and lice began to fall off. But the middle-aged hairdresser wore a cool, professional look on her face as she solemnly combed out the girl's hair.

Fumio was dressed formally in a long-sleeved kimono of silk gauze which Hana had hurriedly had made at Takashimaya in Osaka. The two women then walked up to the portrait studio. Fumio had until then been practically paralyzed with embarrassment after having her mother see the slovenly life she led. Upon entering the studio, however, she began to grow suspicious. When the picture-taking session was over, Fumio asked, somewhat belatedly:

"Mother, is this a marriage-interview photograph?"

"Yes," replied Hana brusquely. So openly did she show her displeasure that Fumio was rendered speechless.

Hana ordered ten prints each of the photographs of Fumio in a kimono with a design of paulownia and phoenixes tied with a sash of embossed brocade. One pose had her standing facing the camera, showing her from head to toe; another showed her at an angle facing forward; and a third, at an angle from the back. Hana left instructions for the prints to be forwarded to Wakayama. Hana and Fumio then made their way out of the department store and set out briskly for the Tasaki mansion.

"Thank you very much for coming out to welcome me," said Hana to Mrs. Tasaki by way of a greeting.

"Is that you, Fumio? What a delightful surprise! Why, you look lovely!"

Seeing the girl for the first time dressed up so formally, Mrs. Tasaki stared in wide-eyed surprise. Hana explained that they had just come from having Fumio's formal photographs taken. Mrs. Tasaki thought to herself that Hana was after all provincial. The latest coiffure with the hair coming down over the ears would have been far more becoming to Fumio, who was rather large. Nevertheless, she complimented Fumio.

"What an exquisite kimono! Fumio, it's so much more pleasing for a young girl to behave like a lady."

As far as Mrs. Tasaki could judge, Fumio did not care in the least about her appearance. Generous girl that she was, Fumio was also of a carefree disposition, and even when she visited the

Tasakis, she did not change into more formal attire. Every time she saw Fumio, Mrs. Tasaki would draw her attention to her casual appearance, but even she had failed to get the girl to change her habits.

The beautician had powdered her face lavishly, and so Fumio was appropriately made up for paying a formal call. Mrs. Tasaki mentally compared Fumio with her mother and discovered that there was a striking resemblance in their features. Nonetheless, it amazed her that the two women impressed one so differently. The glowing beauty with which the forty-nine-year-old Hana was endowed was entirely lacking in her twenty-one-year-old daughter.

"I wanted above all to have Fumio marry before she turned twenty-one. However, it was difficult to accomplish this, since I was in Wakayama and Fumio was here in Tokyo."

Hana did not disclose the fact that there had been a proposal from Hidaka. Instead, she tactfully asked Mrs. Tasaki for her help in finding a suitable husband for her daughter.

"Why, of course. Please let me have the formal photographs of Fumio," said Mrs. Tasaki in a youthful-sounding voice, although she was more than ten years older than Hana. Hana did not take Mrs. Tasaki's request for the photographs seriously, as she had only spoken to her out of politeness and had no real intention of enlisting the woman's help.

The two women—one speaking in the Tokyo dialect and the other in the Wakayama dialect—chatted for a while longer. Utterly bored, Fumio looked away. She was feeling wretched, for the sash had been tied much too tightly around her chest, making it difficult for her to swallow the sweets which had been served.

Politely refusing the invitation to stay to dinner, Hana and Fumio returned to the Muraki-ya. No sooner had Fumio entered her room than she began to remove her long-sleeved kimono. She was on the verge of making insulting remarks about the silly attire. However, seeing that her mother was silent, she thought it best not to say a word. After slipping into her informal kimono, Fumio noticed her mother was seated properly in a corner of the room. She looked down at her feet and saw the Takashimaya folding case, into which she knew she had to fold away the layers of kimono she had thrown off. They were damp with perspiration, and so the proper thing for her to do would have been to air them on a clothes rack overnight before putting them away. However, she was too careless to remember this. As she folded first the silk gauze underrobe, then the silk gauze long-sleeved kimono, Fumio felt utterly disgusted with so impractical an outfit. Was she not trying to break away from the wretched condition of women in the past, who, dressed in such confining robes, had been unable to express themselves? Nevertheless, intimidated by her mother, who never questioned the past, Fumio was unable to express her defiance. As she folded the kimono in a careless manner, she thought of how she would love to have her mother see the revolutionary gym outfit which the Ochanomizu Women's College had recently adopted. The paper case rustled as she stuffed the garments into it.

Now that she had done what was expected of her, Fumio rose to her feet. Feeling ill at ease in the same room as her mother, she began to rearrange at random the books in her bookcase. Suddenly glancing back, she saw that Hana had opened the paper case and was neatly folding the long-sleeved kimono. Fumio stood perfectly still as she watched with intense aversion the elegant movement of Hana's hands. A girl who rebels against her mother usually finds it unbearable to realize that she is no match for the older woman, and Fumio was no exception. Biting her lip, she gazed down at her mother with a strange, piercing look.

After all the trouble they had gone through, the photographs of Fumio, which were forwarded to Wakayama, were of no immediate use. Fumio firmly told her father, who had made his way to Tokyo upon his wife's return home, that she absolutely refused to have anything to do with an arranged marriage.

"The thought that my marriage would unite our family with

that old Hidaka family fills me with revulsion. If you force me to go through with the marriage interview, I swear I'll become a newspaper reporter and earn my own living. It'll be a good chance for me to prove that equal rights means economic equality as well."

The ten sets of photographs were passed on to interested parties and by autumn a number of proposals had come in from the main branches of distinguished families and important landowners in Yamato and Shikoku, all of which were rejected.

"What is a landowner? Father, you're a landowner, and so the blood of a landowner runs in my veins. What a disgrace! Landowners have for generations stashed away in their storehouses the wealth resulting from the hard labor of tenant farmers and have thus led a life of idle luxury. Besides which, I have grave doubts about the Seiyūkai. Isn't it just a group of wealthy landowners?"

"Don't joke like that. Why, look at all the work I do! Every group I've organized—whether it's the Water Utilization Association or the Citrus Fruit Association—has been with the welfare of the farmers in mind. I'm kept busy every single day carrying out my duties."

"You know, Father, I really respected you when I was in Wakayama. I thought then that through politics you were striving to bring happiness to the people. But my thinking has changed since I came to Tokyo. Father, if you are sincere about wanting to go into politics, you have to start from scratch."

"That's nonsense!"

"What is politics? The old Seiyūkai split into the Seiyū Party and the new Seiyūkai. What was the reason for this division? Wasn't it a fight for power among its members? The people have been excluded altogether from politics."

"Fumio. Let's discuss this calmly. You keep talking about politics, but I'm not a member of parliament . . ."

"Mother says that you'll be a minister of state one day. A minister of state is a politician, isn't he? You're a politician, all right."

"Don't say such cruel things! I'm not the great man your mother thinks I am."

Keisaku, who had no trouble directing the members of the Prefectural House to do as he wished, had a difficult time indeed handling his daughter.

"You were absolutely right, Hana. We made a terrible mistake sending Fumio to Tokyo. When I told her I was taking her back with me, she said we should think of her as having left home permanently."

"If that's so, why did she send a telegram asking for more money?"

"What? Has she already sent a telegram?"

"It arrived just before your return."

After her graduation from the Girl's School, Kazumi remained at home and devoted herself to mastering the home-making arts. Utae, her younger sister, did not seem to have any interest in continuing her formal studies after leaving school. The Matanis received a request from an old Yamato family asking for Kazumi if Fumio were not available. Keisaku and Hana were at a loss, as it sounded like an excellent match for Kazumi. However, they feared that Fumio's future would be dark indeed if she, the eldest daughter, were not married off first.

"Please go once more to Tokyo to fetch her home."

"She wouldn't come—not unless I dragged her home bound and gagged."

When she parted with her daughter in Tokyo, Hana had instinctively sensed that Fumio's rebelliousness was raging like a storm inside her. It was now beyond her power to force her daughter to return home. Whenever Keisaku and Hana found themselves alone, they spoke of Fumio and went to bed without deciding what to do with her. People from good families still frowned upon the career woman. Hana had been familiar with the term "old maid" for many years. The thought that her daughter would become a career woman and eventually an old maid nearly broke her heart. Night after night she lay awake, listening to her husband's even breathing. Kazumi and Utae, constantly reprimanded for no good reason, were puzzled by their mother's strange behavior, little knowing that Hana was going through menopause and was therefore unable to keep her irritability under control.

One morning a personal letter arrived from Mrs. Tasaki addressed to both Keisaku and Hana. Written on rolled letter paper in an elegant hand was a conventional greeting. Mrs. Tasaki then mentioned a bright young man by the name of Harumi Eiji, an employee of Shōkin Bank where their son-in-law worked. A friend of their son-in-law since they had been students together in the First High School and Tokyo Imperial University, he often visited the Tasakis. Whenever Fumio happened to visit while he was there, she had observed that the two young people got along very well. She had discreetly investigated the Harumi family and found that the family was in no way inferior, although they did not own as much property as the Matanis. Moreover, the young man's character was pleasing and his future extremely bright. Her husband had said repeatedly that if Eiji were to be the bridegroom, he would be delighted to serve as go-between. Mrs. Tasaki concluded her letter by saying that ever since she had been asked by Hana, she had been on the lookout for a suitable husband for Fumio.

At the breakfast table, from which rose the delicious smell of white *miso* soup, Keisaku finished reading Mrs. Tasaki's letter and rubbed his eyes with the back of his hand. He was over fifty and was turning gray. His face, with its strong chin, suggested a dignity which was in keeping with his age. Using his chopsticks to help himself to some pickled radish from the bowl in the middle of the table, he brought the radish directly into his mouth and crunched it noisily.

Hana had been taught a different set of table manners. When one helped oneself to anything from a large serving dish, one first placed the food on a small individual dish before putting it into one's mouth. Hana frowned with displeasure at her husband's rough and ready manners. They would soon be celebrating their silver wedding anniversary, but the degree of refinement of the Matani family had yet to reach the level of the Kimotos. Feeling very irritated, Hana read the letter which her husband had handed over to her.

"He sounds like a promising young man."

"I wonder if a person born and raised in Tokyo and a girl like Fumio could be happy together."

"I personally would not want Fumio to marry a man who is not from these parts."

"We'll have to think seriously about how far away she'll be, if she marries him."

Both Keisaku and Hana were opposed to the match. Nevertheless, they could not very well turn down this proposal unless they had a better offer or one which was likely to be accepted. In view of the goodwill that Mrs. Tasaki had for them, it would be extremely awkward to reject the offer after having mentioned the business to her in the first place.

"Hana, you answer her letter."

"I'll try my best."

However, before Hana could do so, they received a special delivery letter from Fumio. She had dashed off carelessly on the envelope: "Mr. Keisaku Matani. Personal." Her husband was not at home, and so Hana broke the seal of the envelope. She was completely taken aback by what Fumio had written in bold strokes on three sheets of stationery. Here and there—between such phrases as "the wretchedness of each day," "freedom in love," "freedom in marriage," "the new age," and "the passion of youth"—was written the name Harumi Eiji. Hana read the letter through, scarcely believing her eyes. Fumio had by chance met her ideal man. This man, Harumi Eiji, was a close friend of the Tasaki son-in-law. After hearing from Mrs. Tasaki that Eiji regarded her with special kindness, she had spent many a sleepless night tormented by a passion which welled up from the depths of her being. Eiji was a promising young man who dreamed of going abroad. There was no doubt in her mind that they were compatible in every way. She was informing her father of their love, hoping that he would give them his blessing. If he turned down the young man after looking into his family background, she could not predict at this point just what drastic step she would take. The tone of her letter was threatening.

"This is tragic! She is really infatuated," declared Keisaku, amused by the letter.

Noticing Hana's look of distress, he turned serious, stating that since he was planning to go to Tokyo for business, he would leave a little early and personally speak to Mrs. Tasaki about the whole affair. Hana cast her eyes downward and in a thin voice beseeched him to do so. Once again Hana was tormented by feelings of deep remorse that Fumio had not been married off immediately after her graduation.

Mrs. Tasaki greeted Keisaku in Tokyo. The first thing she said was that Fumio had definitely made up her mind. Therefore, there was no other way to settle the matter than to allow the couple to marry. Smiling sweetly, she explained that everything had taken place just as she had described it in her letter. The two young people extolled equal rights and freedom in love. However, they had been brought up in a society where the position of men and women was not equal. Neither Eiji nor Fumio had ever been intimately involved with anyone else of the opposite sex. In her opinion, they were made for each other.

"I really think they make an ideal couple."

Mrs. Tasaki wore a triumphant look on her face. Keisaku could not help but feel that here indeed was a politician's wife. After listening once again to a detailed description of Eiji's personal character, he became quite enthusiastic about the match. Mrs. Tasaki took care of all the arrangements and personally saw to Keisaku's meals during his stay. One night, Keisaku invited Eiji and the Tasakis' son-in-law to a restaurant. At first, he had doubts about Eiji, a fair, good-looking young man who seemed highly intelligent. Nonetheless, Keisaku, who was practically a teetotaler, was quick to approve of the man when he saw that Eiji was a strong drinker.

The elaborate wedding ceremony which united the Matani and the Harumi families was held in the Imperial Hotel in Hibiya on February 21 of the following year. Tasaki Yusuke, who had been appointed minister of agriculture on the seventeenth of that month, and his wife served as the official go-betweens. The guest list for the wedding. which united the eldest daughter of a man of influence in Wakayama and the second son of a poor family of samurai lineage of Tokyo, was most impressive. The family status of the Harumis was certainly not inferior to that of the Matanis, judging from the relatives of the family who offered their congratulations. For the most part, the relatives were government officials and scholars. Among the friends of the Matani family who spoke on behalf of the bride's family were members of the peerage in Wakayama and members of parliament.

The mother of the bride had every reason to be completely satisfied with all the arrangements. Nevertheless, Hana was not altogether happy and bowed her head in embarrassment throughout the Western-style banquet. Not to be outshone by the magnificence of the wedding garments, clothes she was unaccustomed to fitting over her ample figure, the bride sat next to the groom with her head held high and listened attentively to the speeches. The attitude of the bride and that of her mother were indeed a study in contrasts.

Eiji's father was an architect, but his stern countenance gave him the appearance of a scholar of Chinese classics. A stubborn old man, he looked as though he could easily tackle the young couple head on if necessary. On the other hand, Fumio's mother-in-law was a tiny woman with soft features. Hana was greatly relieved that Fumio had not married the eldest son. It would have been a disaster for such a kind and gentle mother-in-law to live together with a bride as rebellious as Fumio. Hana could just imagine the uproar in the household if Fumio found herself confronted by anyone who argued back at her. Fortunately, Eiji was the second son. If he continued to work for Shōkin Bank, which specialized in foreign exchange, the couple would be spending a great deal of time abroad, thereby avoiding serious discord in the Harumi family.

Under the glittering chandeliers, the white tablecloth appeared especially dazzling. Hana recalled the details of her own wedding following the long journey to Musota, part of the way by boat and the rest of the way in a palanquin. How different was her daughter's wedding! Moreover, Fumio had ignored altogether Hana's wishes. All that Hana had done was to select her daughter's dowry and order her bridal kimonos and trousseau.

Hana had of course been as extravagant as she pleased in getting Fumio ready. Less than half a year had elapsed since the exchange of engagement presents, and so Hana had not been able to order a dowry as elaborate as her own. Nonetheless, she felt that the least she could do was to order all the kimonos her daughter would ever need for both daily wear and formal occasions. She had several outfits made for each of the four seasons and they would last for the next twenty years, even if Fumio did not look after them properly. Hana was completely satisfied, because she had personally seen to all the details that went into the making of the kimonos. Since the wedding of the Crown Prince the year before, phoenixes and embossed chrysanthemums headed the list of kimono designs currently in vogue. The dowry items, from cushions and bedding to the canvas chest covers, had the chrysanthemum design. Phoenixes were displayed along the lower half of the kimonos.

The Harumi crest, consisting of double arrows on a tortoise shell, was most appropriate for descendants of a samurai family. Inquiring about the crest for the women in the family, Hana had been told by Eiji's mother that it was a plum-blossom crest. She had the kimono dealer weave curtains with the two contrasting crests, but they did not harmonize well, the crests having nothing in common. A family crest with this kind of arrow indicated the

Mōri family line, while the plum blossom indicated a family related in some way to the Sugawara family. In the maternal line of the Harumi family, might there have been a descendant of a family with a plum-blossom crest? But even while Hana was considering this possibility, she decided on the ivy crest for her daughter.

Hana was fairly certain that Fumio's mother-in-law would not be fussy about the bride's crest, for Fumio was marrying the second son. In choosing the ivy crest, Hana was probably expressing her hope that her proud and independent daughter would cling to her husband like ivy. She may also have been expressing her unhappiness, as the marriage had been arranged with hardly any thought given to her wishes. Vibrant colors in the urban style had been selected for Fumio's long-sleeved kimono. It was customary in Wakayama for the bride to wear black at the end of the ceremony; however, Fumio wore instead a celadon green kimono of Yūzen silk embossed with colorful ivy leaves. The kimono, decorated tastefully with embroidery and gold thread, was truly magnificent.

In spite of all the effort Hana had put into the bridal garments, they failed to impress the guests. On the contrary, the guests were overwhelmed by the ample proportions of the bride, who, in contrast to the stylish bridegroom, was five foot four inches tall and weighed 150 pounds. Fumio's failure to impress the guests was no doubt due to the fact that she was unhappy about having to dress up so elaborately. Fumio lacked altogether the ability to feel at ease in a lovely kimono. Eiji had said that Japanese women were at a disadvantage at parties given abroad because of their small build. Hana sighed and wondered whether Eiji had chosen Fumio because of her impressive size.

The home of the newlyweds, in Ōmori, south of Tokyo, was a little too extravagant for a mere bank employee and his young wife. It had been bought by the Matanis, who had agreed to provide money for monthly expenses and the salaries of the maids. Eiji was virtually an adopted son-in-law from the financial point of view. But it was not at all unusual at this time for promising young men in the diplomatic corps, the Ministry of Finance, the Bank of Japan, and Shōkin Bank to marry girls whose dowry came in the form of money. Both Keisaku and Eiji regarded the financial arrangement as being a matter of course. As for Fumio, she was far too busy to question the arrangement. Beside herself with excitement, she tossed aside all the principles she had upheld for so long. In spite of all her boasting, she was, after all, a girl who had never experienced hardship. She had regarded with distaste the thought of marrying the son of a well-established family and had chosen for herself a man with no property. As far as she could see, there was no contradiction in their becoming the owner of a new house that had been bought by her parents.

While the young couple were on their honeymoon, Hana returned with her husband to Wakayama. She felt thoroughly depressed and quite unable to feel a mother's joy in seeing her daughter safely married. Aware of Hana's emotional state, Keisaku was very solicitous. He would invite her to join him in the dining car and would occasionally turn to address his wife as he viewed the scenery from the window. This was probably his way of making amends for having sorely neglected her for so long.

"Eiji appears to be a strong drinker," commented Hana, expressing her anxiety. Her statement was totally unrelated to what Keisaku had been saying to her.

"He is, all right. I wish I could drink like that."

"You should have cautioned Fumio. A young man shouldn't drink too much."

"Don't worry. A man who loves his drink will never get in trouble with other women."

Keisaku ordered cider or tea at banquets, because he could hardly drink a half pint of saké. Nonetheless, he had a scandalous record of amorous dallyings. The men gossiped about him, marveling that he could make passes at women by simply fortifying himself with tea. Rumor had it that his wife had learned about his indiscretions and that he had been forced to reform. He was remarkably good-natured about it all. Actually, Hana had never rebuked her husband to his face. Nor had she ever, in a fit of jealous rage, confronted and challenged any of the geishas with whom her husband was amorously involved. Keisaku had probably embroidered the facts to amuse his companions, thus starting such gossip.

"What a fright I had when she found out about my affair. I can't look her in the eyes any more. Come and see what it's like at my house. Why, I'm treated like an adopted son!"

Keisaku was amused by his own stories. But as his view of life became more and more optimistic, Hana grew increasingly gloomy.

"Look! That's the River Ōi," cried Keisaku and he began to hum the well-known tune about the river. Still in high spirits over his daughter's wedding, he was very much conscious that he was traveling along the Tōkaidō with his wife. Hana, however, found it impossible to match his cheerful mood.

"What a drab river!"

Along the Tōkaidō, they passed a number of rivers—the Tenryū, the Kiso, and the Yodo. At night they finally arrived in Osaka. None of the rivers had the depth and beauty of color to charm Hana.

"Dear."

"Yes. What is it?"

"I don't think I've seen any other river as beautiful as the Ki."

"You're probably right," said Keisaku, rather bored; he tapped his mouth with his hand as he yawned.

Shortly after their return to Musota, Kōsaku's daughter fell into the Narutaki River and was drowned. Misono, who had turned eighteen, set out one spring morning and failed to return home that night. Ume was frantic with worry and Kōsaku was livid. The next morning they were notified that their daughter's body had been found. Suicide was out of the question, and the autopsy showed that she had not been murdered. It was generally believed that she had suddenly slipped and fallen into the river while strolling along the river's bank that evening. However, the Narutaki flowed between Sonobe and Kusumi, and it was thought strange that on that particular night Misono had been strolling along the banks of a river located some distance away from Musota. The villagers, their voices hushed in fear, said the poor girl had probably been possessed by a fox. There actually was a place in Musota known as the Fox's Grave. According to the old folks, it was haunted. And yet no one had ever died as a result of being possessed by a fox.

A funeral for the only daughter of the branch family, taking place immediately after the wedding of the eldest daughter of the main family, was enough to make even people who were not blood relations feel uneasy. Summoning a ricksha, Hana left at once for Shin'ike and saw to the details of the funeral, substituting for the girl's grief-stricken parents. Appropriate words of consolation eluded her. Finding it painful to look at Kōsaku, who in his grief stared at the floor and was oblivious to her presence, Hana kept herself occupied and gave instructions to the servants dispatched from the main house. In deference to the main family, the villagers came to offer incense. However, Hana found herself too busy to sit quietly with the other members of the bereaved family.

Hana felt sure that the grief-stricken Kōsaku, mourning the death of his only daughter, would look up at any moment and impale her with one of his sarcastic comments. Strangely enough, she, for her part, had completely forgotten the ill-feeling she had harbored against her brother-in-law all these years and was at a loss as to how to console him.

Hana remained in Agenogaito until after the funeral service. She had been away from her old home for quite a while. When the Matanis moved to Wakayama City, the Matsuis, a young couple, had come to look after their house. Mr. Matsui was employed in the Prefectural Government Office.

"You must be simply exhausted. After all, you've only just returned from Tokyo."

"Not at all. It isn't physical fatigue, you know. It's just my mind that's distracted by all this anxiety. The sensation is really quite strange."

A low-watt electric light bulb hung from the ceiling of the kitchen. Having made plans to return to the city the next morning, Hana relaxed as she and the Matsuis peeled the tangerines that had come from a tree which grew in the grounds of the Masago-chō mansion. The tangerine was as big as a summer orange, but the peel was of a lighter, more delicate hue. Held in the palm of one's hand, it was much lighter in weight than a summer orange and was shaped differently at the top. Grown in the southern part of the prefecture, almost exclusively in Tasukawa in Arida County, it was the best variety of tangerine. The fruit itself, which Hana was very fond of, was small; it was also tender and delicately sweet. As soon as she moved to Masago-chō, she had had a branch grafted to the tree in the back garden, which from the year before had begun to bear the delicious fruit. She had earlier asked someone to take some of the tangerines to Kōsaku and his wife. At Shin'ike, however, she had been unable to say anything to Kōsaku and had spoken to Ume only. In the end, afraid of offending the grief-stricken couple in any way, she had brought the fruit back with her to Agenogaito.

"It's delicious!" exclaimed Mrs. Matsui after tasting it.

"They were at their best about a month ago—so much juicier."

As she slipped a piece of tangerine into her mouth, Hana reflected upon the hectic month she had just lived through. The loneliness experienced by a mother who had given her daughter away in marriage was like the bittersweet but dry taste of tangerines that were no longer at their best but were still pleasing to the palate.

Later that day, Hana lay down in bed and suddenly felt intensely lonely. She now realized that Fumio was a member of another family. She had once deeply regretted allowing her daughter to leave home and letting her attend Tokyo Women's College, but that emotion was not at all like this empty feeling. Despite Fumio's rebelliousness and harsh words, there had been a strong bond between mother and daughter which had been severed once and for all.

Hana once again recalled the events of twenty-five years earlier. She understood with utmost clarity Toyono's reason for not having made the formal visit to the new bride and not having attended the banquet. If Fumio's reception had been held at the Harumi residence instead of at the Imperial Hotel and if Fumio had married the eldest son, Hana would have felt doubly forlorn. She tried to alleviate her wretchedness with these thoughts which whirled through her head, but they made her feel all the more miserable. Tears began to trickle down from the corners of her eyes.

Hana wept silently for some time. She then collected herself and went to the lavatory. The weather was already warm, and so even at night the corridor did not feel cold against the soles of her bare feet. On her way back to the bedroom, a strange light in the garden shrubbery caught her eye. The Matanis had been in the habit of leaving the shutters open from April on, as sliding glass doors had been installed along the inner corridor. Hana paused and focused her eyes on a bluish white light which moved slowly along the base of the greenery. It was the body of a huge snake which appeared to be at least two inches in diameter. Neither its head not its tail was visible But its scales glittered as it moved. This must be the white snake which made its home in the ridge of the storehouse at the other end of the garden, Hana thought. She had often heard from Yasu and the villagers that this snake was the true master of the Matani household. Nonetheless, Hana had not seen it with her own eyes in all these years. Feeling neither frightened nor squeamish, she wondered why the snake alone appeared so vivid when everything else— the trees, the stone lantern, and the garden rocks—was indistinguishable in the darkness.

Hana reported the incident upon her return to Masago-chō. Keisaku remarked:

"Oh? I've seen it just twice. It's huge, about six feet long. But it's gentle and wouldn't harm a soul."

Looking miniscule in the thick bedding, Yasu had her eyes closed.

"Did you really see the snake? I've seen it twice. It's about six feet long. But it's perfectly harmless. There's no danger in letting it live in the storehouse."

Yasu repeated the story ad nauseam. She was nearly ninety-one years old and completely senile. During the past year she had been confined to bed much of the time. She expressed her deep regret that she had been unable to attend Fumio's wedding in Tokyo. Then, as though she had forgotten completely about the wedding, she remarked to Hana that unless they quickly found a husband for Fumio, her marriage would be delayed. This delay would result in grave consequences.

Yasu had been startled when first informed of Misono's death, but three days later she had forgotten all about the tragic drowning. This was probably because she had never been very close to Misono. The old woman took great pleasure in talking about her girlhood memories and the first few years after becoming mistress of the Matani family. She promptly forgot whatever she was told, but the white snake was an exception. She never seemed to grow weary of relating the incident to the maids who looked after her and to her three married daughters, who came to visit her.

"Mother's telling the story about the snake again," reported the eldest daughter, who had married into a family in Nishinoshō. She herself was old enough to have grandchildren and her wrinkled face was the exact image of her mother's.

"Not again! Every time I visit her, she repeats that story."

"Hana, do you think her end is near? This is a sure sign of senility."

She then told Hana that, according to family tradition, the appearance of the snake foretold a death in the family.

"Surely it appeared because of Misono's tragic death. Mother's still very healthy."

"Hana," said Yasu with a sigh. "I am truly grateful to you for treating me so kindly. In my old age, I've complained to you whenever I felt like it. No matter when I die, I'll die a peaceful death. I prefer you to my own daughters and feel more at ease in your company."

"You can't mean that."

"Oh, yes she does. Mother says so all the time."

Hana bowed her head in silence. A wave of happiness swept over her. A woman who succeeded in winning the affection of her mother-in-law had the family under her control. Any woman would be proud of such an achievement.

And yet Hana would probably never have complete control over her own daughter. On the morning of the seventh day after Misono's death in the river, Hana set out by ricksha for Musota. Inserted in her tea green sash, which she herself had tied, was a letter from Fumio received five days earlier. It was the first letter from her daughter since her wedding. Overcome by nostalgia, Hana had unsealed the envelope, only to have her eager anticipation melt into disillusionment.

Fumio's letter, which began with a masculine salutation, attacked Hana as before.

> I have married a mere bank employee, but his future is bright. He and I will not be shackled to the past, since he is not from a distinguished family with an impressive name and farmlands handed down from generation to generation. Our motto is 'a modern life-style.' Therefore, I am returning the many useless items included in my dowry.

Was it necessary for Fumio to be so blunt and cruel? She might have said that since some of the things in her dowry were not needed and would be in the way in their tiny new home, she was sorry but she was returning them. There was a world of difference in the two statements, even though they meant the same thing. Fumio added that she was sending the things to Musota; and, the day before, Mr. Matsui had notified Hana of their arrival.

Before making her way to Shin'ike, Hana entered the gate of the Agenogaito house to see what had been returned. Small green buds were burgeoning on the branches of the persimmon tree. It was spring and Hana's heart grew tranquil.

"What a lovely day," Hana said cheerfully. Mrs. Matsui was sewing near the entrance to the house.

"I'm sorry to trouble you with all these things."

There were several carelessly packed crates and parcels in assorted shapes and sizes, all wrapped in straw matting. They had been left untouched on the concrete floor of the entrance. Hana immediately summoned two tenant farmers and had them unpack the crates and parcels. The following items appeared: a decorative mirror stand lacquered in the Kyoto style; a china chest for the sitting room; a complete set of gold lacquer perfume containers; a wickerwork trunk into which were stuffed Fumio's long-sleeved bridal kimono and a long scarlet underrobe of figured crape; and a koto.

"Oh, dear. Look at that wicked crack!" Mrs. Matsui knit her brows and wiped with a towel the damaged part of the priceless lacquered box.

"These were packed all wrong in the first place. The cord wasn't even tied tightly," muttered one of the men indignantly.

"Please bring them in here after you've dusted them off," requested Hana weakly. When the men had left, Hana smiled wanly at Mrs. Matsui.

"Would you please help me put the things away in the storehouse?"

"I'd be happy to," Mrs. Matsui replied. An experienced seamstress, she suggested that the kimonos be aired before being stored away.

"That's a good idea," said Hana. In her wretchedness, she

moved about sluggishly. Mrs. Matsui, however, was hard at work. After quickly opening the paper cases, she spread out Fumio's wedding kimonos in one of the larger rooms.

"This kimono is really lovely. What perfect taste! The villagers are so sad they weren't able to see Fumio's wedding. Madame, may I show the neighbors the kimonos?"

"No, surely not. It wouldn't do to have the main house in a joyful mood when the branch family is in mourning."

The koto which had been returned was the very one Hana had brought with her from Kudoyama. The gold lacquer design along its side panels was old-fashioned. If it could talk, it would have much to say to anyone who plucked its strings. This was the koto Hana had played for Fumio in the storehouse.

Hana vividly recalled the time she had struck the back of Fumio's hand causing her to bleed. She had given the instrument to her daughter because of the unpleasant memory associated with it and she had hoped that Fumio would one day develop a taste for elegance. Hana was therefore stunned and filled with great sadness to see the koto back here.

"Madame, we could put these things away when you come back from Shin'ike. Won't you please join us for a light meal before you go?"

Mrs. Matsui went off to prepare dinner. Hana seated herself in front of the koto and, surrounded by the gorgeous kimonos, wondered what Fumio's children would be like.

"I wonder," Hana said listlessly as she took up her chopsticks and mechanically brought the food to her lips.

"Yes?"

"I've been terribly worried lately."

"You really haven't been looking very well."

"I wonder if Fumio is barren."

Mrs. Matsui, who was not from Musota, did not know Fumio at all and was totally ignorant of the long-standing feud between Hana and her daughter. Not knowing the circumstances under which part of the dowry had been sent back, she gaily laughed and emphatically denied that Hana had anything to worry about.

"Madame, you shouldn't think of such a possibility. Why, it's less than a month since the wedding!"

Hana realized how foolish she had been and smiled wryly, although she continued to feel uneasy.

Hana's anxiety, however, proved to be groundless. In early summer she received word that Fumio was pregnant and that the baby was due in December.

"That was fast," remarked Keisaku, beaming happily. Hana's joy upon learning that she would soon be a grandmother was no less than her husband's, and she promptly sent her daughter some motherly advice. Addressing herself to Eiji, she requested that Fumio be allowed to return home for her first child, for she truly felt that it was the wisest policy. She then asked Fumio to come home to make a pilgrimage to Jison-in, reminding Fumio of the ancient practice of presenting breast charms.

A letter arrived from Fumio by return post.

> I am entrusting the birth of our child to the gyne-cology ward of the Japanese Red Cross Hospital in Aoyama Takagi-chō which is fully equipped with modern facilities. This is in keeping with the modern age. I beg you not to confuse the child from the time of his birth with superstition.

Fumio's letter did not acknowledge Hana's goodwill. She had not taken into consideration the fact that "our child" was Hana's grandchild as well. However, Hana no longer grieved over her daughter's coldness and was quietly resigned to the fact that Fumio was now a member of another family. After making a pair of breast charms for her daughter, Hana, together with her youngest child, Tomokazu, set out for Kudoyama which she had not visited for well over ten years.

Hana and her son left their home in Masago-chō in a ricksha and made their way to Wakayama Station where they boarded a sooty train on the Wakayama Line. They traveled eastward along the banks of the River Ki to Hashimoto where they were to transfer to another train. Along the way they passed Iwade, Kokawa, and Kaseda, places which Hana would never forget. At each of these places her wedding procession had stopped to rest and each one brought back fond memories.

Tomokazu sat next to his mother. He moved his big body and shifted his legs. Now in his fifth year at Wakayama Middle School, he was planning to leave for Tokyo the following year. Hana had brought him along in order to give him a good chance to see more of the River Ki. It was clear, however, that he was bored by the seemingly interminable train journey.

"Look, Tomokazu. See how beautiful the Ki is," cried Hana.

"But it's such a long way to Kudoyama, isn't it?" The boy showed no interest at all in the scenery.

They had left Wakayama City that morning. Having arrived in Hashimoto in the afternoon, they still had an hour to wait before the arrival of the train on the Kōya Line of Nankai Railways.

"Let's go down by the riverside," suggested Hana. She walked down the slope with the happy look on her face of a woman visiting her beloved parents.

On a map the Wakayama Line appeared to be laid out along the course of the River Ki; however, it was only occasionally possible to catch a glimpse of the blue waters of the river from the train window. Tiny villages and rice fields extended on both sides between Kaseda and Hashimoto. At this time of year, the fields were gradually turning gold and the waters of the river were at a very low level. Hana could scarcely suppress her boundless affection for the Ki.

"I can hear the sound of the river," Tomokazu cried excitedly from where he stood on the pebble-strewn riverbank. The Ki here, near Nara Prefecture, was narrower than it was at Musota downriver and so the stream was far stronger. The surface of the river was a tranquil blue, but underneath the surface the current swept the waters along with such force that the whole riverside reverberated with an unusual booming sound that rattled the bones of Hana and her son.

"I traveled down this river in a boat when I first came to Musota."

"Yes, I've heard about that."

Hana wanted to talk about the past, but the maids had already told Tomokazu about the elaborate wedding procession. Mother and son stood silently and gazed a long distance downriver. A ghostly, bluish haze rose from the water and appeared to tint the autumn sky. Not a cloud was in the sky.

Considering it her duty as a mother, Hana made her way to Tokyo when Fumio was pregnant. She remained at her daughter's side and helped about the house. After recovering from morning sickness, Fumio—though she did not have any feelings of nostalgia for her old home—developed a craving for certain Wakayama delicacies. For breakfast she had white *miso* soup and Wakayama pickled radish, cut lengthwise in the manner of Ki province. As it was the season for *bariko*, Hana had brought a large quantity of the dried fish for the Harumis. Fumio grilled two of the fish three times a day and ate the entire fish, tail and all.

"How I'd love some Kada sea bream, Mother. It's delicious raw or in soup. I'm really tired of the terrible-tasting fish we have here in Tokyo."

"I think it's the ocean current," Hana answered. "I've never had any really delicious fish in Tokyo. The Kada fish are raised in the ocean near Naruto, and so they're nice and firm. They're so tasty in *sushi* as well as in other dishes!"

"You're quite right! How I'd love to have some *sushi* from home. Please ask Father to bring some with him when he comes to Tokyo, Mother."

"All right, dear."

Ever since the wedding, Fumio had worked hard to be a devoted wife. Now that she was pregnant, she felt utterly exhausted from her efforts to please her husband and behaved like a spoiled child with her mother. Hana was greatly relieved to see her daughter being her old self again and responded with ease to her interminable chatter. Nonetheless, when Hana urged her to clean the toilet, Fumio flatly refused.

"That's a silly superstition! In this age of science, all you have to do is follow the instructions of the obstetrician."

Fumio added that prenatal care was far more effective than cleaning the toilet, in order to have a pretty child. Every inch of space in her bedroom was covered with photographs of Rudolph Valentino and Mary Pickford.

"I concentrate on the photographs of Valentino, as I'm planning on a boy. Eiji says that if the baby turns out to be a girl it should look like Mary Pickford, the movie actress. And so he brought home those photographs."

It amused Hana to listen to Fumio explain with obvious displeasure the presence of the photographs of Pickford. She realized that Fumio too was capable of being jealous. However, Hana could not understand the so-called "prenatal care" which called for putting up photographs of movie stars with red hair and blue eyes. It would have been far preferable to put up portraits of Kabuki actors, such as Eisaburō and Fukusuke. At least they were Japanese. But ever since their wedding, the main form of entertainment for the young couple had been the latest foreign films.

Kazuhiko, Fumio's first son, was born in late December. Lying on immaculate white sheets in a room in the Red Cross Hospital, Fumio proudly announced to her mother, who had come to visit:

"I'm not superstitious, but I've had a beautiful baby boy."

For a brief moment there flashed through Hana's mind an image of the white breast charms on which she had written "Fumio age 22." However, she did not think it necessary to mention the offering she had made at the Miroku Hall. Fast asleep in a small crib next to Fumio's bed was the newborn baby whose soft, little body was bundled in a white comforter.

"He has a straight nose. Don't you think he's handsome like his father?"

"I suppose he takes after Valentino."

Fumio was very excited because it had been decided to send Eiji abroad in late spring of the following year. The family would soon be crossing the sea to a foreign country. Fumio spoke to her mother of her future plans of raising her little son to be modern in every way.

But all Hana would say was:

"I'll just wait and see how he turns out."

Eiji's first foreign assignment was the Shanghai branch of Shōkin Bank. In late spring of 1926—following the demise of Emperor Taishō and Yasu's death—the Harumis set sail from the pier in Kōbe Harbor and crossed the East China Sea.

> That I should be crossing the sea to go to China a generation after you traveled down the River Ki is significant. Unlike the blue of the Ki which is changeless throughout the four seasons, the sea is constantly changing from indigo to green then to a serene blue. As we approached Shanghai, however, the waters turned a murky, yellowish brown. The blue of the Ki cannot be compared with the many colors of the sea. I have spoken to Eiji about naming our second son Wataru.

Judging from her first letter from Shanghai, Fumio, married for a year and the mother of a baby boy, seemed to have mellowed considerably. But Hana had to forget about Fumio for a while and attend to other important matters.

Kazumi was engaged to the son of the Kusumi family, an old Yamato family, who had sought her hand for some time. The wedding was scheduled to take place in the spring of 1927. Hana took great pains to see that no mistake was made in uniting the two families. She was determined that her second daughter's wedding would not be like Fumio's: outwardly elaborate but actually very simple in the eyes of a long-established family.

"It wasn't nearly as hectic when we had our daughter marry a poor student," sighed Keisaku, observing the chaotic wedding preparations.

"If you think this is troublesome, you'll never be able to think about the weddings of the other children."

"True. I can't very well tell them to choose their own mates and elope, can I?"

Keisaku could joke in this manner, but he was having problems of his own. Tasaki Yusuke, who had announced that he would turn over his constituents to Keisaku, had encouraged him to run in the coming election. Keisaku, who was fifty-three, looked at his wife and smiled wryly.

"If I had wanted to become a member of parliament, I'd have run twenty years ago. I have every intention to end my career as Matani Keisaku of Wakayama. My dream is to develop the various industries of Wakayama and improve the water and land resources so that Wakayama will never be at the mercy of Osaka. I mean, of course, the Water Utilization Association and the Prefectural Agricultural Association."

"Everything has turned out just as you planned."

"Precisely. Hana . . ."

"Yes, dear?"

"You've always built me up, saying that I'd one day become a minister of state. I never shall, you know."

"Don't say that. Even now I think that you are as capable as any minister."

"What a difficult woman you are!"

"To me, you're a man who could have easily become a minister but who chose instead to devote himself to Wakayama."

"How well you put it!" Keisaku laughed.

Keisaku was fully aware of the fact that he had come this far because of Hana's encouragement. Half of his life had been spent sailing down a smooth river with an elegant wife at his side who had always conducted herself with dignity.

"Hana."

"Yes, dear?"

"I've been thinking of taking formal lessons in the tea cere-mony."

"Why, that's splendid!"

"Have the detached cottage renovated into a tea ceremony cottage and never mind the cost."

Hana had been getting together a group of ladies, including Baroness Nanaura and the governor's wife, to practice the tea ceremony and had formed a fashionable circle of high society women. She immediately got in touch with her cousin, the may-or's wife. Without any delay, Hana began to make plans for the renovation. For a time, she lost herself in a dream of luxury. Once the extravagant tea cottage was completed, the Masago-chō mansion would serve as a meeting place for the ladies.

As this dream was slowly being realized, the National Diet was dissolved in early 1928. Anticipating a general election in February, both the Seiyūkai and the Minseitō began a vigorous election campaign. Keisaku, who headed the Seiyūkai in Waka-yama, found himself having to decide on an immediate course of action.

"It's ridiculous to run for parliament at my age," Keisaku de-clared, with a wave of his hand.

However, he could no longer decline to run after Tasaki Yusuke appointed him a member of the election committee.

"Hana, it looks as though I'm going to become a member of parliament after all."

"It was inevitable under the circumstances."

Keisaku had just returned from a meeting at which it was de-cided, in consultation with the party headquarters, that he would run in the coming election.

On February 20, 1928, Matani Keisaku was elected a member of parliament. Keisaku had been able to concentrate on his elec-tion campaign, since all business matters had been entrusted to his secretary, Otake, who had been with him since he entered the prefectural government. Keisaku received an overwhelming majority of the votes cast. He had raised the necessary funds by selling some of his rice land in Musota. This was not at all surprising, for he had long practiced the policy of investing his own property to promote new plans sponsored by his various associations.

"You know, Hana, I bought my fame with money," he admitted with a sad look on his face.

"Nonsense!" said Hana reproaching him. "It's the land, rich with the spirits of the Matani ancestors, that has given birth to Matani Keisaku. If you must insist that you bought your fame, it was with the land," she declared with conviction.

Shortly afterward, they received lavish gifts from Shanghai to commemorate the election victory. Keisaku received a T'ang ink stick of fine quality and Hana, a luxuriously soft sash of Chinese damask. They also received a letter from Eiji.

Unlike Fumio's letters, Eiji's letter was carefully worded. With polite turns of phrase, he solemnly congratulated Keisaku upon his victory. Now that Keisaku had been elected in the First General Election, it was a new dawn for the Japanese nation.

"He and Fumio are so much alike. They both love to exaggerate," Keisaku said.

"Dear, you ought to read the letter carefully. It isn't clear what he means by the 'new dawn for the Japanese nation.' He could be referring either to the First General Election or your election victory."

"What a cynic you are!"

"But Eiji is thoughtful."

As a member of parliament, Keisaku was asked more often than before for samples of his calligraphy and on many more occasions he took up his brush to write Chinese poems on thick colored paper. Eiji and Fumio had doubtless sent him the ink stick anticipating these requests. Under the bright light, Hana scrutinized her sash with its checkered design on black, a design which had been chosen by Fumio. It pleased her exceedingly that even Fumio had matured into a thoughtful woman who was able to select a sash for her mother.

"It's perfectly natural for a woman to settle down a bit when she's expecting her second child. Didn't you yourself suddenly change after Fumio's birth?"

"Don't be absurd!"

"Yes, you did. Think back on it."

"I wonder."

But Hana had no time to reminisce. She was now worried about Fumio's second pregnancy of which they had been informed by Eiji. The Harumis had Chinese maids to serve them and were surrounded by foreigners. Was it possible for Fumio to have a safe delivery in a strange land? Hana thought of sending them the money for a trip back so that her daughter could have the baby in Japan. According to Eiji's letter, however, the baby was due in late April or early May. Fumio's pregnancy was therefore too advanced for her to make a safe journey home by sea.

"It's a boy. Both mother and child fine. Harumi."

They received this telegram on May 4. Two months later they received a letter and a photograph of Eiji, Fumio, Kazuhiko, and their second son, Shin. Eiji looked stylish, dressed in a white linen suit and wearing rimless glasses. Fumio was seated in a chair carrying Shin who was dressed in a newborn baby's outfit. She wore the latest fashion: a sleeveless dress with an open neckline and frills on her right shoulder and a cloche hat which covered her ears.

"They're all so dressed up," sighed Keisaku.

"Fumio has lost some weight. She must have had a difficult delivery," Hana observed.

Hana tried to read some meaning into Fumio's thin face. However, her daughter's arms and chest were still broad enough and there was no real sign that Fumio, now twenty-five years old, was growing weak. On the contrary, large lively characters, like those she had written as a college student, pranced gaily through the letter, which had been enclosed in an envelope. She wrote that the character for Shin was a slight modification of the first character in the compound meaning "general" in honor of Keisaku's victory in the general election. They had forgotten altogether Wataru, the name they had earlier agreed upon while crossing the East China Sea. Fumio described in detail what life was like in a concession in Shanghai and occasionally included some Chinese words she had picked up for a touch of humor. Now that Fumio was separated from her mother, her remarks were no longer caustic. At the close of her letter, however, she proudly announced that Eiji was receiving a service area allowance and that, as a result, his salary was as high as that of a lieutenant-general of the army. In a postscript she explained that the fine ink stick they had sent earlier was worth fifteen yen in Japanese currency, and the damask sash, seven yen. In Japan, Eiji's monthly salary had been eighty-two yen which was by no means a meager sum. However, after marrying Fumio, his entire salary was used up by daily expenses.

Fumio ought to have written:

"Thanks to you, we are now able to lead a life of luxury on Eiji's salary alone. Please do not worry about us."

Instead, she wrote:

> Eiji does not have an impressive family background nor does he own any farmland, but he is able to provide well for his wife and family.

Hana was no longer upset by Fumio's attitude. Nonetheless, she felt bad about their having spent all that money on such expensive gifts and thought of sending an equivalent value in goods. Fumio's outfit was an imitation of the way Clara Bow, the American movie actress, dressed; it was then considered the height of fashion among the ultra-modern girls of Japan. But Hana regarded it as being so immodest she could hardly bear to look at the photograph. Without delay, she made her way to Takashimaya and bought two formal kimonos of silk gauze and matching sashes which she sent to Fumio. However, these articles of clothing were sent back by return post.

> Freshly distilled saké has to be poured into a new leather bag. Similarly, Western-style clothes are the most suitable for a modern life-style. Your presents can only be interpreted as criticism of my attire. In Shanghai, I shall be wearing the same clothes all year round. I am therefore returning your gifts. However, I appreciate all the trouble you went through.

Three photographs were enclosed together with the letter. One had been taken at the tennis court; it showed Fumio at Eiji's side, holding a tennis racket. Fumio had written on the back: "Have taken up tennis. Sunburned and very dark. The sun in Shanghai is insatiable." The second photograph was of Eiji in a sports cap; he was carrying Kazuhiko, who had a child's version of the same cap perched on the back on his head. Eiji had his cheek pressed against his son's. The last photograph showed Fumio in a dress of loosely woven linen carrying Shin, who had grown quite a bit. She was smiling casually.

Fumio appeared easygoing to some, self-centered to others, but in the photographs she seemed happiness incarnate. No longer feeling hurt, Hana put the silk gauze kimonos and sashes away in the bottom of the paulownia chest in the drawing room. When she had the chance, she would transfer them to the storehouse of the Musota house where Fumio's wedding kimonos had been put away.

The Masago-chō mansion was located in the heart of the city, but the garden was spacious and the trees and plants grew tall. In the lingering heat of summer, the cicadas chirped ceaselessly, as though they were desperately staving off the approach of autumn. Hana, who was fair-complexioned, did not perspire much even in summer. But, troubled by the piercing cries of the cicadas, she recalled the strange words "the sun in Shanghai is insatiable."

Hana's sensibility was such that she could not tolerate such vulgar phrases. "What offensive words!" she thought disapprovingly. She tried to get into a more cheerful mood by working on the plans for their first tea ceremony which was scheduled for early autumn.

In autumn they received a telegram from Shanghai which said: "Shin critical. Fumio." Even though her grandson was dying, it was not possible for Hana to hurry over to Shanghai. So unexpected was the news that Hana, holding the telegram in her hand, was at a loss what to do. Keisaku was away in Tokyo for a session of the National Diet. Moreover, Kazumi, who had married into the Kusumi family, had neglected a cold which she had caught in early autumn when the weather had suddenly grown cold. Her condition showed very little improvement. The mental strain was all that Hana could endure. Three days later Hana received another telegram, saying, "Kazumi critical. Kusumi." Hana hurriedly got her things together and rushed over to Yamato but she was too late. Her daughter had already died of pneumonia.

When Utae arrived with a set of her mother's mourning kimonos, Hana studied her face, fearful that she bore the sad news of Shin's death. However, Utae kept her head lowered, ashamed of showing her mother her tear-streaked face. Following the funeral of the young bride, held only a year and a half after the wedding, the Kusumi family carried out the ancient practice of putting on display in the sitting room the items of the bride's dowry according to the list presented at the wedding. The Kusumis said that they would keep only the wedding kimono and sash and return everything else to the Matanis.

Hana presented appropriate souvenirs to Kazumi's mother-in-law, sisters-in-law, and maids in the Kusumi household. Then, entrusting the packing and delivery of the dowry to others, she departed. Stepping out of the gloomy house and into the bright autumn sunlight, she suddenly felt dizzy. Kazumi's remains were now contained in a small urn. Realizing that on the forty-ninth

day of mourning Kazumi would be buried in the Kusumi grave-
yard and that not even her spirit would be returning to the
Matani home, Hana's wretchedness was such that she could not
shed a tear. As Kazumi's mother, all she could bring back was
what remained of the dowry; she could not bring back a single
bone of her daughter's body.

Fussed over by Utae and Tomokazu, Hana returned to the
Masago-chō mansion. Removing her slippers at the entrance,
she turned to the houseboy who greeted them.

"Is there a telegram from Shanghai?"

"Yes . . ."

Hana saw at once from the way he hesitated that word had
been received of her grandson's death. Her foot missed the stone
step as she fell forward in a faint.

When Hana came to, she was lying down in the living room.
Kōsaku was seated nearby.

"Oh, it's you. How kind of you to have come all this distance."

Hana struggled to sit up, but Kōsaku made her lie back.

"Hana, you should lie still at a time like this. You'll only stum-
ble and hurt yourself if you try to get up."

"Kōsaku."

"Keisaku is still in Tokyo."

Hana began to shed tears of sorrow. Never in all these years
had she wept in anyone's presence. Now, however, she buried
her face in the pillow and wept soundlessly. Kōsaku watched her
grief in silence. He looked much older than Keisaku, as he had
turned gray sooner. His eyebrows, gray hairs prominent, were
absolutely still, a sign, it seemed, that he was crying inwardly.
These two middle-aged parents had both experienced the heart-
breaking loss of a daughter and were incapable now of hiding
their feelings.

Fumio was experiencing the same despair in Shanghai. She
wrote a rambling letter describing the events surrounding the
death of her second son. The gist of her letter was that the grief
resulting from the loss of one's own flesh and blood could only

be understood by parents who had experienced a similar loss. It dismayed her to be writing a letter of this nature to her mother who had successfully brought up five children. The tone of the letter suggested that Fumio had lost all her strength. Still grief-stricken, Hana had not yet informed Fumio of Kazumi's death.

In the summer of the following year, the bank assigned Eiji to the New York branch. This time the Harumis decided that Eiji would go without his family. One reason for this decision was that Fumio was pregnant again and had expressed a fervent desire to have the child born in Japan. She also wished to remain in Japan until the baby was able to walk. A second reason was that they thought it unwise to disrupt Kazuhiko's education. Eiji wrote to the Matanis asking if he might leave his family with them for three years. Before Hana could send a reply, the Harumi family arrived in Kōbe and quickly made their way to Waka-yama, for, once a written order was handed down in Shōkin Bank, the families were relocated within ten days.

Fumio confessed to her mother that she felt a deep sense of guilt that she had caused the death of her son through negligence. The feeling of guilt was unbearable.

"You may have lost a daughter, but Kazumi married and had her moment of glory. Moreover, you were not in any way re-sponsible for her death. In my case, I actually watched Shin fall ill and die. I feel the bitterest remorse when I think about his tragic death."

"But Fumio, I too have experienced deep remorse. My grand-mother once told me that a bride should never have to travel to her new home against the flow of the River Ki. But I paid no heed to her words and sent Kazumi to Yamato. It's too late now to do anything about it, but I can't help feeling that I was to blame for her death."

"I didn't know of such a superstition."

"As for little Shin . . ."

"What about him?"

"I went to Kudoyama and made an offering of breast charms at Jison-in when you were expecting Kazuhiko. But I was so busy when you were pregnant with Shin that I didn't even send someone else in my place. I blame myself that the baby wasn't given a chance to grow up."

"Mother . . ."

Fumio's eyes opened wide and she held her breath for a moment, but she said nothing more. A few days later she asked boldly, albeit self-consciously:

"Mother, how do you make a breast charm?"

Using her cotton handkerchief, Hana showed her how it was done.

"Are you thinking of going to Jison-in?"

"Yes. It may set my mind at ease."

Fumio rose to her feet and walked away. She had a strong constitution and did not seem to suffer from morning sickness. That very evening she showed her mother the charm she had finished making.

"Mother, will this do?"

Fumio, who was clumsy with her hands, had made gigantic charms, bulging and unattractive. Following the death of her baby, Fumio had grown so thin that she was a mere shadow of her former self, but the charms she had made were larger than her breasts had ever been, even when she was nursing her first-born.

Hana could not very well say that the charms would not do simply because they were clumsily made. The mere fact that Fumio, who had even had the maids darn Eiji's socks, had taken up a needle and thread for the sake of a child yet to be born was worthy of praise.

"Yes, they'll do very nicely."

Hana brought out her inkstone case and set it down in front of Fumio. Fumio removed the elaborate cover decorated with gold lacquer and looked down at the two ink sticks lying next to the inkstone, one of which was the ink stick she had sent from Shanghai. Fumio studied the expensive ink stick for a long moment, then took up instead the Japanese one and began to grind some ink. The T'ang ink stick had reminded her of the time she had been pregnant with Shin.

Hana watched to see that the ink was of the proper consistency.

"Let me write the characters," said Hana.

Fumio silently turned the inkstone case toward Hana. Hana wrote "Fumio age 26" on the huge charms. When they were hung up in front of the Miroku Hall, they overshadowed all the others. So large they could not be held in the palm of one hand, Fumio's charms dwarfed the others, all of which were small enough to be easily gripped. Fumio had stretched her tall body and hung the pair from the highest point on the pillar. They looked for the ones Hana had presented in praying for Kazuhiko's safe delivery, but the older charms had been exposed to the elements for so long the characters on them were no longer legible. There were also some funny-looking charms with cotton protruding from a tear in the *habutaé* silk.

Upon their return home, Fumio described enthusiastically their temple visit.

"I can't say that I believe in the efficacy of the offering, but I feel so lighthearted. I think it would be wrong to do away with superstition altogether."

Fumio still insisted on rationalizing everything she did.

The situation could have been extremely awkward for Fumio. She had always derided tradition, so eager had she been to follow a modern way of life. But Hana did not wish to humiliate her daughter, and so, instead, she criticized her dress:

"Can't you do anything about that ugly dress? You look so untidy. Remember that we have visitors all the time."

"I don't care what people think," retorted Fumio.

On New Year's Day of 1931, there was an unusually heavy snowfall in the east of Japan. Even in the west it began to snow after the lunar New Year, and in Wakayama there was snow on the ground, a very rare sight indeed. The snowfall was not as heavy as it was in other parts of the country, but there were about three inches of snow on the ground. It was an extraordinarily heavy snowfall for the region. As people offered their traditional New Year's greetings, they would say: "Snow for a rich harvest," a phrase which had never before been used in the region. The residents of Wakayama City were in high spirits.

Lying in a room in the Japanese Red Cross Hospital in Takamatsu-machi, Fumio gazed out of the window at the snow.

"The snow's too dazzling. My eyes are beginning to hurt."

Recalling Yasu's eye ailment, Hana grew alarmed and quickly drew the curtains to darken the room.

"Mother, how is the baby?"

"It's doing fine, so relax and don't worry."

Fumio's baby, born a month prematurely, had been placed in a strange box called an incubator and was being taken care of by the nurses in a separate room. It had barely uttered a cry when it was born and was as yet unable to suckle milk on its own.

"Neither the patron deity of Jison-in nor the breast charms were much good, Mother."

"What are you saying? Go to sleep now. You'll grow weak if you don't get some rest."

"Is the baby that weak?" Then suddenly sitting up, Fumio cried: "I haven't lost it, have I? Not again . . ."

"Hush, Fumio! Didn't the doctor tell you that the baby will be all right?"

"Please open the window. How can I think about anything pleasant in a dark room?"

Hana let in some light. Looking at the snow which had begun falling again, she changed the subject.

"What do you think about the name Yukiko? Harumi Yukiko. Isn't that a lovely name?"

"I think you should take a look at this." Fumio drew out an envelope from under her pillow and handed it to Hana. It was a letter from New York. Hana read the sheet of stationery on which ten boys' names and ten girls' names were written. Yoshihiko,

Fumihiko, Akihiko, Toshihiko, and Hidehiko were some of the boys' names; and Toshiko, Yōko, Chikako, Etsuko, Hanako, and Kazuko among the girls' names.

"By the way, Mother, please go to Mr. Kinoshita and have him choose the best name for the baby before the seventh-day ceremony."

Fumio looked down as she shyly made this request.

Mr. Kinoshita was a diviner who knew about directional taboos, gave advice on the building of houses, and selected names for children. Hana often went to him when she had a problem. Once she consulted him when Tomokazu came down with a strange illness. Fumio, who had never believed in divination, was now asking her mother to have Mr. Kinoshita choose a name for the baby.

Seven days after its birth, the baby, still inhaling oxygen inside the incubator, was given the name Hanako. The name, although pronounced similarly, used a character different from Hana's name.

"It's a lovely name," commented Kōsaku, who had come to visit his niece in the hospital and to extend his greetings to her child.

PART
III

PART
VII

LOOKING DOWN AT the lotus leaves in the moat, Hana and her granddaughter crossed the first drawbridge and found themselves in the grounds of Wakayama Castle. Suddenly the castle tower disappeared from view, a phenomenon—an intentional one—that was part of the art of fortification. Outside the castle, the white-walled, three-storied tower could be seen from a great distance. However, here within the castle grounds, even though the approach road was built on a steep incline, the tower was barred from their field of vision by tall stone walls. On their right, an ancient camphor tree was putting forth young shoots.

"Grandmother, are those cherry blossoms?" asked Hanako in a high-pitched voice.

"No, dear. They're peach blossoms."

To Hanako, the blossoms were very exotic, and so she gazed steadily at the peach grove on her left. The peach blossoms were of the late-blooming variety that would be bearing tiny fruit in early summer. The petals, a sickly shade of pink, were tougher than those of cherry blossoms. The pink blossoms seemed to tint Hanako's pale complexion. Hana tugged at her granddaughter's hand.

"You should be able to see some cherry blossoms from the top of those steps."

"Really?"

Hana suddenly felt very sorry for her grandchild, whom she had not seen for six years. After her birth in the Red Cross Hospital, Hanako had been taken along to the various bank branches to which her father was assigned. She was now in the third grade, but she was altogether unfamiliar with the four seasons of Japan. Hana caught a fleeting glimpse of Fumio in this child who could not distinguish between cherry blossoms and peach blossoms. It was quite possible that Hana's daughter, who had rebelled against everything Japanese, might have planned to raise her children in a land of eternal summer, thus alienating them completely from Japanese tradition.

"Didn't you see the peach blossoms next to the display of dolls on Girls' Day? In fact, most of the blossoms arranged in the alcove until fairly recently were peach blossoms."

"But I had a fever and spent most of my time in bed. I had no chance to enjoy the blossoms."

It was not merely because Hanako, who was now nine years old, did not speak in the Wakayama dialect that she sounded precocious. The child was tall and thin as a result of having been born prematurely; and she was sick so often that she rarely went to school and spent much of her time reading in bed. Her conversation was unusual for a girl her age and often startled Hana. Nevertheless, Hana was greatly relieved that Hanako had not inherited Fumio's rebelliousness.

Following the campaign launched by Margaret Sanger, an American advocate of birth control, Fumio had had two abortions after Hanako's birth. However, she suddenly decided to have another baby in her late thirties, claiming that she was merely going along with the national policy. In fact, she had realized very clearly a mother's function when she found herself pregnant again after so many years and had wanted very much to have the baby. Together with Hanako, she had made her way back to Japan from south of the equator on a sea voyage which had taken all of two weeks. Upon her arrival, she had had an emotional reunion with her eldest son. The Harumis had decided to give their son a traditional education, and so Kazuhiko had been left with his grandparents. After five years in New York City, Eiji had been transferred to Batavia, then the capital of Java in the Dutch East Indies. Both Eiji and Fumio had agreed that the baby should be born in Japan. It was for this reason that Fumio had returned to Japan with her daughter.

As in the past, there was a constant stream of visitors at the Matani mansion in Masago-chō. Keisaku had been reelected member of parliament for the past eleven years; moreover, he had been an active member of the Wakayama Agricultural Association for a good twenty years. Besides being a member of the

House of Representatives in Tokyo he held many titles: president of the Wakayama Agricultural Association, director of the Wakayama Immigration Association, president of the Wakayama Livestock Union, president of the Wakayama Sericulture Association, president of the Wakayama Shipping Union, president of the Farmers' Insurance Union. These titles were not merely honorary, for Keisaku had personally established and encouraged the growth of these organizations.

Keisaku did not allow his body to grow weak as the years went by. Following the outbreak of war with China in the previous year and the establishment of the Konoe Cabinet, which was supported by the bureaucracy, the influence of the political parties had declined sharply. Nevertheless, Keisaku endeavored to work diligently for the good of Wakayama Prefecture rather than actively oppose the growth of a "military Japan."

"Father, are you still active in the Seiyūkai which has done absolutely nothing to check the growth of Japanese fascism?" asked Fumio bluntly.

"I wouldn't put it that way. The situation was such that all I could do was look after the welfare of my constituents," Keisaku replied guardedly.

Democracy and liberalism were looked upon as embryos of Communist thought. Therefore, the government made scapegoats of all left-wing power groups which took an antiwar stand. In the provinces, the National General Mobilization Act gave extensive powers to the military and the bureaucracy and intensified the war effort.

Fumio, still a liberal at heart, understood clearly the seriousness of the situation in Japan from reading the newspaper.

"Really, Father. Why, even the Socialist Democratic Party dances attendance on the military!"

"You can't reason with those in power who shout at everyone to keep silent. The situation has worsened since the February Twenty-sixth Incident."

"What do you think will happen?"

"I really can't say."

As a schoolgirl, Fumio had never seen such a gloomy look in her father's eyes.

"What is Father thinking about, Mother?"

"I'm afraid I don't know. When he's with me, he just laughs and says that he has the welfare of Wakayama to look after."

"What do you think about the present state of affairs, Mother?"

"What does Eiji say? It must be easier to view Japan objectively when one is in a foreign country."

"Naturally he's vehemently opposed to fascism."

"But isn't Java a Dutch possession? What do the Dutch, who are at loggerheads with Germany, think of the Tripartite Alliance?"

Hana's incisive questions prompted Fumio, who had led a carefree life in a Dutch colony, to stop and consider her own situation. Experiencing her first Japanese winter in years, Hanako was ill most of the time. Fumio remained unusually quiet awaiting the birth of her child, and she was kept extremely busy nursing her daughter.

Nonetheless, the Matani home was as hectic as ever, and Hana was at the center of a whirlwind of activities. She already had several grandchildren, but she handled the complicated business of running a large household with such spirit that she was the envy of many a younger woman. She was called Soong Mei-ling behind her back, so much did she remind people of Madame Chiang Kai-shek. However, no one was openly hostile toward Hana, and Hana, for her part, conducted herself as elegantly as ever.

Keisaku had departed for a ten-day trip to Tokyo and things had become somewhat quieter at home. So it was that Hana had thought of viewing the early cherry blossoms and set out hand in hand with her granddaughter. She and Hanako were the only passengers in the trolley car as it made its way to Wakayama Park. When Hanako expressed her wish to see the castle, Hana changed her original plan and headed for the castle tower.

On this particular Sunday afternoon, the castle was not as lively as it was during a festival, but stalls selling special rice cakes in the shape of pine cones had been set up. It was pleasant to see people going to the zoo and children running out of the playground.

"Look at this tiger," said Hanako, coming to a sudden stop.

There, before their eyes, was a life-sized statue of a tiger, which looked as though it had just crept out in front of them.

"Long ago this castle was called the Castle of the Crouching Tiger in a Bamboo Enclosure. A statue of a tiger was therefore cast in its honor."

Listening with interest to her grandmother's explanation, Hanako continued to study the statue.

"There's something very odd about this tiger. Oh, now I know! Grandmother, its legs are funny."

Hanako pointed at the unnatural position of the tiger's forelegs and hind legs, all four stepping forward simultaneously.

"You are observant, Hanako. When the statue was completed, people made a great fuss over the unnatural position of its legs."

"Why didn't they have the statue recast? Isn't it wrong to put on display anything which is not quite right?"

Hana gazed gravely into the eyes raised up toward hers.

"Some people are amused by silly mistakes like this."

"I find it amusing myself and it doesn't bother anyone."

Hanako's white teeth gleamed as she smiled happily. Hana was pleasantly surprised by her granddaughter's quick-witted response. Fumio would have investigated thoroughly any mistake. Hana felt immensely relieved that Hanako was so different from her mother. She felt that she would like very much to see personally to her granddaughter's upbringing, and she recalled her own childhood when she had been brought up by Toyono.

The second gate leading to the castle tower came into view as they reached level land. Here the two sat down on a bench to catch their breath after the exhausting climb up the steep road. Wakayama Castle had been built high above the city where there was no danger of it being flooded. They turned and looked out over the grove of cherry trees which appeared white and hazy.

"Are those cherry blossoms?" asked Hanako, sounding disappointed. Growing up in a foreign land, she had picked up information about Japan from different sources, such as her parents, picture books, and her teachers at the Japanese Elementary School. According to these various sources, the beauty of the cherry blossom, which was a symbol of the national character of Japan, was far more spectacular than this. Hanako, who was accustomed to tropical flowers, did not appreciate the pale pink blossoms, which she thought were rather insipid.

"The double cherries will be at their best toward the end of the month, so let's come back to view them then," suggested Hana by way of consolation. She bought two tickets and passed through the gate with Hanako. They cut across the courtyard and made their way to the entrance of the tower. Turning to their right in the dark, they ascended the tower.

The tower had been originally built for warfare, but there was no trace at all of a castlelike atmosphere. The thick wooden frames visible here and there in the dimly lit tower were not impressive. The light streaming in through the small square windows filtered through the dust kicked up by the visitors to the castle, one of the national monuments of Japan.

"The air is terribly dusty. I'm afraid my tonsils will get swollen."

"Let's climb up to the top. We'll be able to see all of Wakayama City."

Hana had second thoughts as they struggled up the steep stairs. This spring outing was altogether too taxing for a sixty-two-year-old woman and her nine-year-old grandchild. Hanako, who was delicate in constitution, looked pale for a time after arriving at the third landing. Hana, too, felt shaky and was certain that she would tire her legs and back. However, the view from the top was truly breathtaking. On a clear day, one could look over the entire plain to the mouth of the River Ki.

"Look, Hanako."

"What a lovely shade of green!" cried Hanako as they both

arrived at the top. Hanako tried to describe to her grandmother the difference between the vivid green of the tropics and the delicate green of Wakayama.

"There's the ocean. Grandmother, which direction is south?"

"Beyond that point."

"Then Father is way over there in Java."

Hand in hand they strolled around the outer edge of the tower. Worrying about the child being up so high, Hana held her granddaughter's hand tightly. Hanako laughed.

"It's all right, Grandmother. There's wire netting all around the edge," Hanako said, gently rebuking her grandmother in a grown-up manner.

A ribbon of celadon green flowed to the northwest. The city extended to a point just this side of the river. A vast expanse of green lay beyond the river.

"Take a good look, Hanako. That's the River Ki."

"What a lovely color!"

The rivers in Batavia were a brilliant blue. Hanako was thus enchanted by the celadon green of the Ki.

"That's Musota over there, where your mother was born."

Hanako looked in the direction her grandmother was pointing. Slowly surveying the peaceful village surrounded by rice fields, she suddenly asked:

"Where was I born?"

"In the Red Cross Hospital your baby brother was born in."

"Oh? How very dull!"

Hana did not know what had prompted Hanako to make this disparaging remark.

So exhausted were they on the way home that neither of them could utter a word. Hana fully realized the awkward position her granddaughter found herself in. This child saw Japan with the eyes of a foreigner and was always discovering something new, such as a particular shade of green or blue and the blossoms of cherry or peach. On the other hand, her grandchild was not really a foreigner. She was a Japanese who had no links with Japan's heritage.

"It's perfectly natural, Mother. After all, she isn't even familiar with the changing order of the four seasons: summer, autumn, winter, and spring. The four seasons come in that order only in the temperate zone."

"Now I know why Eiji left Kazuhiko in Japan. When all of you return to Java this summer, Hanako will forget all about the cherry blossoms. What a pity!"

"You shouldn't feel sorry for her, Mother." Suddenly feeling angry, Fumio became argumentative.

"Japanese away from Japan are extremely self-conscious about being Japanese. You never know when you are being observed by a foreigner. The Japanese embassies and consulates tell us to conduct ourselves properly so as not to embarrass Japan. The education provided abroad by the Japanese Elementary School implants the true spirit of Japan in the children and carefully teaches them to be proud of being Japanese. Hanako is not to be pitied!"

Hana and Fumio were sitting in the sun on the veranda on the south side of the house sewing some more stitches onto a good luck "thousand-stitches" belt. Hana was fixing in place a five-sen coin. Pulling a needle threaded with red cotton, she replied slowly:

"I suppose you're right."

Irritated that her argument had fallen on deaf ears, Fumio snatched the belt away from her mother. Fumio's sewing was as clumsy as before, but even she worked on the belts. She drew the needle through the next dot, pressed the needle against the material, coiled the thread around the needle, then pulled the needle through to complete a tiny red knot. As an officer of the Women's Patriotic Association, Hana received almost daily orders for these belts. Except for women born in the Year of the Tiger, one woman was allowed to sew only one stitch per belt. Hana had Fumio, the maids, and the ladies who came to visit her sew one stitch on each belt. She herself set aside the five-sen coins, which had a hole in the center, and carefully attached them to the belts.

"Five sen is considered lucky. It means 'to cross the death line'."*

"It has nothing to do with luck! The coin simply helps to ward off shrapnel, that's all."

Hana sighed softly as she waited patiently for Fumio to finish her knot. She then gathered up the belts and rose to her feet.

"How is Hanako feeling?" she inquired.

"She's feeling fine now."

"Well then, I'll ask her to help with these."

Hanako's tonsils had begun to swell the very evening of their excursion to Wakayama Castle and she had developed a high fever. Fumio, who had lost her second son and who knew how sickly Hanako was, was beside herself with worry as she nursed her daughter. Three days after the outing, the fever had abated. Fumio was, therefore, feeling greatly relieved.

"Mother, please keep Hanako company for a while. I'm going to take Kazuhiko along with me to . . ."

"To where?"

"To the castle."

Fumio, who had not yet abandoned her tomboyish ways, had been dying to climb the castle tower after hearing about the excursion. Three months earlier she had had a difficult delivery; this time the baby had been late in making its appearance. Her recovery, however, had been rapid and she was thoroughly enjoying her first spring in Japan in years. Kazuhiko, who was in his third year at Wakayama Middle School, felt embarrassed by his mother's childlike enthusiasm as they set out for the castle.

> Sleep, sleep
> A child who sleeps will grow.
> If you go to sleep

*Five sen (gosen) exceeded in value four sen (shisen). However, when a different pair of characters is used, shisen means "death line," and so five sen came to be interpreted as "crossing the death line (to safety)."

I'll dress you in a red kimono;
If you stay awake
I'll dress you in a striped kimono.

Matsu, the daughter of one of the tenant farmers, had come to look after Akihiko, Fumio's baby boy. The girl was singing a lullaby to while away the time, as Fumio had made it clear to her that she was not to carry the baby all the time. The girl, knowing nothing about helping in the kitchen of a busy household, was of no assistance to the maids.

Slipping past the baby's room, Hana made her way along the corridor to the detached cottage where her granddaughter was resting. She had with her the "thousand-stitches" belts.

"Hanako," she called softly as she opened the sliding door. Her granddaughter was lying in bed. The girl looked up at Hana in surprise.

"I'm sorry, dear. I shouldn't have wakened you!"

"No, you didn't, Grandmother. I had my eyes closed, but I wasn't asleep. I was listening to Matsu's singing."

Hanako was a pathetic sight indeed with a white bandage wound around her neck. Nonetheless, she greeted her grandmother cheerfully.

"What have you got there?"

While her grandmother explained to her the significance of the belts, Hanako studied them closely. Dressed in cotton flannel pajamas with a print of baby bears, she sat up slowly and reached out for one of the belts. Her curly hair was sticking out in all directions and her red lips lent her pale face a touch of color. She had lost all trace of her precociousness and looked extremely young sitting there in her pajamas. Hana taught her granddaughter how to sew a knot on a "thousand-stitches" belt.

"Some of the belts have tigers painted on them, Grandmother."

"It's said that tigers travel a distance of a thousand miles and back, so they're used in wishing men good luck in battle. That's why only women born in the Year of the Tiger are allowed to sew the number of stitches equal to their years."

"Really?" asked Hanako. "Oh well, the legs of this tiger are in the right position to allow it to run."

"Oh, Hanako!"

Recalling the bronze statue of the tiger at the castle, the two of them laughed.

"Where does a soldier wear his thousand-stitches belt?"

"Around his stomach."

"Are the five-sen coins used to protect him from bullets?"

"That's one reason for the coins, but . . ."

Hana again explained that five sen symbolized a soldier's safe return. Hanako listened with her eyes aglow. Her lips parted slightly and she laughed, amused by her grandmother's explanation. Hanako expressed a desire to attach a five-sen piece to the last belt Hana had been working on. Hana therefore took out a coin from her purse and handed it to her. The girl carefully sewed the coin on the belt. Hana's only regret was that her granddaughter, like her mother, was clumsy with her hands. Nevertheless, Hana smiled and gazed fondly at Hanako's profile.

Keisaku had been detained in Tokyo on business. Two nights before his expected return, a long-distance telephone call was put through to the house in Masago-chō. The telephone jangled loudly through the house, its occupants having retired for the night. Hana awoke with a terrible premonition. She jumped out of bed and dashed out into the corridor. The houseboy who had answered the telephone turned to her and said that the call was from Tokyo.

Hana took up the receiver.

"Hello. This is the Muraki-ya in Tokyo calling. May I speak to Mrs. Matani? Mr. Matani has . . ."

"Hello. This is Mrs. Matani. What has happened to my husband?"

"He suddenly fell ill. He's in a critical condition."

"What is it? A heart attack?"

Keisaku had collapsed in the Muraki-ya. Hana quickly gathered her things together and went by car to Osaka. She boarded the first train bound for Tokyo the following morning, but even then she did not make it in time. Not even Tomokazu, who worked for Mitsui Products in Tokyo, had been at his father's side when he breathed his last.

Keisaku had died of a sudden heart attack at the age of sixty-six.

The death of Matani Keisaku, one of the prefecture's most senior politicians, was reported fully in the Wakayama newspaper.

The caption in bold print under the picture of the bereaved widow pressing a handkerchief to her eyes read: "A moment too late. Mrs. Matani in tears." And then the following rather hackneyed remarks: "I am unable to think clearly and feel that this is all a terrible nightmare. I cannot believe that he is really gone." These words, so unlike Hana's speech with its old Wakayama expressions, did not seem to reflect her true feelings at all.

Kōsaku rushed over to Masago-chō and received an endless line of mourners. His white hair stood out most conspicuously above his black crested kimono. Sorrow pervaded the entire mansion. Keisaku's photograph, displayed in the alcove, was enveloped in the smoke rising from the incense. The man in the photograph seemed to be gazing at the mourners.

Mr. Otake, a member of the Prefectural House who had been his secretary when Keisaku was Speaker of the House, took care of the formal details of the funeral. Fumio worked diligently to serve as a model for the maids to emulate. The tall woman in Western-style clothes frantically dashing about the house carrying some object or other was indeed a sight to behold.

"Fumio, do you have an outfit ready for the funeral?" asked Utae worriedly as soon as she arrived. Fumio's younger sister had married into an Osaka family.

"No, I don't. I'll borrow something."

"But it'll be difficult to find a woman the same size."

"Stop nagging me. What's important now is the fact that Father is dead, not what to wear to the funeral."

Fumio then wove her way through the mourners who were

milling about, before disappearing from view. She had just returned from abroad and knew little about the kitchen, for all her life she had taken no interest in housekeeping. She was therefore of little help. Worried that Fumio was getting in everyone's way, Utae was about to call her away. However, Kōsaku stopped her, saying, "Let her be. She has her own way of expressing her grief."

Keisaku's body arrived in Wakayama City in the afternoon of the following day in a funeral car hooked onto a train from Tokyo. The crowds of mourners who came to see the coffin pass, stricken by the blank expression on Hana's face as she walked behind her husband's body, were unable to offer words of condolence. But Hana bowed politely to each one she recognized.

The coffin was brought into the mansion and arrangements were made for a private family service to be held late that night. After it was decided that the official Buddhist-style funeral would be held three days later, Hana summoned Utae to her.

"Is something being done about an outfit for Fumio?"

Fumio was wearing a black wool suit. It was baggy around the hips and knees, as she had been sitting on the floor and running about the house in what had once been a tight skirt. Fumio had been only partly correct in declaring that as long as she wore black it would do for the funeral.

Hana had hardly had any sleep for three nights running and there were signs of tiredness around her eyes and neck. Everyone fussed over her. They laid out the bedding and made her lie down. However, when Fumio checked in on her a while later, Hana had disappeared.

Fumio slid open the door to the detached cottage where Hanako was sleeping.

"Yes, what is it?" cried Hanako. Being a light sleeper, she woke up straightaway. Flustered, Fumio said:

"I'm sorry, dear. Do you happen to know where Grandmother is?"

"No, Mother."

"Never mind. It's late, so get back to sleep."

Fumio hurried out of the room. She did not want to get others involved, but no one had seen Hana. Fumio searched desperately in one part of the house and Utae in another. Fumio then noticed a light in the storehouse which was supposed to be deserted and quietly opened the door. There sat Hana with bent shoulders, her back turned to the door.

"Mother, what in the world are you doing? We were frantic with worry wondering where you had gone!"

Fumio peered over her mother's shoulders and saw that she had her sewing box open. A black mourning kimono was spread on her lap.

"It's for you. I'm letting down the hem."

"Mother, I'll do that. Please go to bed and get some sleep," cried Fumio, raising her voice in anger. Tears streamed down her face as she got Hana to her feet and snatched the mourning kimono from her. The full impact of her father's death, which she had managed to suppress all this time, had suddenly struck her. Turning pale, Hana looked on silently, and then stole out.

The funeral service was held on a cloudy spring day. Baron Nanaura headed the funeral committee and the head priest of Daidō-ji in Musota conducted the service. With hundreds of mourners in attendance, the funeral of Matani Keisaku was truly impressive. The coffin was surrounded by floral wreaths sent by Nakajima Chikuhei, the president of the Seiyūkai, and other notables in government and society. Elaborate floral arrangements had been sent by the associations in which Keisaku had been very active. They were on display along the pathway from the mansion all the way to and along the road in front of the house where the streetcars ran, lining both sides of the street like a grove of trees.

Dressed in a morning coat with a black band on his sleeve and pin-striped trousers, Seiichirō was seated uncomfortably in formal Japanese fashion next to his mother in the place set aside for the principal mourners. Seated unobtrusively diagonally behind him was his wife, Yaeko. A very beautiful woman, Yaeko had come as a bride from an old Iwade family. She was wearing a black kimono which enhanced her beauty, making her stand out even more strikingly among the other mourners. However, no one addressed her, the new mistress of the house, as Madame Chōkui, as her husband was only an employee of the Osaka central office of Sumitomo Bank who had bought a house in Osaka.

The relatives of the deceased were represented by Kōsaku and his eldest son, Eisuke. Ume, who had been confined to bed with a liver ailment for the past year, did not attend the funeral. Tomokazu was seated nearby; wearing a navy blue suit, he looked like a typical salaried man. He was twenty-eight years old and had just become engaged to the daughter of a member of parliament from Kyoto. Utae had brought along her eldest son, an unruly little rascal. This turned out to be a disaster, for he constantly demanded her attention. Sighing, she looked enviously at Fumio's son, Kazuhiko, who was seated very properly. Then, suddenly realizing that her son had slipped away, she got up to look for him.

Hanako had a white bandage around her neck and was dressed in a sailor's costume which had been hurriedly bought the day before. Dark colors did not suit her at all because of her pale complexion. She had no clothes appropriate for the funeral and so they had had to rush to Takashimaya to buy a ready-made outfit. Hanako was slender and had long arms and legs. She kept pulling at the sleeves, which had three white stripes around the lower edge, since she felt that they were too short. Her collar fit poorly, and the white bow in front was an eyesore. Hanako was not deeply affected by her grandfather's death, as she had rarely found herself in the company of the busy man. By way of reprimanding her daughter for fidgeting, Fumio said:

"Take a good look around you, Hanako. The Meiji and Taishō eras of the Matani family have come to a close with Grandfather's death."

These words were not directed exclusively to her daughter. Fumio was merely expressing her thoughts at that moment. Feeling uncomfortable in her black crested silk kimono, she wore a set expression on her face. She was concentrating more on her father's photograph in its black picture frame, which had been placed on the altar covered with a length of white material, than on the words she would have to say to the mourners who came to offer incense.

Hanako was suddenly overwhelmed by the solemnity of the occasion and swallowed hard. She had been pampered all her life. Nonetheless, here she was confronted by the fact of death for the first time and not able to cling to her mother's sleeve as she had always done before.

Besides friends and acquaintances, numerous other residents of Wakayama who had had no direct association with Keisaku came to offer incense. It was obvious that the funeral would not be concluded according to schedule. Hanako felt that the white smoke which rose interminably as the priest solemnly intoned the sutras would remain forever in her memory.

Indeed, Hanako's ties to the Matani family were once again severed as if by the very smoke rising from the incense. Hanako, being a delicate child, was almost certain to develop a fever and end up in bed whenever her mind had been affected profoundly by an event, such as her grandfather's funeral. Already weakened by tonsillitis, she developed a serious case of pneumonia and was not even able to get out of bed to be present at the ceremony held to mark the forty-ninth day of mourning.

When Hanako finally recovered, she realized that her grandmother had moved out of the Masago-chō mansion and had returned to Musota. Moreover, the day was fast approaching when the Harumis would be returning to Java, where their father awaited them. Hana was not there to see them off when their ship left the port of Kobe.

"Why didn't Grandmother come to see us off?" asked Hanako. Fumio was somewhat taken aback by her daughter's question.

"After all, we'll be returning to Japan in two years. We won't be separated for very long."

"Really?"

"If you're worried about Grandmother, why don't you write to her? Now that she has more time to herself, she'll probably answer your letter."

Suppressing a smile, Hanako looked up at her mother. That very day Hanako began keeping an illustrated diary. Fumio put it together upon their arrival in Batavia and mailed it to her mother.

When Hana returned to live in the old house in Musota for the first time in seventeen years, she turned the room in which she used to lacquer Yasu's teeth into her private sitting room. When guests came she would open all the sliding doors, and if the visitor happened to be someone close to her, she never failed to take out Hanako's diary.

"This is a game called deck golf at which that delicate child won first prize," said Hana to Kōsaku. Kōsaku was seated on a cushion placed on the threshold between the room and the veranda.

"Fumio and Hanako together formed a team, so it wasn't Hanako alone who won the prize."

"It was probably Fumio who hit the ball; she's still a tomboy at heart. I wonder if Hanako will be all right after romping about on the deck like that in the wind."

"Of course. She'll never get well if you keep worrying about her health like her mother does."

"You know, Kōsaku. Now that I've seen Hanako I feel tremendously relieved."

"Why do you say that?"

"Well, I was wondering what I would do if she turned out to be as rebellious as Fumio. But Hanako strikes me as being perfectly normal."

Kōsaku laughed. One of his front teeth was missing. His white

summer kimono with a splashed pattern, sewn a trifle too wide
for him, covered his thin, bony shoulders like a stiff, sleeveless
ceremonial robe. It was badly wrinkled from the collar down.
Hana, knowing that Ume was sick in bed, wondered whether
he had taken it out of storage and worn it without first airing it.
Kōsaku often came to visit Hana now that she was back in Agenogaito, probably seeking some diversion from the dreariness of
having a wife with a protracted illness at home. Hana felt that she
had to entertain him with pleasant conversation.

"Hanako is such a gentle child. Look at this drawing of hers."

" 'Blossoms I Remember.' A very poetic title."

"She drew this one stormy day when she was immersed in
memories of Japan. She has distinguished between peach blossoms
and cherry blossoms by using different colors. Look at this
drawing, Kōsaku."

Not knowing much about flowers, Kōsaku was not especially
interested in the drawing and ignored Hana's request.

"Now that Keisaku is dead, you have no one to boast about.
Do you intend to brag about your granddaughter from now on?"

Kōsaku's words sounded far more cruel than he meant them to
and hurt Hana deeply.

Hana wondered if Kōsaku were indirectly criticizing her eldest
son for not having amounted to much. So completely overwhelmed had she been by Keisaku's funeral that she had lived
in a daze in the ensuing months. Now, however, she was painfully aware of the fact that she had nothing left that was really
hers.

Reflecting upon recent events, she realized that her first big
loss was the Masago–chō mansion, which she had sold. Highly
respected in Wakayama City, Hana was popular and had her
own responsibilities which would have made it possible for her to
lead a full life in the city had she wanted to. A large part of the
Matani land had been used to finance Keisaku's election cam-
paigns, but it was still possible for her to lead a life of leisure
on the income from the land. Nonetheless, Hana had quickly

and resolutely moved to Musota, wishing to remain Matani Keisaku's Hana. It would have gone against the grain for her to have become an active woman of the modern age. To act on her own instead of wielding power in her husband's shadow went against all the womanly virtues she still believed in so staunchly. Hana felt that it would be unseemly for her as a widow to be a leading figure in such women's groups as the Women's Patriotic Association. To her way of thinking, there was something wretched about a strong, intelligent woman who did not stand at a man's side.

Hana had another reason. She would not have sold the house, so full of memories of her husband, if she had felt that it would one day have been of use to her eldest son. Kōsaku had been entirely correct in stating that she had nothing to brag about now. She had long ago given up any hope of transferring her own strength to her son.

Seiichirō was nearly forty and was employed in the Osaka central office of Sumitomo Bank. He and his wife were very happy, but they had no children. Hana's two daughters had children, but they were not Matani grandchildren. Hana often complained that she did not have any grandchildren by her sons and was terribly disappointed that Seiichirō was not eager to have children of his own. In fact, he had recently remarked that he would like to have Tomokazu's son inherit all that was his.

Hana had dedicated herself to the family all her life and therefore regarded it a grave sin for the eldest son not to have children in a patrilineal family. Her son, however, was very casual about the entire matter. Even Yaeko seemed unconcerned about being childless, apparently not taking seriously the idea that the foremost duty of the wife of the eldest son was to bear children. All Seiichirō required of his wife was that she look attractive. Yaeko therefore dressed up more elaborately than before and boasted that when she went shopping she was bombarded with leaflets by members of the National Defense Women's Society proclaiming that "Luxury is our enemy."

Yasu had entrusted Keisaku entirely to Hana. As for Hana, she restrained herself from reminding Yaeko that her foremost duty as a wife was to look after her husband. Seiichirō was just an ordinary bank employee. Hana felt that she could not blame his lack of ambition on his wife, as he had apparently put little effort into attaining a higher position.

Hana was puzzled by her son and had no idea what his dreams and ambitions were in life.

Eiji was also a bank employee. Hana thought the way he boasted about his hopes and dreams was lacking in taste. However, Eiji's ambitions took his wife into consideration. There was nothing of this in Seiichirō. He had absolutely no intention of looking after his father's constituents and going into politics, and not wanting to be overshadowed by his father's fame, he had no ambitions concerning the world of business. Hana was at a loss what to do with all the energy she had until now expended on her husband.

Reflecting upon the past, Hana lacked the audacity to determine to what extent her efforts had helped her husband. Nonetheless, she had been extremely fortunate to have had for a husband a man like Keisaku who had devoted his entire life to the welfare of Wakayama Prefecture.

Keisaku's dedication to the pursuit of one goal in life had bound Hana closely to him. She remembered that years ago she had been fleetingly attracted to Kōsaku. Dispassionately studying her brother-in-law, she tried to imagine what it might have been like had she been the wife of such a passive man. Kōsaku was clever and had, to a certain degree, a mind superior to that of his brother. After the hills had been turned over to him, Kōsaku had worked hard to plant trees, thus increasing tremendously the value of the land. He was a shrewd man. All his life he had been a bookworm and had obviously been more farsighted than his brother in predicting the great changes they had lived through. Nonetheless, Kōsaku had not lived for anyone besides himself.

Ume, the only woman in Kōsaku's life, had not truly savored

the rich fulfillment she herself had known, Hana thought. During her husband's lifetime, Hana had been extremely careful in her behavior toward her brother-in-law and had even convinced herself that she disliked him at one point. Nothing now remained of her former attraction to Kōsaku. Yet Hana bore no ill-feeling toward Kōsaku, even though in all these years he had given nothing of himself to anyone.

Hana had no idea how Kōsaku was interpreting her long silence. He rose to his feet and abruptly announced that he was leaving.

His clogs had been placed side by side an inch apart on the stepping stone at the entrance. The surface of the clogs had been wiped clean with a damp cloth. Being excessively fastidious, Kōsaku took note of this.

"You have a very efficient maid."

Nodding happily, Hana said:

"Yes, I know. Let me introduce her to you." Clapping her hands, Hana cried:

"Oichi!"

A small middle-aged woman came tripping daintily from the kitchen and bowed when she saw Kōsaku. She was fair-complexioned and almost too elegant to be a maid.

"I serve my mistress as best I can."

Oichi's speech was crisp and pleasing. Not even Kōsaku could have found fault with her.

At the time of Keisaku's funeral, a number of women had come to offer their assistance. Among them was one woman who stood apart from the rest because of her extraordinary diligence. Long after the funeral Hana remembered the woman with the neatly tied sash. When she asked an acquaintance about her, she was told that her name was Oichi and that she had been born in the city. When she was of marriageable age, her family had gone bankrupt. She had never married and now lived alone. As she was skilled at sewing, she did some work for professional seamstresses and gave sewing lessons to the young girls in the neighborhood. When Hana asked Oichi to become her personal maid, Oichi consented at once, adding that she would never regret working for a woman like Hana. For some reason the two women had taken an instant liking to each other. Oichi, who was still a virgin, was obsessively fastidious. This pleased Hana exceedingly. Even after being told that they were to live in Musota, Oichi was quietly resigned.

As she explained all this, Hana slipped into her clogs and walked with Kōsaku as far as the gate.

"You're very lucky. There will be terrible times ahead, so you must have people around you that you can trust," warned Kōsaku with a grim look on his face.

The incident at Nomonhan of 1939 had just occurred, and the Japanese public had not yet been informed that the invincible Japanese Army had been defeated by a Russian tank corps. Even Hana was aware of the turbulence in the international scene.

"I suppose you're right," said Hana.

"I know I am."

"Will there be a war?"

"The China Incident is war. The Hiranuma Cabinet can no longer keep the situation under control. It's fine to read Hanako's diary, but you should also read the newspaper," said Kōsaku in parting.

Without looking back, he passed through the gate and headed for home. His thin kimono billowed in the wind, suddenly filling out the outline of his retreating figure. His thin legs, which showed below the hemline of his kimono, made his tall, gaunt figure appear even more forlorn.

"Oichi."

"Yes?"

"Kōsaku said that there's going to be war."

"Really?"

"Yes, he did."

"Well, he's probably right."

"What makes you say that?"

"In my opinion, a man of intelligence who remains idle can see into the future far better than ordinary people who have to work."

"So you agree with him."

Just as Kōsaku had predicted, Britain and France declared war against Germany in September, and World War II officially began. The repercussions were swiftly felt in the world of politics in Japan. In 1940, Saitō Takao's antimilitary speech was vehemently attacked when Naval Commander Yonai Mitsumasa came into power, and it was not long before the political parties gave way to the military. The Tripartite Alliance was signed by Japan, Germany, and Italy. An organization called "The Imperial Rule Assistance Association"—which brought together the bureaucracy, the left wing, and the political parties—was established. This development surprised even Hana whose knowledge of politics was limited. The word "emergency," which Hana felt described the situation perfectly, was widely used. A healthy state of equilibrium no longer existed. Hana privately questioned the authority of the military to pressure the government into a war against such powerful nations as America and Russia.

Very worried about the Harumis who were in Java, Hana viewed with great interest the international situation and often expressed her anxiety in her correspondence with Hanako. Fumio wrote back, reporting that anti-Japanese feeling among the Dutch had intensified. She also mentioned that Eiji was having great difficulty negotiating foreign exchange and that even the Javanese were becoming hostile toward Japan.

Fortunately, Eiji was transferred to the bank's main office in Tokyo early the following year. The Harumis arrived back at Yokohama Harbor and presently settled down in Tokyo. In a letter to Hana, Fumio announced that they had been able to buy a much bigger house than the one they had had in Ōmori. Fumio, whose self-assurance would probably have been undiminished if she had lived to be a hundred, invited her mother to come and see how successful her husband was, even though he had not inherited property from his family.

Hana ignored her daughter's cold remarks. At about this time, Java was hemmed in by the ABCD Encirclement—made up of the American, British, Chinese, and Dutch armed forces—and all Japanese assets in Southeast Asia had been frozen. Japanese-American foreign relations were on the verge of collapse. On December 8, a communiqué was issued from General Headquarters: "The Imperial Army and Navy at dawn of the eighth entered a state of war with the American and British forces in the West Pacific."

> We, by grace of heaven, Emperor of Japan, seated on the Throne of a line unbroken for ages eternal, enjoin upon ye, Our loyal and brave subjects:
> We hereby declare war on the United States of America and the British Empire. The men and officers of Our army and navy shall do their utmost in prosecuting the war. Our servants of various departments shall perform faithfully and diligently their appointed tasks, and all other subjects of Ours shall pursue their respective duties; the entire nation with a United will shall mobilize their total strength so that nothing will miscarry in the attainment of our war aims.*

The Imperial Rescript declaring war moved profoundly the hearts of the Japanese people. The pacifists had no other recourse than to become loyal and brave subjects.

Tomokazu, who was planning to be married immediately following the period of mourning, had already received his draft notice. Upon receiving an appointment, he entered the Army Management School as a military cadet. In the spring of 1942, Tomokazu, dressed in his army uniform, was married in an austere ceremony held in the Kudan Military Assembly Hall. As for the bride, she wore a kimono with a simple design. The photograph of the bride in her bridal hood and a black long-

---

* McNelly, Theodore. *Sources in Modern East Asian History and Politics* (New York: Appleton-Century-Crofts, 1967), p. 151.

sleeved kimono filled Hana with feelings of regret for a long time after the ceremony. There was also an air of loneliness about the photograph, for the groom's father was missing and the wedding guests in attendance were not as impressive as those who would have been present at the height of Keisaku's influence. A glance at the photograph conveyed the forlornness associated with the wedding of a second son. Most unbearable to Hana was the painful reality that such an austere wedding had been the fate of a member of the Matani family.

"You're so old-fashioned, Mother. Don't you realize that a state of emergency exists throughout the entire world? The institution of the family is about to be totally abolished."

Dressed in trousers that had been Eiji's golf knickerbockers, Fumio was on duty as a member of the Neighborhood Association. She held in her hand some circulars on the assignment of soldiers' comfort kits and on air raid drills and appeared to be in a highly agitated emotional state. She had once been a staunch liberal. However, with the outbreak of war she had been completely transformed into a brave woman supporting fully the Japanese cause. But Eiji had spent many years abroad and was very pessimistic about the war.

"Everyone talks about the Greater East Asian Co-prosperity Sphere, but the countries under Japanese military control have been thrown into utter confusion, Mother. If we were honest, we would call it the Greater East Asian Co-poverty Sphere."

"These are terrible times indeed. I'm afraid one thing simply led to another."

"But the war will soon be over."

"What makes you say that?"

"I'd be called a traitor if I said this outside the house, but I know Japan will be defeated in the end."

"Then it must be true."

"Has anyone else said the same thing?"

"Yes. Seiichirō. Kōsaku also said Japan would be defeated and was roughed up by members of the Young Men's Association."

"That doesn't surprise me."

"Fumio isn't the only woman who keeps hoping that the war will end in victory. It's far more gallant to do one's best to win than to do nothing at all because one is so certain of being defeated."

Eiji stared from behind his glasses. He had caught a glimpse of Hana's courage, which Fumio had inherited. Since becoming his wife, Fumio had demanded much of her husband. She also possessed the tremendous will to make her husband live up to her ideal concept of a husband rather than merely observing him and gauging his ability. Despite her rebelliousness toward her mother, Hana's blood ran in her veins.

Hana had made her way to Tokyo for Tomokazu's wedding and was staying with the Harumis. The house was indeed much larger than the one in Ōmori. Nonetheless, the housecleaning had been sadly neglected, for the maids had been commandeered. The sitting room on the second floor, prepared for Hana in great haste, was in a mess. There were no flowers in the vase in the alcove. Hana picked up the vase to study it in detail and saw that it was of fine porcelain. It was yellowish white with an indigo design and reminded her of Sung vases and Korean porcelain of the Yi Dynasty.

"It's Sawankhalok porcelain," explained Hanako, who followed her grandmother about like a shadow. The art dealers told us that it had been dug out of an old grave in Java. I interpreted for my parents in Malay when they bought the vase."

Hana realized at once that it was in fact highly prized Thai porcelain called Sunkoro by Japanese antique collectors. It came as a surprise to her that Eiji and Fumio had begun to take an interest in antiques. Hanako opened a cupboard in the split shelf and announced:

"We have lots more."

To entertain her grandmother, Hanako took out the objects one by one. She had her listen to the clear, bell-like sound that the porcelain gave off when she flicked her fingernail against it.

"What a beautiful sound!"

"It's peculiar to Sawankhalok objects. This particular piece is Balinese. It's colorful all right, but it doesn't give out that musical sound."

Hanako laid out a number of Sawankhalok plates, bowls, and vases and tested them again and again for the sound. At first she flicked the objects simply to amuse her grandmother, but gradually she was carried away by her own interest in old ceramics.

"Has Sawankhalok porcelain always given off this bell-like sound?"

"I would imagine so. It's really lovely."

Flicking once more the outer rim of a plate and listening intently to the sound, Hanako said solemnly:

"Grandmother, do you realize that there were people who lived in this world centuries ago?"

Hana marveled that Fumio, who had been trying to cut herself off so completely from the past, should have a daughter with a genuine affection for things of the past. She had been feeling despondent since her son's wedding, but she suddenly felt her spirits lifted.

"You're entering Girls' School next year, aren't you?"

"Yes, I am. I'm now in the sixth grade. But I've had a bit of a problem lately."

"Oh?"

"In Java the teachers often told us to be Japanese and I studied hard, never once forgetting that I was Japanese."

"And . . .?"

"And when I returned to Japan I found myself surrounded by Japanese. I feel very strange and don't know what to do."

Hana could not help feeling sorry for her grandchild. She had probably been unsuccessful in making friends with her classmates who had grown up in Japan. Trying to cheer her up, Hana said brightly:

"Hanako, let's go shopping. Let me buy you a kimono, since I'll be leaving soon."

"A kimono?"

Hanako's eyes sparkled. Partly because of having lived abroad and partly because of Fumio's convictions, Hanako had never even worn an informal summer kimono before. She envied her friends during her second New Year in Japan, but the nation was at war and Hanako, spoiled as she was, was not one to press her parents into buying her clothes.

Hanako was truly beside herself with joy. Not wanting to overlook a thing in the kimono department of the Mitsukoshi department store in Nihombashi, which she was seeing for the first time, she peered into every corner. Nevertheless, these were critical times and the kimono department which strictly observed the prohibition on luxury had lost its former gaiety. Displayed on a manikin was a bridal outfit to be worn in the second part of a wedding, consisting of a narrow-sleeved kimono over which was worn a garment resembling an underskirt. The manikin struck a defiant pose. The silk crapes and thin brocades had been pushed into a corner. However, instead of the cheaper dyed material, some expensive pongee, whose subdued color had prevented it from being banned, was placed in a display case.

The sale of kimonos of figured silk had obviously been banned. Hana, who was not known in Tokyo as she was in Osaka, could do no better than select a roll of silk crape with a design of white peonies on a darkish pink ground. When she stretched the material across Hanako's back, the pink color brightened the girl's white cheeks and camouflaged her pale looks. Hana then bought a roll of Ōshima pongee for a haori to go with the kimono. The pongee was ten times more expensive than a roll of silk crape, but Hanako, who knew nothing about the true value of kimono material, preferred the silk crape with the peony design and clasped it tightly to her as they left the department store.

The two women made their way out between the stone lions standing guard at the main entrance and strolled down the street. As they approached the Nihombashi intersection, they were stopped by a middle-aged woman whose kimono sleeves were tied back with a sash on which the characters "Japanese Women's Association" were written. The woman, who was wearing a dark kimono and had her hair drawn back in a bun, said in a dry voice:

"Please read this."

There was not a flicker of emotion on her face as she handed Hana a leaflet. Printed in bold letters on paper the size of a post-card were the words:

> We must fight to the finish! Please shorten your kimono sleeves at once!
>
> The Japanese Women's Association
> Tokyo Branch

"What does it say, Grandmother?" asked Hanako, trying to read the words. But Hana shook her head and tucked the leaflet into her sash.

"Hanako, let's go home."

Hanako romped about in the taxi they had taken, enjoying its luxurious atmosphere, and thought back to her life in Java when her family had a private car. Hana, on the other hand, was deep in thought. Twisting a white handkerchief which she had taken out of her one-foot-three-inch-long sleeve, she wondered how material cut off from kimono sleeves could possibly be of any use. That sort of pedantry was more than she could swallow.

Eiji had insisted that there was no need to evacuate his family, so sure was he of Japan's imminent defeat. However, the war situation worsened and the Japanese military persevered longer than he thought they would. Eiji became more pessimistic than ever. Tomokazu, now a second lieutenant, came to visit the Harumis.

"You know, Eiji, Japan no longer possesses a single aircraft carrier," Tomokazu said grimly. He had, in fact, just divulged a military secret.

Eiji looked pale.

"Will we have to fight to the finish on Japanese soil then?"

"Yes. The army is insisting on it, although the navy disagrees strongly."

The war front in the South Pacific was already closing in on the home islands. The Imperial Headquarters had issued a communiqué which stated that Guadalcanal had been the turning point in favor of the Japanese, but most people interpreted the bloody battle as a retreat. Before long the annihilation of the forces defending Attu Island was reported.

People were shouting hysterically: "Fight to the finish on Japanese soil! A hundred million brave lives lost." In late autumn of 1943, Eiji and Fumio finally decided to evacuate their children. By that time half of Hanako's classmates had transferred to schools in the countryside.

Kazuhiko was enrolled in the Literature Department of Tokyo Imperial University. The draft exemption—the last privilege permitted to students—had been extended to the autumn and then terminated. It was therefore not known when college students would be drafted. Fumio, who claimed to care little for the family, nonetheless remained behind in Tokyo with Kazuhiko, in deference to his position as eldest son. Hearing that Utae's children had been entrusted to Hana the previous month, Fumio sent Hanako and Akihiko to Musota.

"Mother, just what is a family?" inquired Fumio unexpectedly.

"I really wonder about it myself at times."

Determined not to start an argument with her daughter, Hana gave an unprovocative answer and continued her work. She was stitching together a sandbag which would eventually be used for fire-fighting purposes. The sand with which the bags would be filled had been fetched all the way from Isonoura by the members of the Young Men's Association and was piled high near the Village Office and in the school ground. Following the first air raid of April 1942, air raid drills were conducted regularly even in the countryside.

"Seiichirō vacated his house in Osaka and is commuting to

the bank from the home of his wife's parents in Kishiwada. Tomokazu's wife fled with her baby to Kyoto. Even Eiji's older brother has evacuated his children to his wife's home. Don't you think that this is all very strange? The only ones returning to the Matani house are Utae, myself, and our children. Mother . . ."

"What is it? And please don't raise your voice."

"It was quite natural to have a matrilineal family in primitive society, don't you think? After all, it's the woman's family one can rely upon in an emergency."

Taken aback, Hana looked up at Fumio, struck by her words. She had analyzed her feelings as a widow's grief, but here was Fumio exposing the real cause of the intense loneliness she had experienced of late. Hana could not tolerate having her eldest son live with his wife's parents. Not wanting to admit to herself that she was a jealous mother-in-law, she had tried to convince herself that Kishiwada was closer and therefore more convenient for commuting to Osaka. Nevertheless, she could not help resenting Yaeko for having snatched Seiichirō away from her. What was more, even though she felt that it could not be helped in view of the times, she resented the fact that Tomokazu had joined the army. And Tomokazu's daughter, who was Hana's first Matani grandchild, had been carried off by Tomokazu's wife to her parents' home. Indeed, as Fumio had pointed out, the heir, the second son, and their families had stayed away from the Matani house. At this critical stage of the war, those gathered about her were her daughters and their children.

The matrilineal line. The woman's family. Hana had observed at first hand this strange phenomenon but had been unable to explain it as precisely as Fumio had. Hana had firmly believed in and had herself lived according to the precept that a woman severed her ties with her parents once she married. As a younger woman, she could never have returned to the Kimotos with her husband, even if a natural calamity had devastated Musota.

Indeed, a great change had taken place. Hana felt that she too had changed. But her own upbringing made it impossible for her to keep up with the times like Fumio. It was one thing for the head of the family to be buffeted around by the affairs of the day, but Hana knew her place was at home. She would remain quietly ensconced in the sitting room until the sturdy beams started cracking and the house itself collapsed.

With two of Fumio's three children, Hanako and Akihiko, and Utae's children Gorō, Yōko, and Etsuko, surrounded by these five grandchildren, ranging in age from five to fourteen, Hana's daily life was once again extremely hectic. To make matters worse, the tenant farmers had been called away to war, and so their wives no longer came to help with the housework. The only one left to help Hana—apart from the old men still living in the quarters near the gate—was Oichi.

"Madame, doesn't it seem as though the house is turning into a kindergarten?" laughed Oichi, who never once showed any sign of displeasure.

Hanako enrolled in Wakayama Girls' School. She set out for the city every morning with her first aid kit slung over her right shoulder and her air raid hood over her left. Hana, Fumio, and now Hanako had all studied at the school. Hana, her hair combed up in a young girl's parted hairdo and dressed in a long-sleeved kimono, had attended the school fifty years earlier. Twenty years ago, Fumio in a hakama with white trimmings had attended the school. And now Hanako, dressed in pantaloons, was studying at her mother's and grandmother's alma mater.

Every morning the students lined up in the school yard for the roll call, the flag-raising ceremony, and the reading of the Imperial Rescript declaring war. The girls then marched in military fashion to their classrooms, where not a book was to be seen. Everyone was a member of the Students' Patriotic Corps. Day after day in the classroom building which had been turned into a sewing factory, Hanako was made to sew collars on khaki uniforms. It was an assembly line method of production: those who sewed sleeves sewed only sleeves, while others sewed only trousers, or pockets, buttons, or buttonholes. All day the girls were kept at this work.

Even while attending school in Tokyo, Hanako without fail used to fall ill once a week and have to miss school. After transferring to Wakayama Girls' School, she found herself spending each day sewing on khaki collars, work which she detested. Her constitution was such that, if she had to do something she disliked, she would conveniently develop a fever. For this reason, she missed three consecutive days of school. When she returned to school, however, she was reprimanded severely by the teacher in charge. He said that if she had been in the army, her punishment would have been a long imprisonment. Hanako was the only one in her group who sewed on collars; therefore, as a result of her absence, there were over a hundred uniforms without collars. Illness was no excuse for being absent, she was told. Japan was now fighting to the bitter end, and anyone who fell ill was showing weakness of spirit.

Because she was so weak, Hanako had been spoiled by her parents. Besides which, she had grown up in a Dutch colony. All this made it very difficult for her to abide by the strict rules of the Students' Patriotic Corps.

"Grandmother, I don't want to go to school any more. If I can't quit, I'm going back to Tokyo," Hanako declared. But Hana, who until now had always been very kind toward her granddaughter, shook her head.

"Aren't you afraid of the air raids?"

"Not at all. I prefer them to the uniform factory. I've had enough of sewing on khaki collars day after day. I'd much rather be killed by an incendiary bomb in Tokyo."

"Hanako!" cried her grandmother. "How can you even think that when the entire nation is fighting a war?"

"But I'm not well. I have a fever."

"If you're that weak, you won't be of much help, so go right ahead and die."

Hanako looked up incredulously, but her grandmother carried on in an offhand way:

"It doesn't matter whether you die here or in Tokyo. I'll serve as witness, so you can die right here."

Hanako grew pale and stared for a long moment at her grandmother. Then, choking back her tears, she dashed out of the room.

"Madame, weren't you being a little too stern with her? She's still crying her heart out."

Worried about Hanako, Oichi went back and forth between the storehouse and the sitting room. Hana ignored her, asking only that she leave the girl alone.

Hanako had run blindly to the far end of the corridor, where the storehouse door had been left open. There she sought refuge. Avoiding the light which streamed in from the second-story window, she lay down in the semidarkness between the rectangular chests. She had been cornered, and, in her desperation, she writhed as she wept. So loud was the sound of her crying that it seemed as if the objects which had been stored away for years in the chests might be shattered into tiny pieces. And so violent was her weeping it seemed as if the heavy air might begin twisting itself into a tornado at any moment.

"Madame . . . she's been crying for over two hours."

"She'll be all right, Oichi."

"What do you mean?"

"A child who can cry like that can't be very sick."

"How true. She wouldn't be able to cry this long without a break if she weren't healthy."

Thus reassured, Oichi made her way back to the kitchen. Thinking that Hanako, who usually had a small appetite, would be famished after crying like that, she cooked an extra cup of rice for dinner. Hanako really was kicking up a din: Oichi could hear her from the kitchen sink. Shaking her head in wonder, Oichi reflected upon Hana's words.

In the spring of 1945 the house in Tokyo which Eiji had bought was bombed and burned to the ground. The family fled to the home of Eiji's aunt. In hot pursuit came a draft notice for Kazuhiko.

"Mother, I told him not to do anything rash, like being the first to charge or trying to distinguish himself. I also begged him to come back alive no matter what," said Fumio, going over with Hana in Musota what she had told her son when she saw him off. Eiji had declared that he would stay with Shōkin Bank until the end, which was, after all, his duty as an employee, and remained in Tokyo. As for Fumio, only once the Harumis had been burned out of their home and Kazuhiko drafted into the army, did she finally join her mother in Musota.

"You were perfectly right. I say the same thing to the young men who come to see me before going into battle. How can one wish anyone's death?"

"Mother, what do you think will happen to Japan? Wakayama is still peaceful, but it's like hell on earth in Tokyo."

"These are indeed terrible times."

Fumio described briefly the situation in Tokyo to Hana, Oichi, and Kōsaku. She finally drifted off into a deep sleep in the bedding spread out for her between Hanako and Akihiko and did not wake up until the sun was high in the sky the next morning. What with being burned out of one place and fleeing to another, Fumio had been in desperate need of rest.

Several days later Fumio was completely rested and finally able to have a long chat with Hana.

"Mother, I can't believe that Hanako is so well! Her legs were never very strong, so we sent her to a school near home in Java. It's incredible that now she's able to go all the way to the city from here."

"Didn't you yourself walk to Wakayama Girls' School?"

"Yes, but I was as strong as a boy. And, of course, in those days we had to walk: there wasn't any public transport then. It must be the country air that has done so much good for Hanako's health."

Hana did not tell Fumio about the way she had told Hanako

to go ahead and die, for it was a time when people were abnormally sensitive to the word death.

Fumio had remarked that Wakayama was peaceful. But, beginning in June, Wakayama City became the target of frequent bombing raids. In the dead of night on July 10, the city sustained a massive bombing attack and was practically razed to the ground. That night was a night of great confusion even in Musota.

"The air raid shelter won't do!"

"Get your things and run!"

"Take to the hills!"

The leaders of the Neighborhood Association ran frantically about the village calling out individual names. Hana held on tightly to Hanako's hand and Fumio and Oichi each took hold of two of the children. They all raced along the footpath through the rice paddies past Shin'ike and in the general direction of Kitayama.

"Look! The city's burning."

"Why, it looks so close! I wonder if the fire will spread to Musota."

"It's hard to tell."

Looking from Musota, Wakayama City appeared like a sea of flames. Within this area of red, the castle became a dark shadow and then itself turned red as the flames flickered up to the tower.

"Oh, the castle . . .," gasped Fumio. In that same instant Hana, too, noticed that the castle had caught fire. The tower was spouting flames which shot up to the sky. Then, a moment later, the castle crashed to the ground.

"Grandmother!" cried Hanako in alarm as Hana, who had been holding her hand, staggered and fell to her knees.

"I'm all right," said Hana in a firm voice.

In the small villages outside Wakayama City that had escaped war damage, the landowners' livelihood remained in a state of collapse long after the surrender. But in the war-ravaged cities people did their best to forge a new life for themselves. Meanwhile, Hana remained idle in Musota.

Utae, whose home in Osaka had not sustained any damage, came immediately to fetch her children and carried back some rice with her. Eiji, whose house had been burned to the ground, summoned his family to Tokyo in the spring of the following year. As for Kazuhiko, he had joined a corps without any weapons. Shortly before being demobilized without sustaining a single wound, he had been digging foxholes along a beach in the Bōsō Peninsula. Eiji became a trustee of Shōkin Bank when it was dissolved. As a result of soaring inflation and frozen bank accounts, he went through a period of hardship, ultimately losing all that he owned.

Juice and sugar were rationed as a substitute for rice and in order to obtain enough food to live on, there was little choice but to barter one's possessions. Fumio, Kazuhiko, and Hanako survived from one day to the next. There had been no time during the hectic war years to have a kimono sewn from the material Hana had bought for her granddaughter. The lovely material had been sent along with their things from Tokyo to Wakayama, then from Wakayama back again to Tokyo. It was traded for food before Hanako had a chance to see it become a kimono.

Hanako went shopping with her mother to Nerima in the west of Tokyo and saw before her eyes the colorful silk crape with its peony design exchanged for a few pounds of barley. She called silently on her grandmother as she watched the brown, gnarled fingers of a farm woman unroll the lovely material and examine the colorful design. Hanako had desperately wanted to keep it as a souvenir of their shopping excursion to Mitsukoshi during the war. The broken pieces of Sawankhalok porcelain lay scattered in the scorched earth. And now this precious gift was about to be handed over to a complete stranger. It hurt Hanako to realize that, young as she was, all that remained now were memories.

"People talk of food, clothing, and shelter in one breath, but don't forget, Hanako, that food is by far the most important of the three."

Hanako would not be consoled—even though she was well aware of her mother's attempts to convince her that it was wrong to be sentimental about a luxurious roll of material when they were practically starving.

"I wonder how Grandmother would feel about this."

"Naturally, there would be other things to sell if we were in Musota. If you had remained there, you would never have had a taste of harsh reality."

Hanako did not wish to face the reality of having to tote barley and sweet potatoes. She expected her mother to express her sorrow at having been forced to sell her daughter's clothing. Her grandmother would surely grieve to learn that the fine material had been traded for food. She would be the best judge as to which was more painful from a woman's point of view: to part with antiques or to part with one's kimonos.

Fumio glanced timidly at her daughter who had sunk into a moody silence. She had traded the kimono material because of the impoverished state the Harumis had been reduced to by the war. Nevertheless, she felt uneasy. Never having formed a deep attachment to her own clothes, Fumio did not feel too sad about parting with them. But, as a parent, it was painful to have to sell that which by rights belonged to her daughter.

Fumio remained silent to avoid further strain in her relationship with Hanako. So distressed was she by the poverty which had forced her to trade clothing for food that she was unable to articulate her feelings.

Before the war, she had been in a position to send not only rice but clothes and bedding as well, Hana thought as she took up the newspaper. She was very much distressed to learn about her daughter's troubles but was also painfully aware of the fact that the Matani family was no longer wealthy. The farmlands had been confiscated, and the tenant farmers released from their obligations.

Landowners without land that they themselves cultivated had to live on rations in the same manner as city dwellers. Seiichirō and Utae came from Osaka to buy rice. The villagers, feeling obligated to Hana, could not very well sell the rice at unfair black market prices, but they were very reluctant to dole out a large quantity.

"Isn't it infuriating, Madame?" asked Oichi in a loud voice. "They say that Matsu's son in Misegaito owns five wristwatches."

"People from the city probably came to trade them for food."

"But there's such a thing as a man's place in society. What good are five wristwatches to a farmer? It's ridiculous!"

"You must remember, Oichi, that the farmers are forced to barter. Blaming Matsu's son will do no good."

"I'm not blaming anyone in particular. I'm just infuriated by this absurd world. These are difficult times, but it's absurd that Madame Chōkui should be eating rice mixed with barley."

"Japan has been defeated in war, Oichi. No one today pays any attention to names like Chōkui and Matani. Some people have had their houses burned down, others have lost a member of the family. Still others have suffered terribly from the atomic bomb. When I think of such unfortunate people, I really have nothing to complain about."

"But Musota escaped war damage. In fact, no other place has become as well-off as Musota since the end of the war. We're near the city and we're near the mountains, and so people come here to buy their rice and they come here to buy timber and they don't even stop to think of the price. The ones who are making money now are the farmers around here and they used to be tenant farmers of the Matani family. But look at them now, the upstarts, declaring that landowners were members of the exploiting class!"

"Fumio said the same thing thirty years ago. That idea isn't exactly new, you know."

"But why must they pick on the landowners? Look at your brother-in-law. He's making a tremendous profit because his trees sell so well. Frozen bank accounts don't bother him in the least. After all, the money he makes is far more than the income of an ordinary farmer. He loaned Hachi, who plans to start a flour mill, some money, and charged him a high rate of interest."

"He's just a shrewd businessman."

"Well, if you ask me, he's crafty. He took all the hills from the main family and then has the gall to come occasionally with some Kada fish and Hidaka eels, with that obsequious look of gratitude on his face!"

Hana was quietly resigned to her fate, but Oichi resented Kōsaku and bore him no goodwill. She went about the house all day long performing her chores with a vengeance, as though her anger had become a source of energy. With only Oichi to run the household, the housecleaning alone took until nightfall. Furthermore, the rice rationed to them was unpolished, and so one of Oichi's duties was to have the rice hulled by a farmer who lived in the vicinity.

"We've been having fine weather lately," remarked Kōsaku, the only caller Hana had these days.

"Do come in," said Hana, greeting him graciously. She was seated on the veranda reading *The Tales of the Heike*. He took off his clogs without a word and entered the house.

Oichi refused to make an appearance when Kōsaku came to call; therefore, Hana rose to her feet and offered him a cushion. As she was about to go to prepare some tea, Kōsaku said:

"I'll have some persimmon instead of that awful tea. This year is specially good for persimmons. They're a beautiful shade of orange now."

He then pulled out two persimmons, one in each hand. He had picked them as he passed through the gate and slipped them into his breast fold.

Hana returned from the kitchen with a plate and a kitchen knife, for she no longer used special plates and paring knives for fruit. In fact, she believed that persimmons were tastier when they had been peeled thickly with a vegetable knife.

Hana wiped the dust off one of the persimmons with a dish-cloth and skillfully pared the fruit. She then offered it to her brother-in-law. Kōsaku helped himself to a piece and chewed on it for a long time. Almost seventy, he had aged quickly; his gray hair and emaciated body had not changed in the least in the past ten years. However, it seemed that his false teeth no longer fit well. It took him ages to chew and swallow the small piece of fruit.

Hana peeled the second persimmon but curbed a desire to sink her teeth straight into it. For it was one thing, she thought, to watch an old woman sucking on the soft, well-ripened sort of persimmon, but it was not at all pleasant to have to watch an old woman struggling to get her teeth through the crisper kind of persimmon. Realizing that the persimmons from the tree with a branch grafted from Kudoyama were altogether too crisp for her to be able to eat, Hana became painfully conscious of the passage of time. Kōsaku stared pensively at the book on Hana's lap. He seemed to be thinking about what to say next.

"That's an old classic you have there. Have you been comparing the fate of the Heike with that of the Matani family?"

"Oh, no. It's just that there's nothing else for an old woman to do but read."

"A number of new magazines are being published now. I'll bring you a few the next time I come."

"Thank you. I'd like very much to borrow a few."

The next day Kōsaku came with two large bundles, one in each hand, and set them down on the veranda. He unwrapped one of the bundles which contained over ten magazines. Besides the new issues of *Kaizō* and *Chūō Kōron*, there were several new magazines, such as *Sekai*, *Ningen*, and *Tembō*. Hana was glad that magazines were being revived, but she was more impressed by Kōsaku's financial ability to subscribe to them. Turning one of the magazines over to check the price, she saw that it was far more expensive than she had imagined. People living in a place like

Musota were not affected as much by inflation as were people living in the city.

"Why are you so surprised?"

"These magazines are so expensive!"

"If you're surprised by the price, you'll be even more surprised by what's inside. We're in for an even worse time than the war."

Before leaving, Kōsaku untied the other bundle.

"I've brought you some eggs. It'd be a shame to let them rot at home."

It was because Kōsaku spoke like this that Oichi felt disgusted. Unable to close his eyes to Hana's impoverished state, he tried to show his goodwill in this manner. Kōsaku had always spoken sharply, as though he felt compelled to be perverse.

"Be sure you're well nourished before you begin reading these magazines. You have to maintain a healthy balance between the spirit and the flesh, you know. These magazines will not provide you with any nourishment."

Touched by his thoughtful concern for her well-being, Hana meekly accepted his presents. Leading an uneventful life with Oichi in the huge mansion, Hana feared that her mind and body had atrophied. With the younger members of the family busy earning enough money to live on, Hana could well understand Kōsaku's strong feelings about the old taking care of each other.

After Kōsaku had left, Hana picked up one of the eggs. She tapped the eggshell with a jade hair ornament from her chignon. Once she had managed to pierce a tiny hole, she quickly broke the membrane with her finger and put the egg to her mouth. The egg white combined with the yellow yolk tasted sweet. As she swallowed the mixture, she felt the nourishment Kōsaku had mentioned run through her body. Hana helped herself to another egg. Having obediently carried out her brother-in-law's prescription, she began to read the first page of *Ningen*.

"Madame, it's dark outside and you're still so engrossed," remarked Oichi, switching on the light as she entered the room with the dinner tray. Due to the food shortage, the wall of formality between the two women had crumbled considerably. Oichi's speech was not as formal as it had been before the war, and Hana addressed Oichi far too politely for a woman talking to her servant. One reason for this change in attitude was that Hana felt apologetic about being unable to do enough for Oichi. After all, she had practically dragged Oichi home with her, never dreaming that she would one day find herself in such reduced circumstances. On her part, Oichi had come to regard her mistress, who had grown old graciously, as a dear friend to be looked after with love and tenderness.

"Oichi, see what Kōsaku has brought me."

"Why, they're just old magazines."

"But I can't afford to buy any. How much do you think a single volume costs?"

On Hana's dinner tray, there were two varieties of bean curd, a sardine and parsley broth, a Chinese cabbage which Oichi had grown, and pickled eggplants. Oichi served Hana rice mixed with barley in a bowl with a morning glory design, serving her just like a maid in attendance upon her mistress. Their relationship was no longer as formal, but Oichi adamantly refused to take her meals with her mistress, however often Hana urged her to.

"Kōsaku brought us some eggs."

"Shall I fry one for you?"

Hana was unable to confess that she had had some raw.

"That won't be necessary, as I have the Kōya bean curd. Please put one in the soup tomorrow morning."

"As you wish. I shall not be having any."

"You're just as stubborn as Kōsaku is. He isn't as bad as you think. He was so worried I would be shocked by the magazines that he advised me to get some nourishment first. He's genuinely concerned about my health. It distresses me to see you so sullen and uncivil when he comes to call."

Hana was not so much lecturing Oichi as speaking up for her brother-in-law. In her own defense, Oichi said curtly:

"It's disgusting to see a widower making a present of eggs and telling a widow who is living alone to get some nourishment."

Hana almost dropped her chopsticks. A chill ran down her spine and her stomach contracted. She very nearly vomited the eggs she had eaten a little while back.

"Madame, you seem to be in pain. Didn't the dinner agree with you?"

"It isn't the dinner. These new magazines are a bit too much for me and they've made me feel a little dizzy, that's all."

Halfway through the meal, Hana told Oichi to lay out the bedding for her. She had not been exaggerating. The magazines were full of erotic stories with many a lurid turn of phrase. Hana had been very shocked.

In an effort to understand postwar Japan, Hana read these magazines and found herself confused and exhausted by their unbridled attacks and wondering why the magazines sold at all. She was both amazed and displeased that Kōsaku bought such trash. Hana found it unforgivable that there should be such a gulf between the intellectual level of the critical essays and the low quality of the fiction in the same magazine. Realizing that the elegance and refinement which she so appreciated in literature had disappeared altogether in modern Japan, Hana felt herself drained of all her vigor.

Ume had died two years after the surrender. Kōsaku now lived with his son, Eisuke, and several grandchildren. As she lay in bed, Hana thought of how her family had changed, of the deaths and of the young additions to her family. She suddenly wondered what Hanako, who was in Tokyo, was thinking about, for among the grandchildren who had lived with her during the war, Hanako was the only one who wrote to her regularly. Eiji, whose heavy drinking had finally taken its toll, had died unexpectedly this past summer. He had lacked the strength to survive in the difficult postwar period.

Dear Grandmother,
How are you? As I write to you from our little house

in Tokyo surrounded by poverty, I wonder why I think back so fondly to the life I led in Wakayama. In those awful years during the war and after the surrender, we had a struggle finding enough food even in Musota. And I was busy in the Students' Patriotic Corps, sifting through ruined houses and growing sweet potatoes. I never even had any chance to enjoy myself in all that time. And yet I look back on Wakayama with great fondness. Is it because I was born there? Or maybe it's because, while life in Musota during the war was just as hard as in Tokyo after the war, Musota is surrounded by all that greenery. I realize, though, sitting here in our wretched little house and going back over those years, that it's not because I've forgotten how much we suffered in those days.

I think that I was happiest in Musota because I was with you. I wonder if that is why I feel so fond of the place, although I don't think that's the main reason. It puzzles me that I should feel so attached to you, for— as Mother is always saying—you are so much a member of the Matani family.

Unlike Mother, however, I do not have any strong feelings against the "family." Mother rebelled so much that you don't need to worry about me feeling the same way she did.

Grandmother, I was reminded recently of the word "atavism." Because of Mother, I was able to be closer to you than any of my cousins. You yourself often said so.

As you know, I'm studying at Tokyo Women's College, Mother's old college. I'm enrolled in the English Department like she was, but I think that my attitude must be very different from Mother's. After all, I'm working my way through college. Since Father's death, I have been receiving scholarships and working part-time to pay for my tuition and clothing. I don't mean to boast; it's considered quite common in Tokyo these days. I mention this only because Mother is full of remorse that even though she received a generous allowance from Grandfather and you, she rebelled against you.

In my study of English literature, I came across the words of T. S. Eliot, who said that "tradition" should be positively discouraged. I cannot understand tradition as he describes it. According to Eliot, tradition negates all that preceded it and will be negated by all that follows. And yet I feel I know what he means when I think of the bond between you and me. The "family" has flowed from you to Mother and from Mother to me.

Please don't laugh at me. One day I shall marry and have a daughter. It amuses me to imagine how my daughter will rebel against me and regard her grandmother with affection. And then, I shall think that, just as people lived in the distant past and will continue to exist in the years to come, however difficult the present may be for me, I must live for tomorrow.

Now I know why I feel nostalgic about Wakayama. I could not have made this discovery or experienced this peace of mind and happiness if I had never been close to you.

Hana wrote a reply to her granddaughter's letter using brush and ink. Instead of writing on beautiful Japanese paper, however, she wrote on ordinary stationery. Hana did not even attempt to explain the special bond between Hanako and herself. She merely described her daily routine, choosing characters so her message would fit on a postcard. Her letter was terse, but the sheer beauty of the calligraphy made Hanako feel that it was brimming with news.

After graduating from college, Hanako found work with a

publishing firm and decided to start saving some of her salary.

"Besides paying for your meals at home, you'll need more money for clothing than you did as a student," argued Fumio. She then asked her daughter what she was saving up for.

"It's for a round trip ticket to Wakayama."

"And just when do you plan to make this trip?"

"I don't have a particular date in mind, but I'd like to go back again one day."

Kazuhiko, who worked for a business firm, was married. Fumio kept a close eye on her bank account and her widow's pension, whose present value was greatly reduced because of the drastic devaluation of the Japanese currency. She felt that she had to be very frugal with her money until Akihiko had completed his university education and had entered a firm. This sacrifice was extremely painful for her. Recalling her own youth, she found it unbearable to be unable to buy her children the things they needed. To make matters worse, she had to rely on them for financial assistance at times.

"It doesn't do any good to talk like that, Mother."

"But I've been thinking things over lately. I was hostile toward landowners because I felt sorry for the people who worked for me. In other words . . ."

"That's right. It was because you were a landowner's daughter and didn't have to work. I work, so I don't have to feel sorry for others who work."

"I didn't mean to seem in any way presumptuous."

Fumio was over fifty years old. She had experienced hardship and the loss of her husband following Japan's defeat and had suddenly aged. She had lost all her former vitality and had no desire to argue with her daughter, who candidly voiced her opinions.

At about this time they received word that Hana had suffered a stroke. Fumio, in response to the promptings of her sons, rushed to her mother's side. However, she returned to Tokyo ten days later after learning that the stroke had been a mild one and that Hana would be all right. Fumio later confessed that she had been completely stunned by the ruins into which the Matani mansion had fallen in the ten years since the war. She had hurried back to Tokyo, because she could not bear to remain in the house any longer. Shortly after the death of his beautiful wife three years earlier, Seiichirō had resigned from the bank and was now living with Hana and Oichi. He was nearly sixty years old. He had stopped working, it seemed, in a vain attempt to uphold the dignity of an old family.

"I felt as if I were looking at the ghostly ruins of an old house," said Fumio in the Wakayama dialect. Hanako listened to her mother, wondering if it were indeed painful to view the ruins of a house in which one had grown up.

When Hana had her second stroke, Fumio received word from both Utae and Tomokazu that this time her condition was critical. There was not enough money for both Fumio and Hanako to make the trip, so Fumio refused to go.

"I've already gone. You go this time, Hanako."

"All right, Mother. I've saved enough money for the trip."

It was the middle of summer, the hottest summer in ten years, and the city pavements broiled under the midday sun. How ironical it was that Hanako was escaping from this infernal heat because her grandmother had fallen critically ill! With mixed feelings of sadness at the approach of her grandmother's death and joy at returning to her place of birth, Hanako left Tokyo on the night train. She transferred to a Wakayama-bound train in Osaka and at noon the next day was walking along the narrow country road in Musota.

In Tokyo, more than ten years since Japan's surrender, modern buildings were appearing everywhere and the city changed face from one day to the next. But Musota appeared unchanged from the time Hanako had sought refuge there during the war. The waters of the River Yu, a tributary of the Ki, gurgling as they always had, flowed between the rice paddies and filled the irrigation ditches which Keisaku had suggested digging to prevent flooding. Wakayama was as hot as Tokyo. As Hanako walked along with her head bowed low, the sun beat mercilessly upon the nape of her neck. The temperature was so high it seemed the puddles of water would begin to boil. But the waters of the Yu were cool and clear. When Hanako stooped down and placed her hand in the water, it felt as cold as melted snow. Hanako wondered how the river, whose waters were drawn from Iwade Dam, had been given its name, which meant "boiling water." Along the way she passed an ox with a basket covering its muzzle, but she had no recollection of having ever seen the young cowherd's face. After all, even a child born in 1945 would now be thirteen. Hanako reflected upon the years which had slipped by since she moved back to Tokyo. In all that time she had not seen her grandmother.

The ancient wooden gate of the Matani mansion was tightly closed. Hanako leaned against the small side gate which opened noiselessly. She was tall like her mother and grandmother and so had to stoop to pass through the gate. When she looked up, all she could see was green. It was as if she were being greeted by the green leaves which were growing luxuriantly on the branches of the persimmon tree inside the gate. They appeared transparent in the sunlight. The heat had drained her of all energy, but now Hanako felt fully recovered. She ran across the courtyard and entered the house.

"Is anybody home? It's me, Hanako," she called out in a loud voice. She could hear the sound of people moving about inside.

"May I come in?" she asked.

"Why, it's Hanako!" cried Utae from the front door. Then immediately she asked:

"But where's your mother? Hanako, didn't she come with you?"

"No, she didn't. Mother isn't coming this time."

"Just like her! She left so abruptly last time we were all taken aback!"

"How is Grandmother?"

Utae's expression grew serious as she explained the doctor's diagnosis. It was only a matter of time now. The right side of Hana's body was totally paralyzed. The best he could do was suggest she rest quietly. Hana herself could no longer distinguish between night and day.

Her mother had described the house as being dilapidated. Hana-ko noticed, however, that the tatami straw mats were new and that an air of opulence—as though money had recently been lavished on the place—pervaded the entire house, which was dimly lit under its old roof. Hana, realizing full well that her end was near when she had her first stroke the previous year, had suddenly begun to sell the objects in the storehouse to an antique dealer. Oichi alone knew about this. Hana had had various repairs carried out in the house and had even had some new cushions made for her guests. Hanako ran into Oichi along the corridor which led to the back of the house.

"How good of you to come! Madame talks about you all the time. She'll be so delighted to see you!"

Oichi was ten years younger than Hana, but she was now seventy and bent with age. She stood there with her body thrown forward from her stomach to her chin as though she were breathing deeply.

"Is it all right for me to go in unannounced? May I talk to her?"

"Why, of course. She's longing to have someone to talk to. Here, let me show you in."

The two women entered Hana's room at the end of the corridor. It had once been used as a sitting room but had now become Hana's bedroom. Even though it was midsummer, the sliding doors were tightly closed and dark curtains had been hung up all around the room to keep out the light of day. As Hanako followed Oichi into the room, her nose was assailed by a smell of hospital, despite the fact that no disinfectant was being used. A small light bulb cast an eerie light across the large room. Hana lay on her side in the middle of the room, which was so dark one could not tell whether or not the sheets were white. In the darkness, Hana's face appeared small and shriveled. Hanako, suddenly reminded of a mummy in a museum, stood still for a moment.

"Madame, Hanako has come all the way from Tokyo," announced Oichi in a loud voice.

"Oh? Is she really here?" asked Hana without moving her head or her quilt.

Hanako was worried that Hana, like Utae, might ask why Fumio had not come, but all Hana said to her granddaughter, who was kneeling down at her bedside, was: "It's you. How kind of you to come!"

Hana's small eyes stared vacantly.

"Hanako. How old are you now? Twenty-seven? You'll make little progress finding a husband on your own. Your mother believes that hers was a love match, but actually she was caught in a trap set by the adults around her. A woman should not become a career woman and remain unmarried."

"Well, I'm certainly not opposed to marriage."

"Your mother was twenty-seven when she had you. She made such a big fuss then, even in front of the nurses in hospital. She cried so much just giving birth to a tiny baby! All that lofty talk about freedom and her attacks on feudal institutions. But when she cried in labor, I knew she would never be a match for the women of the past who stoically bore their pain. I was so amused!"

Hana's face was sadly ravaged by time, but her voice was steady. Hanako, realizing that it would not do for Hana to talk too much, worriedly glanced back at Oichi. How could she silence her grandmother?

"She's like this when she has her eyes open. Please sit with her for a while." Oichi said a few words to the nurse, who was sitting at the foot of the bed massaging Hana's feet, and left the room.

One of the side effects of a stroke is that it produces a vivid recollection of past events. Just when everyone had grown tired of listening to her, Hana had found a new listener; she therefore began to chatter endlessly about all manner of subjects. Hanako learned a little political history and heard in detail about the state of the nation during the Sino-Japanese war of 1894 and the Russo-Japanese War and all about World War I. She was even told that her mother had been born feet first.

"Because of this, Fumio constantly rebelled against us from the time she was a child. If she had been a boy, she might have become an active member of the Socialist Party!"

"You mean the Liberal-Democratic Party, don't you? Remember, she was receiving money from a landowner."

Hana's throat shook as she laughed a metallic laugh. When Hanako's eyes grew accustomed to the dark, she noticed that her grandmother appeared younger than her eighty-one years. There was still a faint trace of her beautiful features and fair complexion, even though her face had withered with age. Her gums had shrunk and so her false teeth forced their way out of her mouth whenever she spoke, making it difficult for her to talk.

"Grandmother, hadn't you better remove your false teeth?"

"Oh, no. It's bad enough that I'm old. How much worse I'd look without my dentures."

Her grandmother must have been a very vain young woman, Hanako thought. She still worried about her appearance even though she was bedridden. Never once had Hana worn pantaloons during the war years; she had insisted on wearing silk kimonos with unshortened sleeves to the very end.

"Fumio, why did you leave so abruptly last time?" inquired Hana.

"Grandmother, Mother couldn't come this time."

Hana gave her granddaughter a strange look.

"Is that you, Hanako?"

As her recollection of the distant past became increasingly vivid recent events seemed unreal to her.

From the day of her arrival, Hanako was in constant attendance upon her grandmother. After becoming ill, Hana had become very self-indulgent and spent money as lavishly as when Keisaku was alive. She presented all her visitors with gifts. Kawaguchi Norio, who had inherited Keisaku's constituency, had become a member of parliament and had been appointed minister of state in the previous year. During one of the minister's visits, Hana instructed Oichi to hand over to him fifty yen for his campaign funds. Hana was totally confused about how the value of money had changed. When someone tried to explain it to her, she refused to listen and stuck to what she had said. She would lose her temper when Hanako was not at her side. Informed that her granddaughter was resting, she complained:

"Isn't an invalid more important?"

Hana took regular naps during the day, which meant that she was wide-awake at night and very impatient with anyone who felt sleepy. It upset her terribly when a person she summoned did not come to her at once. She would then call for all the people she could think of, demanding that they come to her in shifts. Those summoned frequently—and promptly dismissed—were Seiichirō and Tomokazu. Seiichirō depressed her. Tomokazu was far too attentive and only succeeded in annoying her. Instead of listening quietly to Hana, he often scolded her in teacherly fashion for talking too much.

"Why do you keep telling me to be quiet?" demanded Hana defiantly.

"But it's for your own good. You'll tire yourself out if you keep talking like that, Mother. Why can't you rest quietly?"

"I haven't been out of bed for over ten days. I don't feel like eating anything, and I can't see what I want to see. If you tell me not to talk, what in the world have I left to do?"

"Don't think about anything and rest."

"But you need discipline to make your mind a complete blank. Do you think it's possible for someone as sick as I am to sit in religious meditation?" Hana asked angrily.

The doctor had said that it was just a matter of time. He advised the family to restrain Hana from talking, as it would be debilitating for her to talk too much.

"Talk about subjects that won't provoke her. The best thing to do would be to have the person nursing her monopolize the conversation. The next best thing would be to read to her."

In a separate sitting room were gathered Hana's children, relatives, and old farmers and landowners who had been associated with Keisaku. Eisuke from Shin'ike sat among them; Kōsaku, his father, had died two years earlier. They all agreed to read to Hana. Tomokazu shook his head when it was suggested that they read to her the best-sellers Hanako had brought with her.

"Don't you think the stories will upset her?"

Utae agreed.

"Mother is fond of reading modern novels which have been well reviewed. But it would be too tiring for her to concentrate while they were read aloud to her."

Someone then suggested that they read to her her old favorites. They all agreed that this was a splendid idea but were at a loss as to which books to read. After a long pause Seiichirō spoke:

"I suppose we ought to read to her works like *The Tale of Genji* and *The Tales of the Heike*."

Everyone looked a bit dismayed to hear she would be read something in classical Japanese. Some of them had never even read *The Tale of Genji* but were under the impression that it was terribly difficult. Seiichirō suggested another possibility.

"Mother was reading the historical work *Masukagami* before she fell ill."

"*Masukagami*?"

A few of those gathered together in that room nodded knowingly as though they were familiar with the work. It was therefore agreed that *Masukagami* would be read. Misled by the casual manner in which the selection was made, others who had never heard of the classic assumed that it was an easy book to read. Hana's face broke into a rare smile when it was announced that *Masukagami* would be read to her.

A glance at the book which Seiichirō had fetched from Hana's desk was enough to make everyone regret their hasty decision.

The old headman of a neighboring village disclosed the fact that he was an ex-farmer and raised his hands to show how rough they were. It would have been expecting too much to ask such a person to read to Hana, even though he did not actually come out and say that he could not read the text. It was finally decided that Seiichirō, Tomokazu, and Hanako would take turns reading to Hana. Hanako was graciously resigned to being the one to read to Hana all through the night.

"Grandmother, let me read to you."

"I'd like that very much."

An old lamp had been fetched from the storehouse and placed at Hana's bedside so that its light shone on the book. Hana began to read aloud the first page.

> The retired Emperor Go-Toba was the eighty-second emperor since the establishment of the imperial line. His given name was Takahira, and he was the fourth son of the retired Emperor Takakura. His mother, Shichijō-in, was the daughter of Suri no Daibu Nobutaka. When she was known as Lady Hyōe no Suke, she had been in attendance upon Her Imperial Majesty during the reign of Emperor Takakura. Having secretly received His Imperial Majesty's favor, she gave birth to Takahira on the fifteenth day of the seventh month of the fourth year of the Jijō reign period (1180).

The opening pages of the work—like the Bible and *The Records of Ancient Matters*—were extremely boring, but Hana seemed to be listening with great pleasure. Having majored in English literature, Hanako was not very good at reading classical Japanese texts. Nonetheless, she was curious to know more about the author and the content of the work and so took her assignment seriously. When she came across passages she could not understand, she held her breath and read as fast as she could. Now and then she would come to a long string of kana syllabary and not know where to pause for breath. At such times, she recklessly attacked the passage.

"Hanako, I think you read the passage incorrectly."

Speaking in a loud distinct voice, Hana did not hesitate to interrupt her granddaughter. After twenty minutes of reading, Hanako realized how difficult her task was. To begin with, the text was far from simple. Furthermore, Hana was very strict about having the work read accurately.

"I'm completely exhausted. Please let me rest for a while."

"Why, of course," said Hana, who could be reasonable at times.

The nurse, who had been massaging the lower half of Hana's body, had slipped away. Since Hanako could not very well leave her grandmother unattended and go out of the room to brew some tea, she put the book down and sat there idly. Looking over at her grandmother, Hanako noticed that she had her eyes closed, although she did not appear to be asleep. The old woman's hair lay disheveled about her face. In the past Hana had seated herself in front of the mirror and had taken great pains in combing her hair so that not a single strand was out of place. Now, however, her tangled hair appeared as though it had not been combed in days. Instead of feeling repelled by the sorry state of her grandmother, Hanako longed to do something about the situation.

"Grandmother, would you like to have me comb your hair?"

"Yes, please. It's so very dry," responded Hana happily.

The white hair was as stiff as wire from its very roots and refused to stay down even after being carefully combed with a boxwood comb. Recalling that she had seen Seiichirō's pomade in the lavatory, Hanako ran to fetch it. When she returned with the jar, Hana was stroking her hair with her left hand. It was such a thin arm! Fascinated, Hanako watched her grandmother's hand pass again and again through her hair from her forehead back to the back of her head. Hanako held her breath for a long moment, keenly aware of the vitality that Hana still possessed. As she nursed her grandmother, Hanako felt that she saw in her emaciated body a chart of the decline of the Matani family. It astounded her to discover that Hana had not yet lost the desire to make herself as presentable as possible.

Hana's sense of smell was still as sharp as ever. When Hanako removed the lid and rubbed a small quantity of the pomade into the palms of her hands, Hana remarked:

"It smells terrible. What is it?"

"Just some pomade. I thought it would help keep your hair in place."

Hana no longer complained as Hanako rubbed a generous amount of pomade into the white hair.

"Didn't they use a special kind of hair ointment years ago?"

"Yes, indeed. It also had an awful smell!"

As though trying to picture her grandmother as a beautiful young woman, Hanako gently combed Hana's hair so as not to scratch her scalp. Hana was so pleased she plunged into another long soliloquy.

"You've never combed my hair before. Fumio, you're already over fifty. How fortunate you are to have such a fine daughter!"

Hana again confused the two women and spoke to Hanako as though she were Fumio.

"I've always let you speak your mind and do as you pleased. Have I ever failed to send you the money you requested while you were in college and even after you married Eiji? And yet how you ranted endlessly about independence and freedom! Hanako would laugh if I told her all about it. Both Kazuhiko and Hanako are such wonderful children. You must have been a good mother after all. One can never judge whether or not a woman has been successful in life without observing how her children turn out. Fumio, you've always rebelled against me, but I wanted you so much to remain near me. Seiichirō was unreliable. Tomokazu used the excuse that he was only the second son and let his wife run his life. How depressing it was to look after the Matani household all by myself! As a woman grows old, the thing she wants most to do is spend money extravagantly. It was the one thing I had not been able to do in recent years. That's why I've been so extravagant since I had my first stroke and realized that death was around the corner. You probably don't know about the lavish celebration I had after the mats were changed. Now many people come to see me when they hear that I've had a stroke, because they know I'm very generous. You've always disliked the old-fashioned custom of exchanging presents, but it's really great fun."

Hana laughed a laugh that was both throaty and nasal.

"The family fortune began to dwindle from the time your father spent money as he pleased. Even if there had been no war and I had lived frugally, the family fortune would have been exhausted in Seiichirō's generation. The Matani family from which you ran away years ago has already become stuff for the history books. Take a look in the storehouse. All you'll find there are a few worthless objects. The only thing of value is my miniature screen."

The miniature screen was of the sort that was propped up in front of an inkstone for decoration. Hanako remembered helping her grandmother take care of it during the war. Even a large screen of this kind would be only about four inches high. The one in Hana's possession was of exquisite craftsmanship with an elaborate design of jade and ivory. Nonetheless, it was of almost negligible value and so, if sold, would hardly bring in any money at all.

Hana suddenly laughed.

"The storehouse is empty now, you know. Fumio, you often said that you couldn't stand seeing a woman so completely dependent upon her husband and eldest son. You also said that being submissive was ridiculous. But I never thought of myself as being submissive. All I've done was to work as hard as I could. When your father was Speaker of the House, I did my best as the wife of the Speaker of the House. When your father became a member of parliament, I did my best as the wife of a member of parliament. And when Seiichirō entered Tokyo Imperial University, I did my best as the mother of a student attending Tokyo Imperial University. I really tried to do everything I could for Seiichirō until I realized that he was just a pale imitation of your father. There was nothing more I could do."

At what point and to what degree had Hana been disappointed in her eldest son? She remained silent for a while, unable to crystallize her feelings of disappointment. When she had finished combing her grandmother's hair into a neat bun, Hanako returned to her usual place. She used several sheets of tissue paper to wipe off the oily pomade whose smell clung tenaciously to her fingers. The cold night air pierced her body, causing her to shiver.

"Your father once said that he wished you had been a boy. Seiichirō had disappointed him relatively early. After that I did all I could to see that Seiichirō did not disgrace the family. Fumio, I felt so lonely when you ignored my efforts."

In the hectic days following Japan's surrender, Fumio had not had a moment to think about the Matani home. She had of course requested money and had turned over her children to Hana, thus preserving on the surface the natural bond between mother and daughter. All the while, however, she had continued to rebel against her mother. Hana had therefore kept a lonely vigil over the dwindling family fortune. It was difficult for young Hanako to comprehend fully the intense loneliness her grandmother had experienced. As Hana continued her monologue, her teeth protruded from her mouth and a smile spread across her wrinkled face.

"That's why I was so happy when our land was confiscated. I knew then that the Matani fortune could never be restored, so there was no reason to feel apologetic toward our ancestors. Instead of feeling that all I had worked for was in vain, I felt elated and wanted to cry out your name. I gave the excuse that it was for tax purposes and sold all the objects of value. Now that I didn't have to worry about what would happen after my death, a heavy burden was lifted from my shoulders and I was filled with great joy."

Once again Hana laughed.

Indulging a desire which she had held in check all her life, Hana had begun to lead a life of limitless extravagance soon after suffering her first stroke. She had grown cheerful and had lavished money on herself just as money had once been spent freely on her husband, paying no attention to her widowed son. Tomokazu took a dim view of her behavior, but Utae could not help being impressed. As for Fumio, she had simply shrugged her shoulders when she heard about her mother's wild spending. Everyone had misunderstood Hana. Seiichirō, the only one who was unwilling to have his daily routine disrupted in any way, continued to live quietly with his mother. He had resolved to die an idle man, upholding to the end the dignity of an old family.

Hana, however, did not wish to cling tenaciously to her children in the little time remaining for her. She spoke of what would happen upon her death.

"You'll be receiving a great many obituary gifts. But you won't be able to do anything in return. It amuses me no end to think of how all of you will panic after my funeral."

Her gay laughter filled the dimly lit room. Hanako felt keenly the cold night air in her bones. Fearful that her grandmother would be completely exhausted if she continued to talk like this, Hanako took up *Masukagami*.

"Let me continue my reading."

"Yes, please do. Read chapter seventeen of the last volume."

Chapter seventeen. Parting in spring. From the end of the fourth month, the illness of the retired Emperor grew critical and the whole world was greatly distressed. His Imperial Highness was sorely grieved. The prayers and incantations were intensified, but there was no sign they had any effect. The retired Emperor grew steadily worse as day and night people came to inquire after the state of his health. Young courtiers, wearing folded caps, scurried about. Not distinguishing between night and day, they spurred their steeds, obtained from the Bureau of Horses, to far-off Sagano. Upon hearing that the retired Emperor was critically ill . . .

Hanako looked up from her reading and saw that Hana's eyes, nestled in her deeply furrowed face, were open, unblinking, reflecting the dim light from the lamp.

A strange sensation swept over Hanako when she thought of Hana's blood running through her own veins. The spirit of the Matani family still lived within her. There was indeed a powerful bond linking Toyono to Hana, Hana to Fumio, and Fumio to Hanako. Hanako felt that her grandmother's heartbeats were pulsating in her own breast and no longer sought to decipher the cryptic text she was reading aloud. Had the Buddhist priests—who for thousands of years had chanted the sutras before the statue of Buddha, the object of worship of hundreds of thousands of men and women—experienced a similar emotion? No longer did Hanako feel that she was reading the text as a devoted grand-daughter. Believing that this was what was required of her in order to inherit from Hana the vitality of the countless women who had lived and died in the family, she read as one possessed, not realizing that she had raised her voice.

The door slid open.

"Hanako, Mother will be thoroughly exhausted if you read to her like that."

The blurred outline of Tomokazu's face peered into the room. His eyelids were swollen.

Hanako awoke one morning well past noon. As she washed her face with cold water drawn from the well, she suddenly thought about how long she had been away from Tokyo. She was com-pletely exhausted and her eyes were sunken. Hanako reflected upon the life she had been leading as she awaited her grand-mother's death. She took a bite of the tasty pickled radish which was a regional delicacy and thought that she could not be ex-cused indefinitely from her job.

Oichi, all on her own, was busily drawing water, and then throwing firewood into the fire in the stove. A visitor appeared at the entrance. People came to visit Hana daily and after visiting with her, they stayed a while to chat with the other members of the family. Finding themselves generously treated to saké and refreshments, they returned home wearing puzzled looks on their faces. Even the members of the household who had been told by Hana to serve the refreshments appeared perplexed. Hana's illness showed no noticeable change, but the family were worried that her condition might worsen at any time. Meanwhile, they had little to occupy themselves with. Oichi alone was kept busy taking out and putting away saké bottles, lacquerware, and Kutani plates. She popped in occasionally to serve Hanako, who was sitting at the dining table in the kitchen, but did not pause to chat as she rushed around taking out old saucers and tea bowls from the shelves and cupboards. Hanako was familiar with these objects which she had often seen during the war years. Hana was very fond of them and in this dark mansion each object appeared restless. The plates and glasses in Hanako's house in Tokyo all had the quiet air of inanimate objects about them, but here every tea bowl seemed to have a story to tell. This was true of the other things in the house as well: the stout pillars which reflected a somber light, the ceiling, the sliding doors with their large frames and deep grooves along which they ran, and even the badly scratched walls of yellowish brown. Everything in the house Hanako could see seemed to be whispering to her. The very food she had just eaten seemed to weigh heavy in her stomach.

Hanako went into the storeroom and changed into a colorful dress. She had brought with her a number of more sober dresses and had begun to feel depressed after wearing them day in day out. Hanako now had on a cotton dress with a bold print of tropical flowers which fit her perfectly; it also suited better the mood she was in and she soon found herself feeling positively cheerful.

The family members who had gathered in the drawing room had apparently run out of things to talk about. Over and over again they had listened to the same stories and had had enough of them by now. Seiichirō, who sat there among them, a benign look on his face, had not taken part in the conversation.

"Uncle, won't you join me for a walk?"

"Yes, why not?"

Everyone in the room was taken aback, especially since Seiichirō, who rose slowly to his feet, and Hanako in her gaily colored dress made such a study in contrasts.

In Tokyo, it would have been a little too early in the day for a walk, but here the air—free of smoke and dust—felt pleasantly bracing and the strong sunlight pleasantly warm. Seiichirō walked along in complete silence, unaffected by his niece's rather forthright appearance.

"Uncle, how old are you?"

"Four years older than your mother," replied Seiichirō somewhat reluctantly. He would probably have remained silent indefinitely had she not spoken. They strolled leisurely northward along the path through the rice paddies. Hanako inhaled deeply and felt that the blue skies and all the surrounding greenery were being drawn into her lungs. She felt her body immersed in the fragrant air warmed by the summer sun.

"How much longer do you intend to remain single?"

"What do you mean? At my age, no woman would have me."

"You know that isn't true. After all, you're still in your fifties, aren't you? You shouldn't think of yourself as being older than you really are."

"But I'm already fifty-nine. I'll soon be turning sixty."

Not at all amused by Hanako's interrogation, Seiichirō did not answer her seriously. Hanako was five-foot-five and considered tall for a Japanese woman. Her uncle, though endowed with a fine physique, had a weak personality. This good-looking man had done nothing to stave off the family's decline. Hanako could hardly suppress the impulse to shake him very hard.

Nonetheless, she assumed a casual attitude. Placing her hand on her uncle's arm, she drew up closer to his side. The two walked on in silence. Stealing a glance at her uncle, she saw that he was staring straight ahead with a set look on his face. Hanako, aware of how nasal her voice sounded, asked Seiichirō in a teasing tone:

"Uncle, do you spend each day at home doing absolutely nothing?"

"Why, yes."

"Don't you ever get bored?"

"At times."

Hanako waited to see if he would say anything more. However, it seemed that that was all he intended to say.

"What did you dream about doing when you were young? You can't always do what you want to, but you must have once had some goal you wanted to accomplish in life."

"Let me think."

After a lengthy pause, Seiichirō said:

"I guess I've never had any particular goal in life."

Hanako's right arm was sweating profusely under the hemp of her uncle's robe. She had grasped hold of his arm with all her strength. Just when she was beginning to feel rather awkward, her uncle said with the utmost politeness:

"Hanako, please let go of my arm."

Seiichirō walked over to the roadside and turned to face the rice paddies. Slowly he tucked up the front of his kimono.

The sun was beginning its westward journey and white clouds drifted lazily across the sky. The distant woods and mountains melted into subdued colors, and the earth and sky met each other in a graceful diffusion of light. Embarrassed, Hanako walked slowly back along the road they had come down, trying not to listen to the sound behind her. She realized that the head of the household was not affected as profoundly by the Matanis' decline as the women in the family.

Upon returning to Agenogaito, they heard the children making a great deal of racket in the courtyard. As it was summer vacation, Utae and Tomokazu had brought their children along to be with their grandmother in her final days. Not stopping to think of their ailing grandmother resting in her room, the cousins, who had not seen each other for some time, were hard at play. But the commotion they were making was more than they managed normally.

"I wonder if anything's wrong."

"It looks like it."

Seiichirō was as worried as Hanako. Hanako took a deep breath and ran into the courtyard.

"What's the matter?" she asked. She looked down and swallowed hard. A white snake was writhing in front of the storehouse, so weak it could not coil itself up. It was quite something to see this six-foot-long snake helplessly writhing under the midsummer sun. It was difficult to tell whether it really was white or whether it had once been striped but had shed its skin. It had slithered along the rain gutters from the east storehouse to the west storehouse. The dying snake had been discovered after it had fallen to the ground by Hideo—Tomokazu's eldest son and Hana's long-awaited grandson by one of her sons. Little Hideo, who was only four years old, had bravely struck the old animal with a stick.

The white snake—like a white rabbit—had red eyes which stared up at the sky and were utterly expressionless. Hana's grandchildren were not familiar with the story of the snake that lived in the Matani storehouse. They clustered around the dying snake with the typically innocent cruelty of children. Hanako suddenly noticed someone at the gate and looked over in that direction.

"Mother . . ."

Fumio stood there with a canvas bag and a scarf-wrapped bundle in one hand, smiling shyly.

"I'm here," murmured Fumio, like a bashful schoolgirl, and pressed her hand against her gray hair for a moment. Once again she smiled.

Hanako was on her way back to Tokyo that very day. When she crossed Musota Bridge, she felt her body reverberate with the heavy sound of the waters of the River Ki, full from bank to bank even though there was a water shortage in Tokyo. The roar of the river from the dam that could be seen upstream was causing the bridge girders to vibrate. Soaring dizzily skyward to the southwest was the dazzling white tower of the newly rebuilt Wakayama Castle. Postwar industrial development in Wakayama Prefecture was controlled by Osaka capital; therefore, plans were made to develop Wakayama City into a tourist attraction. Three years earlier, the decision had been made to rebuild first of all the castle tower.

Thirty minutes later, Hanako crossed Ichinohashi, entered the grounds of Wakayama Park, and quickly made her way up the slope toward the tower. The second gate appeared to be freshly painted and still wet. As in the past, tickets were being sold at the entrance.

The lighting inside the main tower, neglected in the past, was vastly improved. The tower itself was of ferro-concrete. There was linoleum on the floor and displayed in the large glass cases were objects of historical significance that had once belonged to the Tokugawa shoguns. Also on show were famous products of Ki province. After a quick look at the display cases, Hanako, recalling the first time she had come here with her grandmother twenty years earlier, climbed up to the lookout platform on the third floor. Wakayama fanned out below her, rich with greenery as it had been in years gone by.

A large telescope that had been installed in one corner caught her eye. Tourists were looking through the lens and moving the instrument to the left and to the right. Put a ten-yen coin in the slot and one could use the telescope for a limited time.

Hanako waited for her turn. She then fed in a coin and looked quickly through the telescope. Below her lay Wakayama, which had been speedily reconstructed after the war. Looking up, she saw the blue sky. Finally getting the instrument under control, she focused the lens on Musota and could even make out the Matani mansion in Agenogaito. It was not much more than a dot but was still clearly visible.

On this side of Musota, the River Ki appeared smooth and tranquil, giving the impression its waters were perfectly still. The river was a lovely blend of jade green and celadon. Hanako slowly turned the telescope downriver and was impressed that the color was the same. The ugly smokestacks close to the mouth of the river loomed into her scope of vision. The huge factory of Sumitomo Chemicals, funded by interests in Osaka, spread out slightly to the north of the river's mouth. Keisaku's dream had been to develop both waterworks and agriculture so that Wakayama would not be ruined by outsiders. But the war had destroyed his dream. Disappointed to have the magnificent view marred by an ugly factory, Hanako stepped back from the telescope. The forest of smokestacks rapidly receded into the distance and beyond them lay the ocean.

Hanako heaved a sigh of relief and in that instant the telescope clicked: the lens cap had automatically closed. She moved away from the telescope and gazed for a time at the vast, mysterious ocean whose color changed as the sunlight played upon the waves.